IN SEARCH OF

MOBY DICK

IN SEARCH OF

MOBY DICK

Quest for the White Whale

Tim Severin

G.K. Hall & Co. • Chivers Press
Thorndike, Maine USA Bath, England

This Large Print edition is published by Thorndike Press, USA and by Chivers Press, England.

Published in 2001 in the U.S. by arrangement with Basic Books, a member of Perseus Books, LLC.

Published in 2001 in the U.K. by arrangement with Little, Brown & Company.

U.S. Hardcover   0-7838-9362-0   (Nonfiction Series Edition)
U.K. Hardcover   0-7540-1557-2   (Windsor Large Print)

The text of this Large Print edition is unabridged.
Other aspects of the book may vary from the original edition.

Set in 16 pt. Plantin.   919.04

Printed in the United States on permanent paper.

British Library Cataloguing in Publication Data available

Library of Congress Cataloging-in-Publication Data

Severin, Timothy.
     In search of Moby Dick : quest for the white whale / Tim Severin.
     p. cm.
     ISBN 0-7838-9362-0 (lg. print : hc : alk. paper)
     1. Melville, Herman, 1819–1891. Moby Dick. 2. Melville, Herman, 1819–1891 — Knowledge — Whales. 3. Melville, Herman, 1819–1891 — Journeys — Oceania. 4. Novelists, American — 19th century — Biography. 5. Sea stories, American — History and criticism. 6. Oceania — Description and travel. 7. Oceania — In literature. 8. Whaling in literature. 9. Whales in literature. 10. Albinos and albinism. 11. Setting (Literature) 12. Large type books. I. Title.
     PS2384.M62 S38   2001
     813′.3—dc21   00-053900

CONTENTS

CUTWATER

'I have seen Owen Chace [*sic*] who was chief mate of the *Essex* at the time of the tragedy; I have read his plain and faithful narrative; I have conversed with his son; and all within a few miles of the scene of the catastrophe.'

HERMAN MELVILLE, *Moby Dick*

With an off-cut of heavy canvas, Owen Chase was hastily nailing a temporary patch over a hole in the bottom of his whaleboat. The hole was fresh, knocked that same hour through the thin cedarwood planks by a swipe from the tail of a whale he had harpooned. It was a measure of Chase's professionalism that the moment the accident happened, he had taken up a hatchet and chopped through the line to free the whale from the foundering boat. While his crew bailed, Chase stuffed three or four jackets into the hole to plug the leak as best he could. Then he ordered his men to row back to the mother ship, the *Essex*. The damaged twenty-seven foot boat had been hoisted aboard as smartly as possible, and now lay upturned on the quarter of the *Essex*. First mate Owen Chase was in a hurry. He wanted to rejoin the other two boats from the *Essex*, including Captain Pollard's, which were still out on the water, and now some distance downwind. They were in hot pursuit of a small pod of whales, and it appeared that the captain's boat had successfully harpooned one of them.

Owen Chase judged it would be quicker to put this makeshift patch on his own boat than to unlash and lower one of the spare boats which were snugged down in stowage. Chase was from Nantucket, like his ship, and he regarded the incident as a run-of-the-mill mishap in the fishery. What happened next, however, was anything but ordinary.

As he was driving the tacks, Chase glanced up and saw a sperm whale, a very big one, come to the surface about a hundred yards off the windward bow. The sea was calm, and the animal lay quietly on the water, spouted two or three times, then disappeared. Noting only that it was an unusually large specimen, perhaps eighty feet long, Chase turned back to his work. Two or three seconds later he saw the animal again. Now it was less than a ship's length away and appeared to be swimming steadily in the direction of the *Essex*. The animal was moving at no more than three knots, and for a moment Chase did not react. Then he took a second glance, calculated the angle of the whale's approach, and realised that ship and whale were on a collision course. Instinctively the first mate called to the helmsman, the ship's boy, to change course. But the manoeuvre was awkward. The whaleship was moving at no more than walking pace. Her main topsail was aback, and she had little steerage way. This was normal practice as it allowed the ship to stay near her boats when they were spread out across the sea. The whaleship had not even begun the turn when the whale suddenly accelerated and rammed the *Essex* head-on. The animal's blunt head struck the ship near the forechains. The impact jarred the *Essex* so severely that it felt as if she had run on to a rock, and she 'trembled like a leaf'. The crew almost fell flat on their faces.

There was a shocked silence. The men on board exchanged glances of amazement. In the interval they felt the behemoth pass under the vessel, grazing the keel. Then the attacker reappeared on the leeward side. The animal lay on the surface, apparently stunned by the force of the blow. Then the whale seemed to gather itself, and swam off downwind. Collecting his own wits, Chase guessed that the *Essex* must have been damaged, and he ordered the pumps to be rigged. Within minutes he could tell that the vessel was indeed taking on water and settling down by the head. He ordered a signal to be made, recalling the two boats' crews.

Scarcely had he sent the signal than Chase caught sight of the whale again. Now it was about a quarter of a mile to leeward, and behaving very bizarrely. The huge animal seemed to be in convulsions. For several minutes it stayed on the same spot, thrashing its tail up and down, whipping up white water, and clashing its jaws together. The first mate turned his attention back to the deck. He urged the crew at the pumps to redouble their efforts and, fearing that the *Essex* was mortally hurt, began to plan the best way of provisioning and launching the spare boats as lifeboats. While his attention was engaged inboard, he heard a crew man shout out, 'Here he is again! — he's making for us again!'

Turning round, Chase was appalled to see the whale charging directly towards his ship. This time there was no mistaking the animal's intention. Its head was half out of the water and throwing up a bow-wave as it came careering down on the vessel. The tail was churning a broad white wake. The charging whale had 'tenfold fury and vengeance in his aspect', was how Chase described the apparition. He shouted at the steersman to put the helm hard up, to swing the *Essex* out of the whale's path. But again the manoeuvre was too slow. The sperm whale slammed head first into the *Essex*, right under her bows. The *Essex* was a 328-ton whaleship, built for endurance, and a sturdy vessel. But the impact from an enraged bull sperm whale was too much. The collision completely collapsed the *Essex*'s bows, and she was doomed. The whale swam off and was not seen again.

Owen Chase remained calm. He knew that the ship was finished, and he ordered the men to stop pumping. The priority now was to launch a lifeboat, so he cut the lashings of the spare whaleboat on the quarter, and his men carried it on their shoulders to the midships where the rail was lowest. Meanwhile the ship's steward darted below deck to retrieve the essentials for navigation: two quadrants and two sets of nautical tables. These items were placed in the whale-boat, with the sea chests of the captain and the first mate, and Chase added two steering compasses which he snatched from the binnacle. The ship had now taken on a decided list. The steward made two trips below, but when he tried a third time, he found water was pouring in so rapidly that he was forced back on the sloping deck. The *Essex* was literally falling over, and the boat crew had scarcely slid their lifeboat into the water, and jumped in themselves, when the *Essex* toppled. She lay there on her side, half-submerged.

Owen Chase's crew were in shock. They rowed clear, and gazed at the wreck of their destroyed vessel. None of them could believe what had happened. Nor could the crews of the other two boats who had abandoned their whale hunt, and now rowed up. The harpooner on Captain Pollard's whaleboat could only croak, 'Oh, my God, where is the ship?' The new arrivals rested on their oars, and there was a long, appalled silence as they examined the hulk before them. The *Essex* lay horizontal, her three masts acting as temporary floats, with the cross trees sticking up out of the water. All were stupefied. Captain Pollard finally summoned up a question: 'My God, Mr Chase, what is the matter?' And Chase gave a reply which was to become a classic of whale lore — 'We have been stove by a whale.'

Owen Chase's description of the destruction of the *Essex* was published the following year, 1821. It appeared under the expansive title, *Narrative of the Most Extraordinary and Distressing Shipwreck of the Whale-Ship Essex, of Nantucket; Which Was Attacked and Finally Destroyed by a Large Spermaceti-Whale in the Pacific Ocean*. One of Owen Chase's sons took a copy of the book with him when, at the age of about sixteen, he too went on a whaling trip to the Pacific. As luck would have it, he showed the volume to a young shipboard visitor during a 'gam'. This was the sociable custom when two whaleships, meeting by chance on the high seas, sailed in company so that captains and crews could exchange news and pay visits between the ships. On this occasion the ship-in-company was an American whaleship out of New Bedford, the *Acushnet*, and the 'gam' took place at the same latitude where the *Essex* had been lost some twenty years before. The young visitor who saw Owen Chase's little book was the future author of *Moby Dick*. 'The reading of this wondrous story upon the landless sea, & close to the very latitude of the shipwreck had a surprising effect upon me,' wrote Melville, and in due course he sent his fictitious *Pequod* to the bottom of the sea by a similar mechanism. He made changes for dramatic effect — notably, the *Pequod* goes down in an instant, sinking vertically so that her mast-heads still flying their flags are the last to disappear beneath the waves. But the main elements of the scene — the slow-moving ship, the dispersed whaleboats, the deliberate charge of the whale, the shocking finality of the wreck — were all foreshadowed when, on 20 November 1820, the battered *Essex* rolled on her side, more than a thousand miles from land.

Herman Melville was not yet twenty-two years old when he 'gammed' with Owen Chase's son. Later he told his London publisher, Richard Bentley, that he had spent 'two years and more' on whaleships, as a harpooner, and so knew a great deal about the whale fishery. This was a gross invention. Melville was in debt, and trying to wheedle a large advance out of the publisher for a book about whaling, and he was stretching the truth in the interests of self-promotion. In reality the author of *Moby Dick* had been working on whaleships for under two years, and only in a very lowly capacity — as a foremast hand. He never had the seagoing experience nor the whale-hunting skills to become one of the hand-picked harpooners, who were treated as petty officers aboard ship. He left the *Acushnet* prematurely, in the less than glamorous role of a deserter. His second berth, aboard the Sydney barque *Lucy Ann*, would have taught him even less about whaling. The *Lucy Ann* was an unlucky ship, no whales were seen, and Melville was merely a substitute crew member taken aboard to make up numbers. His brief voyage ended in Tahiti, when he and most of his colleagues were left ashore as malcontents and mutineers. His final whaling experience was aboard the *Charles and Henry* of Nantucket, seven months between Tahiti and Hawaii, with scarcely a whale taken. After that, Melville never went whaling again.

So where did Melville get his impressive knowledge of whales and whaling which brought us *Moby Dick*? His work is packed with information about the different species of whales, how they breed and migrate, how they respond to being hunted, how they behave individually and in groups. Did he quarry these details exclusively from books like the one Owen Chase wrote? Were the details accurate, who had provided them, and where had these informants got their data? Or had Melville met the real-life models — if there were some — for Captain Ahab and Queequeg the tattooed harpooner while he was on his travels? Maybe he had seen a fighting white sperm whale, or heard rumours of one, when he was a Pacific sailor, however briefly.

These questions fascinated me in the light of my own encounters with great whales. These experiences had usually been at close quarters and from a succession of boats which made Melville's *Acushnet* seem positively modern. For twenty-five years I had made my living by conducting practical experiments into the truths which lie behind the great legends of our culture, and turning my experience into books. Many of the legends had been connected with the sea. I had built and sailed a leather boat across the

North Atlantic to test whether Irish monks could have reached North America a thousand years before Columbus and given rise to the legendary exploits of St Brendan the Navigator. I had also sailed a replica of a ninth-century Arab ship from Muscat on the Arabian Gulf to China to investigate the stories of Sindbad the Sailor; and with a copy of a small Bronze Age galley my crew and I had rowed and sailed the Black Sea and the Mediterranean to look into the geographical realities of the wanderings of Jason and the Argonauts and the places where Ulysses had his escapades during his seaborne odyssey. More recently, with four companions, I had floated on a bamboo raft most of the way from China to North America, to test the theory that sailors from Asia could have crossed the North Pacific, landed on the shores of Central America, and left traces of their visit in the high culture of the Mayans and their forebears.

Every single one of these expeditions had met great whales, either in spirit or — more usually — in the flesh and at very close range. In the legend of St Brendan, for example, the Irish saint beaches his fragile oxhide-covered boat on the back of 'the great fish, Jasconius' — thinking it to be an island. The travellers light a fire, the heat wakes the whale, and the animal begins to move. The monks are terrified until St Brendan calms them with a reassurance that God has sent Jasconius as their ally and friend. So it turns out. Again and again during their wanderings, the

15

little leather boat with its dozen monks land on the back of the peaceable whale, a convenient place to celebrate mass. How this tale might have developed became clear to us fourteen centuries after St Brendan's lifetime. My three companions and I — including Trondur Patursson, a fisherman and artist from the Faeroe Islands — discovered that our thirty-six-foot leather boat, engineless and drifting, was a magnet for curious whales. They came swimming up from the ocean depths, gave a puff of breath, and eased alongside, sometimes only a yard away, to take a closer look. Perhaps the animals thought that our *Brendan* was another whale, a natural assumption given that our vessel was the same length and approximate shape as a middling-sized whale, and covered in thick skin stretched over an open framework which closely resembled a whale's ribcage. A skin boat and a whale might give off a similar sonar echo, attracting the attention of those marine mammals which use echo-location to examine their surroundings or find their companions.

This similarity between skin boat and whale produced one tense moment when a passing pod of killer whales or orcas detected our presence as *Brendan* lay becalmed some 150 miles south of Iceland. We watched the leader of the hunting group break away from the pod and turn towards us. The scimitar of his big dorsal fin cut majestically through the water as he casually swam in our direction to investigate. Three of us aboard

16

Brendan looked on, impressed by the animal's size and his almost swaggering, self-confident approach, but the fourth member of the crew, Trondur the traditional sailor, reacted very differently. He seized an oar and began to lash a sharp knife to the end of it so as to have a makeshift pike. The big orca slid under the boat, passing only a few inches below us, so only a layer of greased oxhide separated our feet from his black and white blotches. Then, with a relaxed puff of air from his lungs, he casually surfaced on the far side, swung back, and rejoined its companions. I had noted Trondur's fierce expression, and asked him why he had been ready to defend against the intruder. Trondur must have thought the rest of us utter landlubbers as he explained that Faeroese fishermen had seen orcas swim up to other whales, particularly if they were injured, elderly or sick, and literally rip them to pieces for food. Trondur had feared that might be our immediate fate.

I respected Trondur's judgement and I believed him. But I also knew that many marine biologists dismissed tales about orcas attacking great whales as being no more than fishermen's yarns. The scientists demanded clear proof of such dramatic events, and doubted that killer whales were sufficiently aggressive or powerful to tackle a fully grown great whale. Rightly, the scientists pointed out that such stories had been doing the rounds for at least 150 years, passed down from one credulous mariner to the next.

One story, often repeated by fishermen, was that the orcas worked together in concert to pull aside the whale's lips and feed on the living tongue. Several years after the *Brendan* Voyage, I came across a series of newly-taken photographs which showed an orca pod harrying a grey whale to its death off the coast of California, tearing mouthfuls of flesh from the stricken animal. The caption noted that the orcas feasted on their victim's tongue. The fishermen, it seemed, were ahead of the scientists in their knowledge of whale behaviour.

During the five months we were at sea in our little skin boat, we saw great whales everywhere: in such large numbers between the Faeroes and Iceland that their presence informed us of our approximate position, because the whale grounds had been used as a locator mark by sailors since Viking times. Off Greenland one morning we filmed a pair of very big sperm whales. Everything was in shades of grey — the overcast sky, the sullen sea, and the two animals, the colour of burnt charcoal, cruising slowly past us on the surface, their big square snouts pushing aside the water like enormous logs. Sixty feet or more in length, they were as big as any sperm whales seen in modern times. They must have been a pair of ageing bulls hunting at the farthest northern limit of their migratory range before rejoining the herds of cow whales in warmer waters. And off Newfoundland, just before *Brendan* made final landfall, we were treated to the unforgettable spectacle of dozens upon dozens of humpback whales, surfacing, spouting, diving and gambolling around us in the late evening light, as if in a triumphant dance of farewell. Delighted, we stood up on the thwarts of the little leather boat to watch the display, conscious that we had seen perhaps ten times as many whales as ships throughout our journey, and we accepted the presence of whales, rather than other vessels, as our most frequent diversions. In fact we were so accustomed to seeing whales that when we glimpsed a blue whale, a monster at least eighty feet long, off Greenland's Cape Farewell, I began to wonder whether we were merely lucky in our observations, or there was some other reason for the extraordinary variety of whales we were seeing. Blue whales are said to be very rare. Marine scientists believe that fewer than 10,000 still survive, and they are too widely scattered across the world's oceans ever to be counted. Fully grown, the blue whale — or sulphur-bottom, as the old whalemen called them — are among the largest animals ever to have lived on our planet. Heavier than the biggest dinosaurs, they are nearly as big as a jumbo jet.

Yet this was not the last blue whale I was to see on my slow-moving experimental voyages, while the other species of great whales bobbed up in the most unexpected places. For instance, the first sperm whale I ever saw, or rather heard, was in the Mediterranean, a polluted and enclosed sea known to be nearly fished out. The creature surfaced in the night, not ten yards astern of the little yacht on which I was sailing, alone at the helm, halfway across the channel between Corsica and Sardinia. The enormous whoosh of breath, expelled so close at hand, made me leap up from the cockpit bench in fright. I peered out into the pitch-black, wondering what on earth was happening. Consulting an old pilot book next morning I read that sperm whales were sometimes met around Corsica, feeding for squid in the deep submarine trenches near the island. And then, twenty years later on our Jason Voyage, sperm whales again appeared before me in the Mediterranean, and in an area where they were less likely to be found — the centre of the Aegean Sea. Here the waters were too shallow, according to marine biologists, for these deep-diving animals to be comfortable. Yet there they were, sperm whales, three of them, wallowing and puffing along, seemingly content.

I began to suspect the reason for the gap between scientific knowledge and traditional sailor lore when I was on the Sindbad Voyage. That journey, too, involved whales from the outset. Sindbad the Sailor, on his first of the seven — some say six — voyages, also lands on the back of a whale. As in the St Brendan story, Sindbad thinks he is on an island. The shore is covered with bushes and sand, and he and his companions go to find a stream to wash their clothes. When the island moves, Sindbad escapes in an emergency lifeboat made from a large wooden washtub. Whales of several species do swim in the Arabian Sea, and their presence has been noted through the centuries. Alexander the Great's admiral, Nearchus, when his fleet was off the coast of Baluchistan, ordered his deck crews to blow trumpets and beat drums as the ships steered their course past huge sea monsters, spouting so close that his terrified oarsmen were scarcely able to row. The early medieval Arab mariners, on whose real voyages the stories of Sindbad were based, also reported meeting whales, whose spouts rose up 'like a minaret. From afar one would think it was the sail of a ship.' And in modern times military pilots flying over the Gulf of Oman have looked down from their cockpits and seen the shapes of great whales casting shadows through the clear water and on to the pale sands below them.

So we too expected to see whales on our own Sindbad Voyage in 1980, and a marine biologist asked to join my crew for the first month. He anticipated that a slow-moving Arab sailing dhow would provide the ideal platform from which to spot whales in an area where they had been little studied. With admirable self-discipline, he arranged to be hoisted to the masthead in a bosun's chair every morning and evening when the sun was not too scorching. From that vantage point, sixty feet above the deck, his head wrapped in a scarf, he scanned the ocean surface with his binoculars, and made notes on a clipboard. He spotted whales, but not nearly as many as did two members of my crew far below him on the deck. Once again it was Trondur, joined this time by Mahommed Ismail, a traditional sailor from the Minicoy Islands off the coast of India. Again and again one or the other would call up to the masthead, and draw the lookout's attention to a whale he had not yet noticed. These alerts became a running joke with the rest of the crew, which the marine biologist took in good part. When the time came for him to leave the ship and return home, he confessed with a wry smile that the one thing he had really learned was not so much the number and type of whales to be found in the Arabian Sea, but that in future he would be more sceptical of the observations of marine biologists when compiling their statistics. He wondered what fraction they saw of the whales that swam by them.

Of course the traditional sailors and whale-hunters had been prone to exaggerate, and their notions could be as entertaining as they were false. A medieval Norwegian writer claimed that mischievous whales deliberately squirted jets of water into passing boats to swamp them, and well into the twentieth century it was believed that a whale's breath was toxic. To inhale a whale's spent air would lead to dizziness and fainting fits, possibly even death. And the fine spray of droplets thrown up in the spout would raise a rash if it fell on human skin. In truth, a whale's breath can smell truly foul, a giant case of halitosis which seems to reflect the animal's recent diet. But it is quite harmless. The early nineteenth-century whalemen were the most experienced group of whale-watchers who have ever lived, and yet they held that a sperm whale's right eye was bigger than the left. Given the choice, they tried to creep up on a whale from what they believed was the weaker side. They also claimed that when a big sperm whale was harpooned and dived deep, it would sometimes lie still, at the full stretch of the whale line, and they would hear mysterious creaking noises issuing from the deep ocean. They could not explain these noises, nor how it was that if they harpooned one whale in a group, the other whales seemed to be aware of the fact even if they were several miles away. This time their observations were, of course, correct. The whalemen simply had no notion that sperm whales were communicating their situation to one another by a vocabulary of clicks and creaking sounds.

Looming up through this confusing fog of whale lore and hearsay was the creature that fascinated me: Moby Dick himself, the great white whale. Scarcely a scientific study of sperm whales did not, sooner or later, mention Moby Dick. He is the whale which forms our popular image of his species, if not of all great whales. Chief protagonist in a classic of American literature, he is embedded in the awareness of millions of readers in the English-speaking world and, in translation, can be found on the book lists of schools and universities from Western Europe to Japan. Just as important for the myth-making, he has been portrayed on the screen again and again. He began silently as *The Sea Beast* in 1926 with John Barrymore as Captain Ahab, and achieved a benchmark presence in 1954 when director John Huston pitted him against Gregory Peck. Forty-four years later, the actor Patrick Stewart was playing the same role for television, in four episodes, and Moby Dick who had begun life for Hollywood as a papier mâché model was now a computer simulation most of the time or, when appropriate, a half-scale motorised creation, but only of his flapping tail. On harbour sides and seafronts around the world, Moby Dick's name has been appropriated by pubs and restaurants; souvenir shops sell him in wooden and plastic miniature, as well as carved and painted on to wooden sign-boards; manufacturers of marine clothing put his outline on their labels. He is modelled in bars of soap. In short, wherever there is a wish to create a romantic, tarred and creaking image of a bygone maritime age, Moby Dick may be invoked. His name has become so instantly recognisable that in March 1997 when a lone, lost sperm whale blundered by mistake into the Firth of Forth in Scotland and was trapped there, the press who followed all (ultimately unsuccessful) attempts to rescue him immediately dubbed him 'Moby' — a name shared by countless pet goldfish.

Yet when Moby Dick first surfaced, the story did not even carry his name. The novel was originally entitled *The Whale* and, rendered down to its bones, it is primarily a magnificent sea adventure. The narrator, Ishmael, is a young man from New York who decides to go on a whaling voyage. He travels to New Bedford, the main American whaling port, where he is befriended by an experienced harpooner, a spectacularly tattooed South Sea islander called Queequeg. The two of them sign aboard the Nantucket whaleship *Pequod*, which puts to sea on Christmas Day with a ragtag, international crew including two more ace harpooners — Daggoo, a huge African negro, and Tashtego, an American Indian. Some days after departure, the captain of the *Pequod* appears on deck, and Ishmael discovers that his vessel is in the hands of a dour, one-legged whalemaster who, rather than hunt for whales in general, is intent on seeking out and destroying Moby Dick, the rogue whale which took off his leg during a previous voyage and is the terror of the whaling fleet. The *Pequod* steers south through the Atlantic and round the Cape of Good Hope while Captain Ahab searches the oceans for his prey. On passage a few whales are taken, and it emerges that Ahab has smuggled aboard his private boat crew of Asiatics, 'Manila men', led by a sinister boatswain called Fedallah. Their task, once Moby Dick is located, is to row Ahab close enough to

25

dart a fatal harpoon into the white monster. *Pequod* sails on across the Indian Ocean and through the Indonesian archipelago where the lurking presence of the great white whale is detected, then out into the enormous expanse of the Pacific Ocean. Finally, in a vaguely defined area south of Japan, the *Pequod* and Moby Dick have their climactic encounter. For three days the struggle lasts. The reckless courage of the hunters is screwed to fever pitch by the demented Ahab who keeps pressing home the attack. Boats are smashed and sunk. First Fedallah is killed, then Ahab, whisked out of his whaleboat by a flying line which catches him around the neck. In a grand finale Moby Dick turns on the *Pequod* herself, slams into the ship and sends it to the bottom of the sea. Only Ishmael survives, clinging to the coffin prepared for his friend Queequeg who has had a premonition that he will die.

The book was a commercial flop on publication in 1851. In New York and London it got mixed reviews. 'An ill-compounded mixture of romance and matter-of-fact,' judged *The Athenaeum* magazine in London. 'Sad stuff, dull and dreary, or ridiculous,' announced *The Southern Quarterly Review* on the other side of the Atlantic. 'The Mad Captain . . . is a monstrous bore.' Other reviewers were more generous. 'Certainly one of the most remarkable of books which has appeared for many years past,' approved *Bentley's Miscellany*, and *John Bull* noted 'flashes of truth . . . sparkle on the foaming sea of thought'. The reviewers locked horns on almost everything — the quality of the writing, the management of the plot, the vocabulary, the characterisations, the book's intentions and pretensions. The features of the novel which seemed to attract universal approval were the whale details. All agreed that the book, its title soon changed to *Moby Dick*, was very good on whales and whaling. The *Atlas* magazine of London summed it up admirably. The book contained 'a mass of knowledge touching the whale — its habits and its history — the minutest details of its feeding and sporting, or swimming, strangely mixed with ingenious and daring speculations on the mysterious habits and peculiarities of the great brute — the whole written in a tone of exaltation and poetic sentiment which has a strange effect upon the reader's mind, . . . at last, making him look upon the whale as a sort of awful and unsoluble mystery — the most strange and the most terrible of the wonders of the deep'.

It was this 'wonder of the deep' — Moby Dick himself — that I wanted to investigate, to find out how much truth there was to his story. I realised that I would have to track him down through both time and space because, after surfacing briefly at the time of publication, the legendary Moby Dick had behaved very like a real whale. He seemed to take a deep breath, and then dive, almost disappearing from general consciousness, and staying down a long, long time. For nearly seventy years few people read the Moby Dick story. It did not help that a substantial stock of unsold copies was destroyed in the warehouse of the American publisher, Harper Brothers, when the building burned down. By the turn of the century the story was so forgotten that Rudyard Kipling, normally so well informed on adventure literature, had not read the book. It took a literary revival built around the centennial of the birth of the man who created him — Herman Melville — to coax Moby Dick back into public view. This made Moby Dick a very rare phenomenon, almost unique in my field of interest: Moby Dick was not a tale that dated back to antiquity or the Dark Ages, it was genuine *modern* myth of the sea. And this provided me with the place to start my quest: I would begin with the man whose imagination had breathed life into Moby Dick, try to see the whale through his eyes, then cross-check my findings with men who still hunted the great sea creatures. If I was lucky and the trail led far enough, I might learn whether there ever could have been a great white sperm whale which attacked ships at sea. What I hoped against hope was that perhaps such a 'wonder of the deep' still existed. I had little idea quite how far my quest would lead me — not just across oceans but down through the consciousness of Melville and into layers of little-known lore about whales and the world's largest fish held by some of the most remarkable and courageous fishermen with whom I have ever sailed.

I decided that the place to begin looking for clues to Melville's genuine experiences — and test them — was the same Pacific island where he had begun his Pacific adventure. And that, in a curious way, also led back to the unfortunate crew of the wrecked *Essex*.

Part One

NUKU HIVA

'The Marquesas! What strange visions of out-
landish things does the very name spirit up!'

HERMAN MELVILLE, *Typee*

The Essex *was not* going to founder immediately. That soon became clear to the men of the three whaleboats. They had time to salvage more supplies. Rowing back to the hulk, they used their hatchets to chop away the rigging. Relieved of the weight of her masts, the *Essex* rolled about two-thirds the right way up again. The vessel was still a derelict, but now the crew could clamber back on her, hack through her deck, and get at her stores. By mid-afternoon they had succeeded in retrieving six hundred pounds of unspoiled ship's biscuit and as much fresh water as they dared carry in their light whaleboats. This was about sixty-five gallons for each boat. They also took a musket, a small canister of gunpowder, and some boat nails, a couple of files, and two rasps, in case they needed to make emergency repairs. They also retrieved the whaleman's traditional standby larder — several live turtles which had been kept captive on the *Essex* to provide fresh meat. When the wind began to strengthen at the onset of darkness, the three boats hung off the lee of the wreck, strung out one behind the other on a long rope, like beads on a string.

During that dismal night Owen Chase had a chance to reflect on the circumstances of the sperm whale collision, and he concluded that the ramming was entirely deliberate. The sperm whale had come at them from the pod that was being hunted; the animal had the appearance of being extremely angry and resentful; and Owen Chase went so far as to surmise that the angle of the head-on charge had been calculated so that the combined collision speeds of the ship and whale had the maximum effect. As for shattering the ship's timbers, Chase had never heard of a whale head-butting a ship before, but he had no doubt that the effect of the blow would be devastating. 'The structure and strength of the whale's head is admirably designed for this mode of attack,' he observed, 'the most prominent part of which is as hard and as tough as iron; indeed I can compare it to nothing else but the inside of a horse's hoof.'

At daybreak Captain Pollard was faced with making an excruciatingly difficult decision. It was clear that the three boats could not stay with the *Essex*. Sooner or later she would founder. The overloaded whaleboats had to try to make land, but which land? The *Essex* had been hit in one of the emptier stretches of ocean on the planet. The nearest known land lay 1,400 miles to the south-west, the remote Marquesas Islands. In the opposite direction the coast of

34

South America was well over 2,000 miles away. Astonishingly, Captain Pollard chose the longer journey. He had his reasons: the shipwrecked mariners' best chance, though it was a slim one, was that they would be spotted by another vessel, probably a cruising whaleship which, as a matter of good business, always kept a sharp lookout. There was also the possibility of chancing upon an unknown island. The Pacific was still poorly charted, and new islands were occasionally being put on the map. In addition, the prevailing wind was in favour of the South American option. But there was also a strong negative reason: the islands of the Marquesas had a bloodcurdling reputation. Among sailors it was said that the islands were inhabited by merciless cannibals. The crew of the *Essex* feared that if they ever reached the Marquesas alive and stepped ashore, they would be taken prisoner and eaten. In view of what subsequently happened, this was among the supreme ironies of maritime history.

The voyage of the three whaleboats was a nightmare. There were twenty men in total, spread as evenly as possible, seven men each in two boats, and six in the one commanded by Owen Chase, which was the oldest. It says much for the first-class seamanship of the whalemen, and the legendary sea kindliness of their whaleboats, that for thirty-one days the three boats stayed together in company and afloat, surviving a bad gale which forced them to run before the wind and heavy seas. Their constant worry, of course, was the dwindling supply of food and water. The officers had calculated that it would take sixty days to reach the mainland, so each man was allowed one ship's biscuit and half a pint of water each day. To eke out these rations the men scraped off and ate the barnacles that began growing on the hulls. They killed the captive turtles, ate the meat and drank the reptiles' blood. Several men tried drinking their own urine. On the thirty-first day they were overjoyed to see a pimple of land on the horizon, a tiny island which they took to be Ducie Island. It was not. It was actually an uninhabited and uncharted spot of land, later to be named Henderson Island, and too barren to sustain anything more than minimal life. They came ashore and stayed for a week, until they had eaten every shellfish, gull egg and wild bird they could catch. The only fresh water came from a tiny spring on the strand which was uncovered at low tide. On this desolate place they spent a wretched Christmas Day, and two days later, leaving behind three men, the maximum number the island's resources could provide for, the three boats set out again, now heading for remote Easter Island.

Amazingly, the three increasingly leaky boats still managed to keep together until, on the fifty-third day of their ordeal, a gale separated them. By that time one man on Owen Chase's boat had died and been buried at sea. A second man succumbed to exposure soon afterwards, and his corpse was also put overboard. But when crewman Isaac Cole went into convulsions and died at four o'clock on the afternoon of the eighty-first day, the three survivors decided to eat what little flesh remained on the corpse. By then they had only three days' supply of ship's biscuit left. With primitive butchery they cut off the arms and legs so they could more easily separate the meat from these limbs. They opened the scrawny body and removed the heart. Then they sewed up the torso, and dropped it and the limb bones into the water. That day they ate the human heart first, and a little flesh. The rest of Isaac Cole's remains they cut into strips, and hung in the rigging to dry. But the meat quickly turned green. So they roasted it. Ten days later, Owen Chase and his two shipmates, barely alive, were picked up by a passing brig, the *Indian* of London.

The fate of *Essex*'s other two whaleboats was even worse. One boat and her crew were never seen again. The remaining boat, under Captain Pollard, now with six men aboard, shared the same agonies of increasing hunger and thirst as Owen Chase's crew, with one difference: they resorted to murder as well as cannibalism. Two men died of exposure and malnutrition, and were eaten immediately. Then the four survivors drew lots to see whose flesh would feed the others. The cabin boy, Owen Coffin, drew the short straw. He was Captain Pollard's nephew.

Another crew member volunteered to take his place. But Coffin insisted on being sacrificed. He was shot with the musket, and the meat from his body kept the others alive for ten days. Then one of them died, without the need for murder, and he too was eaten. It was on the ninety-sixth day after the loss of the *Essex* that the two survivors, Captain Pollard and Charles Ramsdell, who had actually pulled the trigger of the musket that killed Coffin, were picked up by another Nantucket whaleship, *Dauphin*. Her captain was Zimri Coffin and, such was the close-knit world of Nantucket whaling, Pollard and Ramsdell had eaten his kinsman, the cabin boy.

It was little wonder that Owen Chase's book, which so affected Melville, caused a sensation. Quite apart from the cannibalism, it was a tale of small-boat voyaging of epic proportions. Both Owen Chase and Captain Pollard had kept their whaleboats afloat for more than 4,500 miles and survived for a quarter of a year. But it was the gruesome business of cannibalism which really caught the public attention. There were shudders at the awful fate of the men who died naturally and were eaten; revulsion at the murder and consumption of the poor cabin boy.[*]

[*] Oddly enough, the revulsion did no harm to the careers of the survivors. The three men left on Henderson Island were picked up by a ship specially sent to collect them and — remarkably — all eight survivors not only went back to whaling, but all of them became captains of whaleships.

The irony of it all was that if Captain Pollard had decided to make for the 'cannibal Marquesas', instead of heading for South America, probably none of this man-eating would have happened. Anthropologists working on the Marquesas a century later failed to find incontrovertible evidence that the dreaded Marquesans were the anthropophagous devils which their popular reputation once suggested. The dead bodies of warriors killed in their incessant inter-tribal wars were sometimes eaten in order that their *mana* or spirit transferred to the victors, but chance castaways were not regarded as a source of *mana,* and if there was cannibalism, it was not on a massive scale. Generally, the idea of the ravening 'cannibal Marquesans' was an overwrought myth. It was a myth which was still believed long after it had deceived the luckless sailors of the *Essex*, and the man who was most responsible for perpetuating that man-eating myth was Herman Melville. At the height of his writing career he was known, not for *Moby Dick*, but as 'the man who had lived among cannibals'.

So two Melville myths — the white whale and the cannibals — took me to Nuku Hiva, chief island of the Marquesas. It was late September, and the flight from Tahiti, the only air link, had emphasised the remoteness of the archipelago. For three and a half hours the aircraft droned north-east over a seascape entirely devoid of shipping, a empty expanse of intense blue broken only once by a cluster of pale circles and crescents. They were the coral atolls of the Tuamotos, frail excrescences like the lime-casts left by sea worms on the surface of pilings and hulks. From the air you could pick out the dark shadow where a navigable channel broke the circle of a reef, and provided access to the shelter of the aquamarine lagoon. There might be a dozen or so huts dotted along a sandy beach beside a line of palms. But these were fragile homes, never more than twelve feet above sea level and at the mercy of hurricanes and tidal waves.

The Marquesas were different. They rise boldly from the ocean floor, massive volcanic blocks without fringing reefs, their mountain peaks often shrouded in low cloud, dark, steep slopes slashed with ravines and clad with dense green vegetation. There are fifteen islands in all, though only six of them are inhabited, and they break the vast Pacific horizon a thousand miles from any place that might reasonably be called a neighbour. Living in such isolation the native peoples had called their archipelago 'The Land of Men', scarcely acknowledging the existence of other humans elsewhere. They came there centuries earlier as seaborne immigrants, arriving via the stepping stones of Melanesia, Tonga and Samoa. It was from the remote Marquesas, too, that the great Polynesian re-emigration had taken place, when the Marquesas had been the dispersal point for the huge double canoes that had carried Polynesian populations as far as the 'Land of the Long White Cloud', New Zealand. But that outreach seemed to have faded in the Marquesan memory by the time Melville and the other whalemen set foot ashore. Then, the islands were isolated, introspective, and — to the newcomers — alarmingly barbaric.

A French tricolour was hoisted on the flagstaff by the airstrip when I arrived. A landing area had been levelled from rugged volcanic terrain at the north-west corner of Nuku Hiva. It was near the cliffs and exposed to the trade wind, so the flag of France rippled to a brisk breeze. After first discovery by the Polynesian navigators, the Marquesas had been re-named and then ignored by the Spanish, visited by Captain Cook and eyed covetously by the United States and England. A French expeditionary force had not yet finished claiming the archipelago for the Paris government when Melville arrived. And the Marquesas are still, very obviously, a French Overseas Territory. Four young bronzed French gendarmes looked as if they were on summer duty on the Côte d'Azur. Wearing short haircuts, short sleeves and kepis, they cursorily checked the documents of the dozen returning islanders and half a dozen tourists. Everyone was speaking French. I heard not a word of Marquesan. The half-dozen vehicles parked at the small airport building were all made in France and, apart from the police vehicle, rather decrepit. It was clear that as soon as the plane had discharged its passengers, taken on its new manifest, and flown away, everyone on the ground would climb into their vehicles and depart. The airport would be abandoned until the next flight arrived in three days' time. I took the only taxi available, a rusty pick-up truck with tyres lacking much tread. The French tourists had a hotel driver waiting for them, so I was the sole passenger.

The road across the island was abominable. Badly rutted and tortuous, it climbed across the eroded hillsides of Terre desert, the Empty Land, unfit for human occupation. Small plantations of pine trees had been draped across the contours in an attempt to prevent the barren soil from being gouged into even deeper gullies and ravines. The pick-up truck jolted along at no more than fifteen miles an hour, partly because the road was so rough, but also because it was obvious that no one recently arriving on Nuku Hiva needed to be in a hurry. If you had an appointment, the person you were looking for would not be going away, and frankly there was not very much for any visitor to do, nor many surprises to be had. Nuku Hiva was effectively the capital of the Marquesas, but it was still a backwater. It was best to slow down and enjoy the view.

The taxi brought me on to the high central plateau of the island, more empty land, unexpectedly alpine with its pastures and rambling wire fences carried on wooden fence posts, dark brown cattle, and occasional patches of woodland. Again there were no houses, and the horizon was rimmed by dark, forbidding mountain walls, so it was clear that we were crossing the broad crater of an extinct volcano. At the far edge, I was suddenly on the caldera's rim and looking down a mountainside which fell away precipitously to a magnificent bay, far below. Here the sea had invaded a second volcanic crater, a mile wide, taking a massive bite from the edge of the island. The encircling headlands end in two sentinel rocks and on the horizon, framed in the gap, is the outline of a smaller, neighbouring island, Ua Pou. From that height it was obvious that Taiohae Bay makes a superb anchorage, and half a dozen small yachts were at anchor in its shelter to prove it. Three out of every four people on Nuku Hiva live on the inner edge of the bay, and Taiohae town curls around the shoreline in a display of colonial civic planning. Reading from the left, there was the supply jetty and fuel dump, next to them the hospital and the police barracks. In the centre another flag pole marked where the tricolour was hoisted in front of the municipal offices and bank. Then came an irregular ribbon of shops and guesthouses fronting the beach, until the settlement eventually petered out in a cluster of villas and the neatly regimented bungalows of a small tourist development.

Melville had described that same beach in

1842. Then a native village of palm-thatched huts stood on the same spot, and was already the largest settlement on the island. His best-selling book *Typee* is the romantic tale of how he arrives in Taiohae Bay as a wide-eyed and restless sailor aboard an American whaleship. A swarm of dusky South Sea maidens swim out to the approaching vessel, and offer fresh coconuts and themselves to the sailors. Melville decides to jump ship and run away, to explore the delights of island life. He is joined in his escapade by a young deckhand, Toby. Picking the right moment, Melville and Toby slip away from a shore party, and dash off into the woods behind the beach. They must put as much distance as possible between themselves and any pursuit, so there is a punishing journey as the two runaways struggle up into the rugged mountains. They climb precipices, slide down cliffs, huddle in bushes, negotiate ravines, and barely survive the long ordeal. They are heading for a valley of a friendly tribe called the Happars, and they dread that they will stumble into the valley of the Typees, a bloodthirsty tribe who will kill and eat them. The story purports to be a truthful account of what happened to Melville while he was on Nuku Hiva, and he claims that nearly a week is spent on this gruelling escape, until the two hungry and footsore runaways come to human habitation.

To their horror, they discover that they have blundered into the territory of the dreaded

Typees. But instead of being eaten, they are treated with great hospitality. The tribal chief greets them courteously, and they are given food and shelter and shown around the village. Melville, who is lamed by a bad leg, is carried piggyback by a faithful servitor. After a couple of weeks, Toby leaves the valley to go back down to the coast, promising he will find help and send someone to fetch Melville. Left on his own, Melville's idyll becomes even more agreeable. He wins the affectionate attention of Fayaway, a beautiful Typee maiden; they go boating on a small lake; he is honoured by the tribe. For chapter after chapter Melville describes the customs of the natives, their physical beauty, their dress, their diet, their taboos, rituals and festivals, how they build their houses and how they practise the art of tattoo. In short, he puts himself forward as an eyewitness authority on their culture. Then Melville detects sinister overtones. He is banned from a tribal gathering, he finds human bones, and he realises that his kindly hosts are really cannibals. Aghast and determined to escape, he contrives to get down to the coast, and scrambles aboard a ship's longboat that is conveniently at hand, searching for castaways. But the Typee warriors have chased him. They swim out, try to pull him bodily from the longboat. Melville turns and strikes the leading warrior with a boat hook, hitting him in the throat. The man sinks, and when he rises again Melville relates how 'never shall I forget the ferocious expression of his countenance'.

I knew it would be fruitless to check Melville's personal account of the Typees against the native way of life on Nuku Hiva today. When Melville arrived, the peoples of the archipelago were already being overwhelmed by the culture shock which the Australian writer Alan Moorehead called 'The Fatal Impact'. In the 1840s the native population of the Marquesas was approximately 20,000. Eighty years later it had plummeted to just over 2,000. The culprits were the usual ones — disease introduced by foreigners, starvation, emigration, demoralisation, loss of hope. After the 1930s the population began to rebuild slowly, partly as a result of improved medical facilities and partly due to the influx of a handful of European settlers. But Marquesan culture in terms of music, dance, art and social customs was virtually extinct. Today there is a brave movement to try to revive Marquesan culture, but many of the old ways exist only as hazy memory. It is difficult to know what to rebuild. Paradoxically, the main sources available to the enthusiasts wanting to find out what that old culture was like are the travelogues and descriptions written by the early foreign visitors, the vanguard of the destruction.

The sole remnant of Melville's world I expected to find was the geography of Nuku Hiva. The contorted surface of the island had played a crucial role in the adventures he claimed to have had there. He wrote long

46

descriptions of valleys and cliffs, the anchorage and the landing place, the glens and waterfalls. If I could compare these word pictures with the reality of the landscape, then I might begin to understand how Melville's mind transmuted facts into prose, and by what process he could have dreamed up — or known — Moby Dick. And there was always a slim chance that, somewhere on Nuku Hiva, I would pick up the trail of the white whale.

The taxi began the winding descent to the settlement. Now at least the road was metalled, and halfway down, beside three apparently loose horses grazing on the roadside shrubs, we stopped to replace a flat tyre that had succumbed to the early rough going. As we were changing the bald tyre for one which was even more slick, a cyclist laboured uphill towards us. He was the first human we had seen in two hours. A fit middle-aged man on a mountain bike, he waved cheerfully, called a greeting, and standing on the pedals swayed his way around the next corner and was gone. 'The Mayor,' grunted the taxi driver, 'his horses.' On Nuku Hiva everyone knew everyone else.

The first item Melville noted when the *Acushnet* dropped anchor in Taiohae Bay had also been the tricolour of France. It 'trailed over the stern of six vessels, whose black hulls, and bristling broadsides proclaimed their warlike character'. They were the ships of the French flotilla which, in July 1842, were anchored in the bay to impress the local chieftains with the prestige and power of Louis Philippe, the 'citizen king' whose government was adding their islands to his colonial domain.

And immediately Melville stumbles.

He says he arrived on the island fifteen months after he had set sail from New Bedford, and claims he spent the next four months on Nuku Hiva living with cannibal natives. The dates do not match the known movements of his ship, nor the sworn deposition of her captain giving the date when Herman Melville deserted. The records show that the *Acushnet* left New Bedford on 3 January 1841. She cruised south through the Atlantic and around Cape Horn, and after calling at the coast of Peru, made her way via the Galapagos islands (presumably taking on a few of the famous tortoises which, like their cousins the sea turtles, were regarded as a source of food) to make a leisurely sweep across the Pacific, looking for whales. When his ship began to run out of supplies, Captain Valentine Pease diverted to the Marquesas. If the French fleet was in the bay when he arrived, then this was seventeen, not fifteen months after the *Acushnet* left New Bedford. The two-month gap is significant because we also know the approximate date when Melville left Nuku Hiva. The *Lucy Ann*, the ship which picked him up, departed Nuku Hiva at about the end of the first week in August. In other words Melville could not possibly have spent four months on the island, as he claims. At the most he could have been on Nuku Hiva for eight weeks, and the most likely length of time of his stay was, almost exactly, four weeks.

Like his boast to his publishers that he had spent 'two years and more' as a harpooner on whaleships, Melville's concept of time was elastic when it suited him. The title of the London edition of his book, *Narrative of a Four Months Residence Among the Natives of a Valley of the Marquesan Islands*, was a deception.

So, too, was Melville's notion of distance. I spent the next few days staying at a guesthouse in Taiohae and exploring the terrain which Melville described so vividly during his flight into the hills. The start of his escape reads accurately enough. Sneaking out of the back of a canoe shed where the *Acushnet*'s liberty party were taking shelter from a rainstorm, Toby and Melville hurry between the native huts and plunge into the groves of trees at the back of the village. They are heading for the ridge which overlooks the settlement. Halfway up the slope their progress is halted by a patch of dense reeds. Using their sailors' knives they reap a way through, and emerge on the ridge where their silhouettes are spotted from the village by the natives who raise the hue and cry. Toby and Melville scramble onward with all speed. They are determined to reach the highest point of the land, the lip of the caldera overlooking the bay. Three hours later, they are standing there, at the top of an 'immense overhanging cliff composed of basaltic rocks, hung round with parasitical plants' . . . 'The scenery was magnificent,' records Melville. 'The lonely bay of Nukuheva, dotted here and there with the black hulls of the vessels composing the French squadron, lay reposing at the base of a circular range of elevations, whose verdant sides, perforated with deep glens or diversified with smiling valleys, formed altogether the loveliest view I ever beheld.'

His description fits perfectly the view from the caldera's lip. There is even a craggy precipice which resembles Melville's vantage point. It is so sheer that Taiohae's hang-gliding club use it for their launches.

The falsification begins when Melville goes on to describe his adventurous flight across the mountains. There was, he said, a five-day ordeal before he and Toby arrived in the distant valley of the cannibal Typees, and the journey reduced them to extreme exhaustion. The actual topography of Nuku Hiva makes his description and the accompanying ordeal difficult to believe. The valley of the Typees is now called Taipivai, and a well-defined track crosses the saddle of the ridge which separates Taiohae from Taipivai. The route follows the topography, and even to a stranger's eye the natural line is obvious. And should you miss the path, the contours of the land soon bring you back to it. If you insist on staying in the underbrush, which Toby and Melville might have done to avoid detection, it is still

50

not particularly difficult to find a way through to Taipivai by going straight across country. Still more dubious is Melville's claim that it took five days to travel from Taiohae to Taipivai. The allegedly awful home of the cannibals is, in fact, five miles away as the crow flies, and perhaps three times that distance through the bush. But Melville deliberately gives the impression that he lived among the Typees in a place far removed from any chance of rescue. In truth he was no more than five or six hours' walk from the beach where the French had built a temporary fort,[*] and Captain Pease of the *Acushnet* peaceably traded for fruit and vegetables.

I went across to Taipivai to try to fit Melville's description with what the valley had to offer. It was a charming place, steep-sided, narrow, and with a small, clean river rushing down the valley floor. There was a hamlet where the road from Taiohae crossed the river on a small modern bridge. Downstream the high tide could bring small supply boats to within half a mile of the houses. Here were small villas, and their vanilla gardens filled the air with their scent. Upstream

[*] The chief at Taiohae particularly liked a horse the French had brought with them, and an officer exercised on the beach. The chief had never seen a horse before, and asked if he might try a ride. He charged along with such gusto that the French were considerably impressed. It was the start of a trend: modern Marquesans are excellent horsemen, often riding bareback.

the sides of the valley were clothed in mature forest, and the little river ran so quickly over rocky shallows that there was no chance of finding a lake where Melville said he had gone swimming and boating with the lovely Fayaway. There were more farmhouses, some coconut groves, and a small sawmill. The entire valley was on a small, intimate scale, and the only feature still remaining which must have given Melville material for *Typee* was the impressive stonework of a *pae pae*, a megalithic habitation site. Two rectangular stone platforms or *meaes* had been built on a small knoll halfway up the valley's slope. They were guarded by *tikis*, statues of the old gods carved from dark red volcanic stone. The *tikis* had short thick torsos, short arms and legs, and great heavy round heads with bald pates. A few were female, but most were male, and one or two had the heads of serpents. All their worn faces had a blank, forbidding look. It was said that a curse fell on anyone who removed a *tiki* from its present position, and the curse was only lifted after the *tiki* had been returned. A square pit dug into the higher of the two *meaes* was said, ghoulishly, to be a receptacle for the victims' bones after a cannibal feast.

Lucien Kemitite, the mayor on the mountain bike, was sceptical about the cannibal feast. Mayor Kemitite was a driving force within the movement to restore the use of the Marquesan language and culture to the islands, and he had a lively knowledge of Marquesan oral history.

When I enquired about the square pit, he said it was more likely a simple foodstore, but he did provide an example of the curse of the *tikis*. A French tourist had stolen one of the smaller statues and taken it to Paris. As soon as he got back home the thief had fallen very ill, and the doctors could find nothing wrong. Eventually he consulted a clairvoyant who told him that the cause of the trouble was some item he had brought from a foreign land. So he packed up the stone statue and posted it back to the mayor, who replaced it at the *pae pae,* and the distant patient in Paris recovered his health.

I asked the mayor what role in Marquesan culture had been played by great whales, particularly sperm whales. He replied that the Marquesans made no distinction between whales and dolphins, and told me the legend of the brother and sister who once ruled the people of Hatiheu on the north coast of Nuku Hiva. One day the two quarrelled so bitterly that the sister decided to leave the island for ever. Summoning her followers, she left with a flotilla of canoes, but her brother went after her, and begged her to come back. She refused to have anything more to do with him and carried on out to sea, and the brother's canoes began to pursue her. During the chase, every one of the sister's boats capsized, and all the people in them turned into a great school of whales, or dolphins.

This disaster may have been folk memory of a failed emigration attempt following an inter-tribal war, but it did not mean that dolphins thereafter became taboo. If a school of dolphin were seen close off the island of Ua Pou, the people would paddle out in their small canoes and drive the animals inshore by knocking stones together underwater to frighten them. Once they had steered the dolphins into a bay, the tempo and volume of the clattering would increase until the panicked dolphin stranded in the shallows. There the animals could be taken by hand and killed for their meat. Not all the school would be caught. The islanders only took enough dolphin to feed themselves, and let the rest swim free. These dolphin drives, the mayor assured me, were a thing of the past. They had been abandoned twenty or thirty years ago when Ua Pou got electricity and refrigeration was possible, and supply ships began bringing a regular supply of chilled foods so that dolphin meat was no longer needed.

As for a white whale, the mayor did not believe that any such animal existed in Marquesan tradition, nor in fact. Near the islands it was very rare to see any sperm whales at all. Which explained why a large sperm whale's tooth was one of the most precious objects known in the Marquesan tradition. A good-sized tooth was so valuable that an early visitor, a sandalwood trader, successfully negotiated one of the most profitable deals in Polynesian history. For a payment of ten large whale's teeth the local chief agreed that his people would fill the visiting ship with sandalwood, cutting the trees, bringing them down the mountain, floating them out, and loading them. It is said that the fortunate trader sailed off to China where he sold the entire cargo for a million dollars in the currency of the day. Even in Melville's time, when the visiting whaleships had flooded the market with whale's teeth and the value had tumbled, the sperm whale's tooth was still held in high regard. In *Typee* Melville describes how Karluna, a Typee beauty, owns a whale's tooth which is 'the most precious of the damsel's ornaments. In her estimation its price is far above rubies.' Mehevi, the chief nobleman of the Typees, dressed in his finery, wears in his ears two 'small and finely shaped sperm whale teeth'. They have freshly plucked leaves stuffed into one end, and are 'curiously wrought at the other end into strange little images and devices', so they resembled 'a pair of cornucopias'.

Other travellers remarked that the Marquesans liked to carve sea shells so they resembled the tooth of the sperm whale. And modern anthropologists surmise that the shamans, the *tuhunga,* used a single large whale-tooth pendant as a ritual focus to concentrate their powers.

These precious whale teeth must have come either from trade with distant islands or by chance, from the carcasses of dead whales washed up on the shore. Harpoon heads recovered from the archaeological sites are far too small for hunting anything more than fish. So it seemed that I was also out of luck on Nuku Hiva if I was looking to find a prototype for Queequeg, the superbly tattooed harpooner in *Moby Dick*. Only Queequeg's chequerboard face, 'a dark, purplish, yellow colour, here and there stuck over with large blackish looking squares', linked with Melville's direct experience, because Melville writes half a chapter in *Typee* about Marquesan tattooing, most of the information very accurate.

But here again, there was a note of caution. With much dramatic detail, Melville describes how the natives of Taipivai were very keen to tattoo their sailor visitor. They point out that his white skin would make such a perfect canvas for their art. Mehevi also wants him to be tattooed, and suggests suitable patterns. The tattooer-in-chief pursues Melville about the village waving his instruments, the sharp-toothed combs and tapping mallet. Yet somehow Melville avoids the operation — and he does not explicitly state how. It is another example of Melville building up suitably colourful ordeals while 'living among the cannibals', but then sidling away from any clear explanation of how he emerged intact. Certainly Melville had no tattoos to display when he returned to New England and told an intrigued audience about his 'four months' on the Marquesas, though tattoos were already common enough among Western sailors of his day.

So once again, the question arose: where did

Melville get his information if it was not from his brief personal experience? I found most of the answers in the council room next to Mayor Kemitite's office. The enthusiasts for a Marquesan cultural revival were compiling their own collection of literature about their islands. Three glass-fronted cases held an embryonic Marquesan library. There were articles from popular magazines, off-prints from heavyweight archaeological journals, studies on tattooing, travellers' tales both contemporary and reprints, missionary accounts, even South Pacific cookbooks. If the original book had not been available, there were photocopies ordered from the national libraries of France, Australia and the United Kingdom. Browsing through this wonderful hodge-podge of material, I located the origins of much of *Typee*, and some of *Moby Dick*, too. Here were many of the sources that Melville had raided to embellish his own, rather thin, experiences. He admitted a debt to the Reverend William Ellis, a missionary who lived for nearly eight years in Tahiti and Hawaii and wrote about Polynesian ethnography. Melville also made several nods in the direction of Captain David Porter, who published a journal of a belligerent three-year cruise in the Pacific in command of a United States frigate. This cruise included invading the valley of Taipivai at the head of an armed column, and when repulsed, burning down as many of the native houses as would catch fire. And Melville helped himself liberally from the memoirs of Reverend Charles Stewart of the USS *Vincennes**, who paid a less bellicose visit to Nuku Hiva in 1829. Stewart's description of the countryside behind Taiohae Bay reappeared, with very slight modifications, in Melville's *Typee*. And if Melville wanted to remind himself of how dramatic his 'king Mehevi' looked when dressed up in loincloth, cockerel-feathered headdress and tattoos, there was a remarkably similar island chieftain, posing for the frontispiece of the chaplain's book.

And then I chanced upon a strange coincidence. Melville's uncle was a sea captain by the name of John DeWolf who had achieved some fame by crossing the entire width of Siberia, from Okhotsk in the east to the Russian capital at St Petersburg, much of the way by dog-sled. The huge transcontinental journey had been made in the company of an explorer-scientist, a naturalist named Von Langsdorff. The latter had earlier visited the Marquesas as a member of a Russian exploring expedition, and during the marathon trans-Siberian journey he undoubtedly talked about his experiences in the South Seas. Melville was deeply influenced by his glamorous uncle, and indeed DeWolf's second-hand yarns may have inspired Melville's wanderlust. When he came to write *Typee*, Melville quarried information from Von Langsdorff's

---

* On board was a midshipman, Thomas Melville, Herman's cousin.

description of the island and its people, and he cites Von Langsdorff in *Moby Dick* as well. But lurking in the background was someone even more interesting. In the Nuku Hiva library I came across the story of a man who may have been in some ways the model, not for Queequeg, but perhaps for the role in which Melville cast himself, as 'the man who lived among cannibals'. On that colossal trans-Siberian journey DeWolf and Von Langsdorff had been accompanied by a French sailor named Cabri who had lived among the Marquesans for nine years. Cabri was a survivor from the wreck of an English trading vessel. He had been accepted among the Marquesans without being eaten, spoke the language fluently, had a Marquesan wife, and integrated spectacularly. One account said he had two Marquesan children, another credited him with six. In fact Cabri was such an expert on Marquesan culture that he was virtually kidnapped from the island by the Russian expedition to use as a living encyclopaedia.[*] When DeWolf met him, Cabri was being transported to the imperial court at St Petersburg, partly for the savants to interview him, but also

[*] There was another survivor from the same wreck, an Englishman called Robarts or Roberts, who made a living as ship's pilot guiding foreign vessels into Taiohae Bay. He and Cabri did not get on, competing for the favour of the native chiefs, and there is a suspicion that Robarts was an accomplice in arranging Cabri's forced removal from the island.

for the courtiers to stare at him. To European eyes, the Frenchman was a freak, so heavily tattooed from head to foot, including his face, that he later forged a career in France as a living picture show. He appeared in a small theatre, and spectators paid to see the stained work on his skin, and watch him stamp out Marquesan dance steps. Eventually Cabri's rarity value faded, like his tattoos, and he was reduced to travelling around France as little more than a fairground attraction. When he died of pneumonia, his corpse was buried in a secret grave to prevent souvenir hunters from digging him up for his skin.

I thought of Cabri as I watched the young men of Taiohae riding their surfboards on the breakers that rolled on to the back of the beach. They swam like seals, just as Cabri had learned to do during his years on the Marquesas. Then it was a skill little practised by Europeans, and seldom by sailors. So in Russia he had been given a job previously unknown — swimming instructor. He was appointed swimming instructor to the marine corps cadets in Kronshtadt. Melville had noted how well the Pacific islanders could swim, and whaling logbooks record several instances when, in an emergency, a Polynesian crew member dives overboard to rescue floundering whalemen. It is a theme that Melville develops when he makes Queequeg the hero of a rescue off New Bedford harbour. A young man who has been mocking the tattooed savage is knocked overboard by the swinging boom. In a flash Queequeg strips off his clothes, makes a running dive into the sea, locates the drowning man, and pulls him back to safety.

Nuku Hiva is still proud of Melville's visit. Though he did not stay long, and often misrepresented what he saw, Melville is included in the pantheon of artistic geniuses who had made the outside world aware of the islands: Robert Louis Stevenson as writer, Paul Gauguin as artist and Jacques Brel as musician. So there is a monument to the deserter from the *Acushnet*. A great slab of wood stands on edge, close to shore, just beside the shed where the Taiohae canoe club keep their fibreglass racing canoes. Into the dark timber a local artist has carved a relief map of Nuku Hiva, naming the features which Melville wrote about, and marking his alleged track across the ridge to Taipivai. In one corner of the monument is set an oval picture frame. In it is a photograph of Melville, bearded and full of gravitas. In the opposite corner a second identical frame holds a portrait of a younger, thinner, darker man with large, soulful eyes. This is Richard Tobias Greene, 'Toby', fellow runaway and companion in adventure, whom Melville described as 'a strange, wayward being'.

He was also Melville's alibi. A groundswell of criticism began soon after *Typee* was published. Certain readers began to doubt the details he gave in his book. It was pure fabrication, they said. Melville was inventing everything. Then, in the nick of time, Toby Greene surfaced. He had heard about the book, and came forward to verify at least some of the events. He was an independent witness, if not of all the adventures, at least of the first few days among the Typees. His testimony silenced the critics, and *Typee* became regarded as a reliable treatise on 'life among the cannibals'.

This was Melville luck. The same fortunate coincidence helped *Moby Dick*. That story, too, risked being denounced as a wild fantasy from start to finish, particularly the improbable sinking of the *Pequod* by a whale. Then, while the book was at press, an English-language newspaper in Panama carried a report of the sinking of another whaleship, the *Ann Alexander*. Once again the culprit was a rogue sperm whale, and the attack seemed deliberate. There was an eerie similarity with the role of Ahab aboard the *Pequod*: the *Ann Alexander* was destroyed because her enraged captain insisted on completing a running battle with a 'fighting whale'. The animal had already chewed up two of his whaleboats, and Captain Deblois was reduced to attacking direct from the mother ship. He was poised at the rail, ready to hurl the harpoon at the sperm whale, which was almost under the bows, when the animal sank from view. A moment later it reappeared on the surface alongside the ship, charging at high speed towards the hull. The impact burst the *Ann Alaxander*'s lower planks, and she sank. The crew were rescued the next day by another whaleship, and five months later the whale itself was taken. In its head were splinters from the *Ann Alexander*, and two of her harpoons were buried in its blubber.

The coincidence was too apt for Melville to overlook. 'I make no doubt it is Moby Dick himself,' he wrote triumphantly . . . 'Ye Gods! What a Commentator is this *Ann Alexander* whale.' To a man who had consigned his own white whale to fiction, it did seem almost too good to be true. 'I wonder if my evil art has raised the monster,' he added warily.

Melville was a man whose genius worked — above all else — from books and the power of his imagination, underpinned by his own direct experience. My visit to Nuku Hiva had made me realise that Melville had the facility to construct a wonderful façade. He made brilliant use of any materials that came to hand, and artfully revealed the slight framework of his own experience as more than it really was. So if I was to find a real Moby Dick, I would have to look behind Melville himself. I would have to seek out the sources that he had worked from, and check their truth by doing what he did — learning from the men who hunted whales. No one else could tell me what I wanted to know. It did not matter that the whale-hunters' information was sure to be skewed with misconceptions and tinged with superstition. Their continuing myths and superstitions were equally important because I was on the track of a legend.

Part Two

PAMILACAN

'With a fresh wind the *Pequod* was now draw-
ing nigh to these straits; Ahab purposing to
pass through them into the Javan sea, and
thence cruising northwards, over waters
known to be frequented here and there by the
Sperm Whale. Sweep inshore by the Philip-
pine Islands, and gain the far coast of Japan in
time for the great whaling season there'

HERMAN MELVILLE, *Moby Dick*

Tonio had the small, round head of a child — and a cherubic face to match. Under the white-painted cone of his coolie hat, he looked scarcely ten years old. His slight body was in proportion to the face, and he had delicate hands and feet. He stood balancing like an acrobat on the cross-bar of the port outrigger, as the hunting boat skimmed over the wavelets. One hand held the brim of his hat to prevent it being blown off in the slipstream of our passage. His head swivelled ceaselessly, first one way, then the other, then back again. From within the shade of his basket-work hat, his eyes scanned the water, ahead, to the side, and then ahead again. He seemed un-troubled by the reflected glare of the tropical sun which bounced off the sea. He stood relaxed, al-most at the bow of the boat, a yard from the main hull, empty air beneath him, the spray rushing below. From his left hand a long bamboo cane led aft to a short crossbar attached to the rudder. With this, he controlled the direction of the hunting boat. Occasionally, maybe every twenty minutes or so, he switched the tiller bar from his left hand to the right. And then the other hand went up, to anchor down his hat. Otherwise the only movement was his head, and an occasional slight shift of his stance, a repositioning of his small, bare feet. When you looked closely at his ankles, you noticed that the achilles tendon stood proud. Overdeveloped by a lifetime of standing balancing on an unstable outrigger, the two hollows on each side of the tendon were abnormally deep.

Behind Tonio four men seemed overdressed for such a hot tropical day. Like Tonio they all wore loose-fitting shorts or cut-off jeans, so their legs were bare. But their upper bodies were muffled against the sun by at least two layers of shirts. Pando the engineer, who looked after the eighty-horsepower diesel engine, even wore a long-sleeved woollen sweater. All their clothes were excessively patched and worn. All four had their heads wrapped in some sort of cloth. Pando had a T-shirt pulled upside-down over his head, so his face looked out through the hole for the neck. Both Gabriel and Juny, the youngest crew member, also wore T-shirts, tied around their heads. Chubby Adoy at the stern of the vessel sported a vivid red garment piled up in a scarlet turban. Sometimes he put on a pair of imitation Ray-Ban sunglasses which gave an incongruous modern touch. In all other respects, the crew of the boat looked like pirates.

Not one of them sat. They all stood, looking to left and to right, watching the sea. Adoy regularly turned around to scan our wake, and every so often Juny hoisted himself six feet up the stubby little mast. He stood there, feet on the crosspiece, hugging the white and red painted mast-top into his stomach, to give himself a wider horizon and a better angle to stare down into the water. At intervals one of the crew gave a low grunt, and Tonio would quickly glance back from his position near the bows, follow the eyeline of the man, and look at the same spot on the glittering sea. Usually Tonio had already seen the same sea mark, and had dismissed it as unimportant. If not, he would adjust the bamboo shaft, and the speeding hunting boat would curve in to take a closer look.

For their ability to watch the sea, I had joined them, hoping to learn from them. Their eyesight was phenomenal. They could see an insignificant object floating on the water half a mile away. One day it was a small dead squid, not two feet long and barely showing above the surface. They diverted, scooped it up, and ate it for lunch. Another time it was a breakaway fishing float, three parts hidden by the waves. They investigated, hoping to find something attached. They pulled up the float and revealed a short length of line, three hooks and a small fish on each hook. Another free lunch. These men depended upon the quality of their eyesight for their livelihood. They were fishermen who hunted by eye. They were the human equivalent of cruising gannets who patrol over the sea

69

watching for the flash of a sprat, then drop down in a sudden bombing dive. Tonio and his colleagues did the same. When they saw their prey, one of them — Tonio — would leap bodily into the sea and take the fish.

The forward section of the boat, the centre hull between the outrigger floats, was empty, except for a heavy rope. One end was tied back to the main crosspiece, the strongest part of the vessel. From there the rope was flaked down in a free-running zig-zag heap, perhaps 150 metres of it, which was carefully arranged on a duck-board laid across the bilge of the boat. The other end of the rope ended in an even heavier section, a salvaged mooring cable by the look of it, much worn and meticulously braided into a heavy loop. This splice passed through the eye of a massive steel hook with a sharpened point. The hook, sixteen inches long and weighing three or four pounds, now hung loosely over a crossbar near Tonio's bare foot. This hook was cherubic, childlike Tonio's work tool. If the crew saw a target, he would steer towards it, snatch up the hook, and dive overboard, holding it in both hands and out ahead of his body. It would be the action of a second, almost too fast to follow. Pando would have tugged the length of fishing line which cut the fuel to the engine, stopping it. Tonio meanwhile, carried by his flying dive and the weight of the hook, would be on the prey.

Underwater, he had two or three seconds to grapple, place the hook and drive it home. Then another five seconds to swim to the surface and grab the flying outrigger of the hunting boat before the line thundered out, and the boat was torn forward.

Tonio's target was not the gannet's little sprat. His prey was the biggest fish in the world, an animal as long as the chase boat, and weighing up to eight tons. The prey was whale shark. And until three years previously, men like Tonio would have been equally prepared to leap on to the back of a twenty-ton whale, and catch it by hand. They called it 'jumping a whale', and it seemed madness.

There was a felicitous link with Melville in this, too. One of the most effective scenes in *Moby Dick* is at dawn on the day the *Pequod* sails from Nantucket. Ishmael, the narrator, walks along the dock towards the *Pequod* with his friend Queequeg to join their ship. The quay is deserted and there is a thick mist. Somewhere ahead through the murk Ishmael thinks he sees, or imagines, shadowy figures near the vessel. He is puzzled and strains to make out what is happening, but then his attention is diverted by the sudden appearance of an old sailor who, Cassandra-like, issues a cryptic warning about the forthcoming voyage. Ishmael dismisses the warning and goes aboard. He finds nothing untoward, and Queequeg has not noticed anything. Weeks later when the *Pequod* is at sea and sees her first whale, the boats are lowered for the pursuit. The crew have noted how Captain Ahab has a spare boat hanging in the davits near the quarterdeck, and have been puzzled by this unconventional arrangement. Others think they have heard muffled voices in the lower hold of the ship. Then, as the regular crew hasten to lower away their boats, they have an unpleasant shock. Up from their hiding-place below deck appear 'five dusky phantoms'. They are the private boat crew whom Ahab has smuggled aboard to prosecute his hunt for the white whale. The men are Asiatics. They have 'tiger yellow' skin, and when they lower Ahab's boat, they row with such attack that they seem 'all steel and whalebone; like five trip-hammers they rose and fell with regular strokes of strength'. Melville tells us where they came from: they were, he says, 'some of the aboriginal natives of the Manillas'. They were Filipinos. As were Tonio and his crew.

Lory Tan had told me about the 'whale jumpers'. Energetic and prosperous, Lory ran a publishing house in Manila and was enthusiastic about the maritime traditions of the Philippines, which had been little studied. He was also passionate about protecting the magnificent marine environment of an archipelago of 7,107 islands, and had been gathering data for the first field guide to the whales and dolphins of the Philippines. His research had taken him to interview fishing communities the length and breadth of the Philippines.

'You have to go to Pamilacan in the south,' he told me. 'No one in the Philippines can tell you as much about whales as the islanders of Pamilacan. They have been hunting the large sea animals for as long as anyone can remember.'

'Are they still hunting whales?' I asked.

'Not officially. Whale hunting was banned by the government a couple of years ago, and they are supposed to have stopped.'

'You mean they still do?'

'Well, perhaps one a year. It is hard for some of the fishermen to give up the habit. With the help of the World Wide Fund for Nature I am trying to set up a whale-watching base there, and convert the whale hunters into whale spotters for tourists, but it is a slow process.'

'When would be the best time for me to visit the island?'

'In March, the height of the season for hunting whale shark. It is still legal to catch whale shark. You will see something you will never forget. They don't use harpoons. They hook the sharks by hand.'

Lory suggested that I stay on Pamilacan with Nita Bauboj. She lived in a small two-room house beside the beach, and had a tiny cabin for rent. It was no more than four walls of woven bamboo standing on short stilts, a nipa palm thatch roof, a minuscule verandah which faced north across the straits to the much larger island of Bohol. At night the lights on the main island blazed, modern civilisation spread right across the horizon, eight miles away. But Pamilacan could have been on a distant planet. There were four lightbulbs in Nita's house and they glowed erratically for an hour after sunset — only when the island council could afford fuel for the communal generator and the man who ran the machine was not away on a fishing trip. So most of the night was velvet black, and there was no sound except the steady rumble of waves advancing across the coral foreshore at low tide or, when the tide was full, the muffled boom of the breakers falling on nearby sand. The household comprised Nita's second husband Ninoy; her seventeen-year-old daughter, who was a stunning beauty and had a toddler on whom everyone doted; and Nita's son, Walen.

Twenty-two years old, Walen offered to be my interpreter. The language of Pamilacan was Cebuano, which I was finding completely unintelligible. I recognised barely one word in a hundred. But Walen's English was self-taught and rudimentary, and I was doubtful about the arrangement, until I saw Walen at the cockfight.

It was held on Sunday afternoon in the centre of the little island, in a dell where a grove of palm trees provided shade. The cockpit was a square of bare earth surrounded by a chest-high mesh of sagging chicken wire. At least half the population of the island gathered there. They came in twos and threes, men, women, children and dogs sauntering along the footpaths leading to the cockpit. Many arrived at least two hours early in order to squat in the shade, gossip, play cards, or admire the fighting cocks which arrived tucked under their owners' arms like feathered bagpipes. The birds had been pampered all their lives. Their owners — despite their poverty — fed them special grain which could only be bought at a high price, watched over their health, caressed them, treated them as their own children. They poured their hopes and affection into these strutting, raucous birds, and were careful about which contest they were allowed to enter. If another rooster was judged to be too big or powerful, then the match was refused. And when, as inevitably happened, a fighting bird lost and was killed, the owner often had tears running down his face, as he handed the corpse to the victor's owner — to be eaten, a banquet for a family where fresh meat was a luxury.

Betting was central to everyone's enjoyment. Only in the whale shark season were cockfights held. No one had any money at any other time. For most of the year, Pamilacan was virtually a barter economy. Fish and produce were exchanged for produce and fish. Bank notes might arrive unexpectedly, hand delivered by a traveller from Bohol. The cash was borrowed from a bank on the mainland or it came from family members working off the island — the women of Pamilacan had a good reputation as domestic servants among certain Chinese families in Manila. But only whale shark meat brought cash-in-hand. And then a good deal of the money was brought to the ringside, and placed as bets. It was a complex ritual. The audience pressed three or four deep around the chicken wire, their attention fixed on the ring where the handlers of the fighting cocks stood, along with their assistants and the referee. The crowd watched every gesture as the two fighting cocks were held up for inspection, then placed beak to beak, and snatched away from one another, a device to stir their aggression. Which animal would win? Which animal looked in best form? What were the odds on the betting? As the excitement increased, into the centre of the ring strode young Walen, head thrown back, confident, quick-witted, and in control. His gaze swept the audience, he whirled, he held up one hand and called out the odds offered by one owner and his supporters. Arms reached from the crowd. They proffered tubes of rolled-up bank notes, wagging the money to draw attention. Walen took the money, palmed it, and called new odds. Like an expert auctioneer, he repeated the offer, turned to another section of the crowd, adjusted the changing prices, turned back again, encouraged, repeated, cajoled until he was hoarse. He was required to remember who had bet, against whom, for how much, and at what odds. He took no written notes, and would be called on to repeat the performance at the next bout thirty minutes later when all the numbers and gamblers would be different. He was the stake holder and, after the match, the settler of disputes. He was half the age of most of the audience, and yet everyone, from grizzled fishermen to housewives, trusted his memory. Learning a few new words of English and polishing his grammar in order to help me on Pamilacan would be no problem.

The island itself was little more than a raised chunk of ancient coral, a mile and a half in diameter, and roughly circular. The sandy cove where you landed if you had been lucky enough to hitch a ride on an outrigger from Bohol — there was no ferry — was called Chapel Side. Here was a hamlet of about twenty small neat houses and the white-painted chapel to San Isidoro. Guarding the landing beach was a ruined stone tower, triangular in ground plan, known as the Spanish Tower. It was a relic of the days when fleets of sea raiders would appear from the Sulu Sea and sweep through the Philippines, looting and searching for slaves. It was such a regular scourge that the Spanish missionary priests organised a series of signal stations and refuges along the coast. When the pirate fleets appeared — and sometimes they could number hundreds of light fast-moving craft — the populace would take shelter in the forts. The Spanish Tower was now a shell, but its walls of hewn coral blocks still stood to their original height of nearly thirty feet, and Lory Tan and his associates had proposed that it be restored and converted into a whaling museum. Chapel Side itself was ready to please the tourists. It was kept spotlessly clean. At least once a week the community joined forces to pick up and burn the dead leaves and palm fronds which fell to the ground, and to rake the sand. The chapel of San Isidoro was being given a new roof, and a fresh coat of whitewash had been applied to the church's plain façade with its stark cross bolted to the wall and the saint's name written above. Chapel Side was clean and trim and ambitious.

The provincial government had given the islanders just enough cement to pave a track across the coral rocks so they would not have to pick their way over the ankle-turning potholes and ridges. A normal roadway would have been useless as the island was too small for cars or trucks. So the islanders had built themselves a double track. It was like a concrete railway, two ribbons of cement set wide enough to accommodate the wheels of a home-made handcart. From Chapel Side this path climbed to the central plateau of the island. There it levelled off beside one of the island's few shops — a tiny kiosk with a wire-mesh window where you could buy cigarettes, packets of sweets, and warm soft drinks. You knew you were halfway across Pamilacan when you passed the primary school with its basketball court of cracked concrete. A quarter-mile further on the twin ribbons of cement dipped sharply down a slope and brought you to Little Tondo, and there you met the other half of Pamilacan's personality.

Little Tondo was nicknamed after a notorious slum in the suburbs of Manila.

The epithet was rather unfair, though

everyone used it. The reason was really the contrast with Chapel Side. Where the latter had been tidy and trim, Little Tondo was a neglected mess. A double line of thatch houses fronted a beach protected by a coral reef. The huts were neat enough, but very workaday. Their porches were piled with fishing nets, broken engine parts, fish boxes. The desiccated tails of large tuna fish were nailed as trophies to the outer walls. The evil-looking skulls of sharks dangled from strings, mouths open, teeth like bandsaws. There was no organised civic sanitation in Little Tondo. Everyone used the beach as their lavatory, and no one swept the alleyways. But I had seen dirtier and more decrepit villages, and to my eye Little Tondo was really no more than an unashamed working settlement, a fishing community, and a competent one at that. There must have been twenty motorised outriggers pulled up on the beach, or riding at anchor in the shelter of the coral reef. All the boats were well looked after, and well painted. There were no rotting abandoned hulks on the shoreline, and although the fishermen were certainly a rough-looking bunch, they were friendly and good-humoured. Little Tondo, I decided, was a working-class district compared to genteel Chapel Side.

The stench at Little Tondo was overpowering. The catch of manta ray and whale shark was butchered in the shallows in front of the village. Then the chunks of meat and skin were hung up to dry in the sun on lines of wooden racks erected along the beach. The animal flesh dangled there in all stages of decomposition, and the smell wafted through the village. The older meat had shrivelled and merely smelled rank. After three weeks in the sun the outer skin had the texture of wrinkled shoe leather or dirty shrivelled sheets of industrial plastic. They were ugly but not really offensive. The odorous culprits were the fresh cuttings from whale shark. These pieces were very large, up to ten kilos in weight. Whale shark anatomy does not allow the animal to secrete its waste in the normal way, I had been told by a naturalist. The ammonia which would normally pass as urine was retained in the animal's body, in the flesh. The result was that whale shark meat, a day old and dripping its moisture, stank. The smell was as fierce as the territorial spray of a tribe of tom-cats. If you were close enough and down wind, the odour was enough to make your eyes water.

Pamilacan defied a basic rule of human settlement. Fresh water had to be carried from the mainland, ten miles away. Plastic jerry cans were filled from a tap near the jetty on Bohol, loaded on to an outrigger, taken on a wet, choppy journey for forty-five minutes, then carried shoulder-high through the shallows, up the beach and distributed among the nipa palm huts. In the winter rainy season, water could be collected from roof traps, but for much of the year the population of the island, 1,700 people, depended on water from across the sea. The three wells on the island, dug within yards of one another in a small valley, were ruined. The water in them was so brackish that it could only be drunk by cattle, or used for washing clothes. Humans drank it only in emergency, or if they were so very poor that they could not afford to share in the cost of an outrigger going to the tap in Bohol. In past times the wells had given sweet water, but the islanders, who were staunchly Christian, had a story that a Muslim once landed on Pamilacan. He had asked for a drink of water, and been refused. In anger he cursed the wells, and they had turned salt. In truth, the wells had been drained so frequently that the water table had dropped. Sea water had invaded the aquifer. Now, in the dry season, even the supply of tainted water dried up. When I arrived in March, there was nothing more than a gritty puddle of water at the bottom of each of the three well shafts. Small children stood teetering on the lip of each well, each with a chopped-off plastic bottle on a string. They dropped the bottle to the bottom of the well so the bottle fell on its side. A trickle of water seeped in, and they would hoist their prize to the surface, then pour the precious fluid into a waiting jerry can, half a cupful at a time. In the evening the paths leading up from the wells would be marked by troops of little children walking along slowly with jerry cans of brackish water on their heads, the

81

product of hours of patient toil.

The people stayed on Pamilacan, even without fresh water, because they had been born there, and because they could still go fishing. The island's name was the clue to why they stayed. It means 'the place for hunting manta rays'. For time out of mind the Pamilacan fishermen had caught manta ray, the smaller ones with nets, the larger rays by 'jumping'. No one could tell me how or when the jumping technique started. As far I was aware, no one else in the world regularly caught sea animals weighing as much as half a ton in this foolhardy way. When I asked why they did not use a harpoon like every other hunting community I had ever heard of, they gave a devastatingly simple answer: it was more certain to fix a hook by hand, and harpoons were expensive. They were too poor to afford to throw, and perhaps lose, a harpoon.

Walen took me to talk to the oldest fishermen on the island. Amadeo Valeroso was eighty-nine years old, and Francolino Operio was seventy-one. They both lived near the top of Pamilacan's only hill, where the land rose towards the south of the island and ended in a moderate-sized cliff overlooking the sea. Their houses were identical — wooden-sided cabins, the planks bleached pale grey by the sun, raised up on low pilings. Pigs lazed in the darkness under the houses, and a cluster of grandchildren and great-grandchildren scurried off delightedly to fetch the old men. Amadeo and Francolino appeared, equally pleased that someone wanted to hear their reminiscences. Both were very thin. Amadeo walked with a stick and was hard of hearing. Francolino, obviously his good friend, would sometimes lean across to shout loudly as he repeated my questions. Both had started as fishermen in their teens, long before anyone on Pamilacan could afford an engine. Their boats had been outrigger canoes, with a single mast and sail, and four or five men to paddle. They went out with a hook to 'jump' giant manta ray. I asked Amadeo if he had ever tried to catch a sperm whale, and he shook his head.

'But did you see many sperm whale near the island in those days?' I asked him.

'Yes, maybe more than fifty in a season. In April, May and June. I only estimate because sometimes they were sleeping on the sea.'

Sleeping? I asked him what he meant. 'Yes, they must sleep, open on the sea, they go phoeeeow,' and he made a whooshing, whistling sound. 'If you go near the sperm whale you leave distance, maybe twenty-five metres. Maybe he likes floating on the water.'

'Were you frightened?'

'The sperm whale is not really dangerous. He just likes playing with the sea. He does not even mind people looking at him.'

'What was the biggest sperm whale you ever saw?'

Amadeo gestured towards a tree. 'Almost ten

fathoms [eighteen metres], to that coconut tree from here. It was already dead. We found a harpoon in its back. We saw it on the sea, near the Spanish Tower. We tried to eat the meat, but it smelled bad. We had no recipe, not good to eat. Maybe if we had recipe . . .' His voice trailed off.

Francolino, who had been listening patiently, offered a good reason why you did not molest a sperm whale. One day while fishing he had come close to a baby sperm whale lying quietly on the sea. Out of curiosity, he had reached out and touched it with his paddle. He waved his hands in a gesture of amazement, 'Oooh, oooh, more than ten sperm whale come to the surface because I touched the child. They go around my boat, like playing, and I was afraid because maybe that was dangerous for me.'

'What did you do?'

'I threw my paddle, and when it hit a big whale, the whale struck it with its tail. The paddle was split. I was very afraid. And I go away from there as fast as I can.'

I asked whether they had ever seen a white sperm whale in all their years at sea, and they shook their heads. But they had both seen a bursahon.

'A bursahon?'

'A white manta ray. Not the normal black ray we call sanga. The white manta is different.' Amadeo had caught three or four white manta ray in his lifetime, jumping them with a hook.

But they were less than two fathoms across, wing tip to wing tip. They were not real bursahon.

An animal big enough to be nine or ten feet from wing tip to wing tip seemed quite big enough to me, certainly for a small man to tackle, jumping out of a canoe and landing on its back.

'How big is the real bursahon?'

'Four, maybe five fathoms across,' said Francolino.

Amadeo nodded. 'I saw the bursahon which was at least five fathoms across.'

Both agreed that the animal was pure white. And it was far, far too big to catch.

A pure white, giant manta ray was a creature new to me. Of course I immediately thought of the white mass of Moby Dick. Melville establishes the image when Ishmael sets out on his whaling voyage and in his mind's eye float 'endless processions of the whale, and midmost of them all, one grand hooded phantom, like a snow hill in the air'. Whether Moby Dick was all white or part-white Melville never makes entirely clear. He describes 'a peculiar snow-white wrinkled forehead, and a high, pyramidical hump', and a body 'so streaked, and spotted, and marbled with the same shrouded hue that, in the end, he had gained his distinctive appellation of the White Whale'. The animal Melville had in mind was probably inspired by reading a short story in an American magazine, *The Knickerbocker*, in 1839. The piece was called 'Mocha Dick or the White Whale of the Pacific' and it was a yarn about a big bull sperm whale regularly encountered off the coast of Chile. The animal was said to be 'as white as wool', though whether because it was an albino or from old age was not known. It had first been reported in 1810 and, over the years, had successfully repulsed many attacks from whaleships. It had survived so many onslaughts that its back was riddled with harpoons, and a skein of broken whale line streamed in its wake. The whale apparently had learned how to protect itself from his attackers. It swam with its body at such an angle that the harpooners could not strike a vital spot low down near the ribs. Unsuccessful boats were chased back to their mother ships. It was said that Mocha Dick once struck out with his flukes at a whaleboat as it was being hoisted back aboard. The animal was what the whalemen called a 'fighting whale', and Mocha Dick became a challenge for whaling crews to try to capture him. J. N. Reynolds, who wrote the article for the magazine, claimed that when whaling captains met for a 'gam' they would regularly ask 'any news of Mocha Dick?'. Eventually the hero of Reynolds's tale kills Mocha Dick after a fierce battle. The whale proves to be the biggest he ever saw, 'seventy feet from his noddle to the tip of his flukes', and yielded one hundred barrels of oil. In his back were found twenty rusty harpoons.

White whales do exist. A breeding colony of Southern Right whales off Argentina produces one white calf in every ten animals born, though the colour seems to darken later in life. Another species, the beluga, is born dark and then changes colour completely so that the adult animal is milk-white all over. Beluga means the 'white one' in Russian, and although at three to five metres it is only a fraction of the size of a sperm whale, the beluga is toothed, like the sperm whale, and its high-domed forehead makes it look like a miniature, very intellectual Moby Dick. The French scientist and survival expert, Alain Bombard, filmed an albino fin whale in the Mediterranean. A large white whale, with just a greyish blue patch at the back of the neck, and presumed to be an albino, was taken by the French whaleship *Anglo-Norse* in 1951; and a white sperm whale was reported by a Japanese whaleship six years later. Both animals were encountered in the Pacific. And even if Reynolds's Mocha Dick was not really 'as white as wool', it could have been what the older whalemen called 'grey headed'. They noted that the big, solitary bull sperm whales often become mottled in their old age, characteristically with a pronounced patch of white or light grey on the head or lower jaw. Mocha Dick could have been such an animal, lone, wary, and powerful. The French deep-sea sailors had an apt name for them. They called them 'emperors'.

Max Valeroso, the most successful whale jumper in the history of Little Tondo, had also seen plenty of sperm whales, but never a white one. Valeroso is a common name on the island, and I did not know if he was related to the elderly, rather frail Amadeo. Certainly Max gave a totally different impression. You knew at first glance that Max was a man of substance. He carried himself with an air of authority, and had the solid agility of a retired, middleweight prizefighter. He was friendly and approachable but, one felt, he stood no nonsense. He had begun as the poorest of the poor, a humble fisherman who had gone to sea on a hunting boat at the age of twelve, helping his grandfather. Within three years he had graduated to be the 'jumper' on board. It was a major compliment from the other members of the crew. They had the right to pick the most agile and bravest man among them to leap on the prey. Initially, Max had 'jumped' manta ray, like everyone else. This was dangerous enough because the big rays had been known to fold their wings around the man clinging to their back, and then dive deep, pulling down the assailant and drowning him. Max reckoned that in his lifetime he had caught more than three hundred manta ray with the hook. The meat was dried and sold, and he had saved his earnings. He was still only fifteen years old when he tried something even more dangerous — to 'jump' a whale.

The species which the Pamilacan hunters

tackled was the Bryde's* whale or tropical whale. It is a baleen whale very similar to the better-known fin and sei whales. In fact the species was only identified early in the twentieth century as being distinct. Previously it had been confused with the sei or sardine whale, as it has the same long, slim profile. Not that these distinctions mattered to men like Max Valeroso. To them an adult Bryde's whale represented a tempting source of meat. The adult animal weighs between twelve and twenty tons, and Bryde's whales were seen frequently off the island. To most observers a Bryde's whale would have been rather difficult to spot, because when it comes to the surface to breathe, it stays low in the water and shows very little of its head and back above the sea until it begins its dive and curls its lower back above the sea. But to the keen-eyed sea hunters of Pamilacan, accustomed to spotting manta rays several fathoms down, a Bryde's whale was glaringly obvious. For the hunters the whales had a difficult swimming pattern. The whales tend to make sudden changes in direction while feeding, disappear underwater, then surface at quite a different spot and in an unexpected direction. They are also quite fast swimmers. However, they do not stay submerged for very long, and are sometimes rather inquisitive,

* Named after a Norwegian whalemaster and properly pronounced 'breuda' but almost always pronounced 'bride's whale.'

approaching the boats. Occasionally, and sometimes fatally for both men and whale, a Bryde's
whale will indulge in a whole series of breaches,
exploding out of the water almost vertically, all
its body except the tail leaving the water, and
then slapping down with a tremendous splash.
This was the moment when some of the
Pamilacan hunters tried to 'jump' the whale.

'Did you ever get hurt?' I asked Max.

'Yes. Once I had trouble with a Bryde's whale.
When you see that the whale is about to jump,
then you must jump in advance of it, to be in the
right place to put the hook. I put the hook in the
right side of the whale, but I did not expect to let
go of the hook. I slid back to the tail, and the tail
hit my left leg. I was so badly hurt that I could
not even swim. When I came back to the surface,
I shouted to my friends in the boat, and they
came and picked me up. When I get back into
the boat, I said to my crew that we must go back
to the island as I must take rest.'

'When I come to shore I cannot walk, and even
after that I can only walk with a stick. After three
weeks I go back in the boat, but now I run the
engine and am directing the crew. When I say
"Jump!" he jumps, and the whale is caught.
Even until now my leg sometimes hurts from the
blow from the tail of the whale.'

His best year, Max remembered, was when he
was twenty years old. That was the year when he
had caught his personal record, nine Bryde's
whales in a single season, all with the hook.

Overall, during his time as an active hunter he had taken more than a hundred whales by hand. Nor had he squandered his hard-earned money, but invested it in his own hunting boat. Now Max is the entrepreneur par excellence of Little Tondo. He owns four boats, called *ValMax 1*, *ValMax 2*, and so on, and he acts as the middleman for the village fishery. When a whale shark is caught, it is Max who checks the size and condition of the catch, negotiates the price with the lucky fisherman, contacts the meat buyer from Bohol, and arranges for all the able-bodied villagers of Little Tondo to cut up the animal and stow it in little boxes. He makes a substantial profit from each transaction, but he is in no way divided from his community. Max still goes to the cockfight with his own fighting cocks; he is treated as an equal. Watching Max walk away with his prize-fighter's rolling walk, but also the limp from the old whale wound, I could not help feeling that he had earned his success. He had never seen a white whale, neither sperm whale nor Bryde's. But, oddly enough, he had seen the 'bursahon' on one occasion, an enormous white manta ray which had been estimated as seven or eight metres from wing tip to wing tip.

RJ2 was the name of the boat I rode with Tonio and his team. They did not own the boat. It was far too expensive for them. The ultimate owner was an investor in Manila, and the boat, along with *RJ1* and *RJ3*, was named from the initials of the owner's son. There was a local

91

manager for the vessel, and Tonio and the others would take a share in any catch. They considered themselves lucky to have the chance to go hunting, and they were doubly lucky in that their owner was prepared to pay for the diesel fuel to go hunting even when no whale sharks were reported. Most of Pamilacan's boats, and especially those smaller boats belonging to islanders of Little Tondo, could not afford to waste fuel on a speculative hunt. They knew from experience that if whale sharks arrived in the area, they came in groups. So the boats like *RJ2*, funded by wealthier owners, went out as scouts, sweeping the sea, and only when they caught a whale shark would the other, poorer boats scramble to join in the chase.

The hunters are good marine biologists. They know that the whale sharks appear most frequently at a certain phase of the moon — six or seven days after a full moon, so that is when they are especially alert. They do not know, though they probably guess, that the appearance of the whale sharks is connected with the release of huge quantities of plankton from the coral reefs. Then the deep-dwelling whale sharks come close inshore to feed. Waiting for them are men like Tonio.

I spent several days on *RJ2*, cruising the coast. The fishing ground was thirty-five miles from Pamilacan, off Bohol at a place called Jagna, too far for the crew to return home in the evening. So we stayed at a house on the Bohol coast, together with the other hunting crews from Pamilacan, perhaps four or five boats. There were local boats moored off the beach, many of them. But they only caught devil rays and fish, using nets. Only the men of Pamilacan were hook jumpers, specialising in the giant whale shark.

Each morning we would get up soon after dawn, and have a light breakfast of bread and water. One of the crew would have bought or bartered a handful of reef fish from a local fishermen. The tiny brightly coloured creatures half the size of a sardine looked as if they should have decorated an aquarium tank. These small offerings were cleaned, their scales scraped off, and then grilled over a charcoal hearth. It scarcely seemed worth the effort. A couple of pounds of cheap low-grade rice were boiled in a black iron pot, the fish thrown in, and then the sooty pot was carefully loaded aboard *RJ2*. It was all the men would eat during an eight-hour day.

We cast off the mooring lines which tied *RJ2* to a coconut tree. Tonio took up a long bamboo pole to punt the vessel clear, and Pando the engineer fiddled with the fuel line on the diesel engine. When he was satisfied, a whiskery starting rope was wrapped around the flywheel, and the entire crew, except Tonio, lined up and bent down to take hold of the rope. 'Uno, dos, tres,' and the crew heaved, the rope flew up into the air, there was a puff of black smoke, a deep clunking sound, and — occasionally — the engine clattered into life. There was no gearbox, no reverse gear, no hand throttle. Pando controlled the speed with a length of fishing line wrapped round a wooden bobbin.

All morning we patrolled the coast, up and down, up and down, on a beat that extended for perhaps ten miles. The sun hammered down, the water glittered, the noise of the engine blunted the hearing, and the men stared at the sea. Melville had written of the boredom of a whaleship lookout staring for hours at the ocean, waiting for the spout of a whale. It was an ideal moment for a romantic to day-dream, he claimed, until his reverie was shattered by a sudden movement on the water, a mist of spray rising up where a whale had surfaced and expelled the stale air from its lungs. Sperm whales would then wallow before diving again, taking deep breaths for as much as five or ten minutes, each breath sending up the characteristic forward-sloping spout of the sperm whale. What Tonio and his team were trying to spot was something much more difficult — the faintest flicker of a fin, a patch of different-coloured water, slight underwater swirl. Their prey did not have to come to the surface to breathe. It remained totally submerged, and only the very sharpest eyes would see it. I doubted that Tonio and his crewmates had any time to day-dream.

Hour after hour we patrolled. Our track took us along what must have been a fringing reef where the whale sharks might come to feed. We were not alone. Two more boats, ones with wealthy owners, were also on the prowl. They moved up and down in the same pattern as ourselves, and I saw our mirror image — a fast-moving lightweight predatory shape, silhouetted against the sea, the same outlines of 'jumper', engineer, and spotters. We barely acknowledged one another, it was all so routine. Only at noon — no one but me wore a watch, yet the crew knew the time almost to the minute — would we take a break. Pando cut the engine, and mercifully the noise stopped. Tonio flopped down on the outrigger, and stretched out, grateful to ease his legs. The sooty black pot was produced, and the crew gathered round. They ate with their fingers, scooping out their tiny ration of rice. A glass of water, and then there were twenty minutes of relaxation with a cigarette before 'Uno, dos, tres' and the motor clattered back to life.

In four days of patrolling we never saw a whale shark. If we had, Tonio assured me, we would have caught it. The problem was not in the catching of the animal. A good jumper could do that with no trouble. The difficulty was the growing scarcity of whale sharks, and actually spotting them when they were present.

On the fourth day we turned for home. The men wanted to get back to their families, and we had burned up our allowance of diesel fuel. *RJ2* was one of the few boats based at Chapel Side so they dropped me off in the evening, on the beach beside the Spanish Tower. There was a particularly beautiful sunset so I walked back up the hill to where old Amadeo and Francolino had their houses. I stood on the cliff top and looked west, towards Bohol. The sun had sunk to the horizon, and below me another hunting boat was making for home across the low swells. It was going to Little Tondo, and travelling slowly. As its silhouette came across the sun, the boat stood black against a red-bronze sea. A waft of wind brought the sound of its engine up to me. I could hear the variation in the engine's rhythm as first it laboured, then ran easy, then laboured again with the rise and fall of the following swells. It was the sound, Walen had told me, that the community would be waiting for. It was the sound of a successful hunting boat towing something heavy. The boat was now directly opposite me, a mile offshore, and very small. Behind it, perhaps thirty yards away in its wake, I could just make out a thin black crescent emerging from the water. It was the waving sickle of a huge tail, a black shadow. A whale shark was being towed home.

The maw of a whale shark of quite ordinary size can be more than four feet wide. When open for feeding, the mouth assumes a slightly flattened O-shape, and reveals a huge pale tunnel of a throat. Then the mouth looks like the entrance to a road drain. The animal is, of course, a filter feeder. It takes its nourishment by sucking vast quantities of sea water into its mouth, and extracting myriad tiny creatures, mainly the larvae of fish and coral, krill, and other plankton. Occasionally the whale shark also swallows small fish such as anchovies, sardines and squid. But its six thousand vestigial teeth are so tiny that it cannot bite, and the whale shark is considered harmless to man. Yet, underwater, when you see the huge head looming an arm's length away, imagine the gaping road drain, and recall that the animal feeds by suction, you hope fervently that the whale shark keeps its mouth shut.

I was diving with face mask and flippers underneath the hunting boat I had seen towing the captured whale shark the previous evening. The boat was now anchored close off the reef at Little Tondo and the living whale shark was tethered in the shadow of the keel. One rope led from its upper jaw down to an anchor on the sea floor. A second, shorter, rope was attached to a buoy on the surface, and a third rope looped around its tail and was fastened back up to the boat. At thirty-four feet in length, the animal was nearly as long as the boat, and there was no chance that the Pamilacan fishermen could have hauled their giant catch aboard. The crew would not have had the strength to lift the whale shark, and had they been strong enough, its ten-ton weight would have sunk their boat. Even the deadweight of the animal in the water was too great to be towed twenty miles to their harbour. So when the 'jumper' had hooked the shark underwater, he scrambled back on the boat and helped the crew who were doing battle with their monstrous catch. Every time the whale shark dived, the crew slowly paid out the line. When it rose again to the surface, they quickly regained the slack. The struggle might go on for two or three hours before the animal began to tire of attempting to swim free. By then the crews' hands were torn and bleeding. Then the 'jumper' had gone back into the water. This time he carried a knife, and swimming on to the back of the animal he cut a small nick across the fish's spine close to the head. The effect of this cut was to disable much of the fish's nervous system, and numb it. By this technique the hunters arranged for the animal to travel with them. A neat, round hole was cut through the shark's upper lip, a heavy tow line passed through, and the whale shark was led to Pamilacan, swimming behind its captor like a bull being led with a ring through its nose.

Now the fishermen were waiting for Max Valeroso, the middleman, to come out in his canoe to check the size and condition of the animal and offer them a price. As Walen paddled me out for my dive, the mouth of the submerged whale shark appeared on the surface from time to time as it reared its head, attempting to see what was holding it in place. The animal swam in slow, puzzled circles trying to escape its tether, and the mouth made a slow vortex in the water, rimmed by thick speckled lips.

I had never swum close to a whale shark

before. To a novice like myself, the shape of the animal evoked as much caution as did the enormous mouth. The animal is, after all, a true shark, and it looks like one. It has the same tall muscular tail, the long torpedo-shaped body with pectoral fins set low down like balancing vanes, the pointed snout (though this one was much flattened), and the same sinuous movements as it flexes from side to side. It recalls the images seen on television programmes about the predatory sharks such as the great white, mako, and whitetip. The skin of the whale shark also sends an intimidating message. Grey tinged with green, it is marked with a chequerboard of white spangles and pale bands. They bring to mind the tiger's camouflage or the cheetah's spots. I told myself firmly that this animal was utterly harmless, but my involuntary reaction was that this creature was a shark, and that sharks can be lethal.

The animal in front of me was vast. It was a fully grown specimen of the largest cold-blooded species of animal on earth. I had a sense of being overwhelmed by the magnitude of the beast. Behind the enormous flat head, the body of the whale shark extended so far back through the water that its tail was almost lost from sight in the shadowy underwater world. And the animal was very much alive. A round eye looked directly at me. I could see the five gill slits behind the head, opening and closing as the shark pumped water in through its mouth. Occasionally the tremendous tail swayed from side to side. This was a behemoth, and in its own element. Underwater I was the intruder, slow, clumsy, and a fraction of its size. Even with the whale shark tethered in place, I felt as vulnerable as if I had stepped into a narrow stable stall containing a Clydesdale or Percheron. With no intention to harm, a really big animal can simply move sideways and crush you. The whale shark was ten times larger than any heavy horse, and before diving down to look at the whale shark I had seen a single whiplash smack from its massive tail send shock waves through the bows of the huntboat, and tip three men into the water.

I swam closer, peering into the viewfinder of the small video camera I was carrying. I was trying to place the huge head square in the frame. Shafts of morning sunlight striking down through the sea water lit up small blades of brown seagrass free-floating in the current. The seagrass distracted the eye, and still concentrating on the viewfinder, I tried to evade the seaweed and find the whale shark in the frame. The animal seemed to have vanished in the general blue-green background. Suddenly there was a gentle bump. I looked up, and realised that, carried by the current, I had run into the huge mouth, head-on. The watertight lens had tapped the animal on the snout. The whale shark took not the slightest notice. What I had thought was the general sea-coloured background in the viewfinder was actually the huge expanse of head. I realised I had a technical problem: if I tried to film from a few yards back, the lack of visibility made the shark indistinct. If I came closer, the animal was far, far too big to fit in the frame.

The solution was for me to swim along the length of the shark, and back down the other side, pointing the camera from no more than five feet away. I began the circuit, and the animal was so substantial that at intervals I had to bob to the surface, take a gulp of air, and duck back down. The shark continued to ignore me.

I passed the staring eye. It was set in a deep socket, close behind the corner of the wide mouth. In size it was a little less than a tennis ball, and had no lid. To close it, the whale shark rotated the orb and could suck it back into its head. Just behind the eye was a deep round hole, which to a layman looked like an ear. It was in fact the archaic remains of a gill, and behind it were the gill slits themselves. There were five of them, like long gashes in the skin cut by a very sharp knife. They flared and shut regularly as the animal took oxygen and plankton from the sea. Back, back along the body I swam, following three prominent ridges which extended nearly all the way to the huge tail. In places the star-patterned skin was blotched with rust-red patches which I presumed to be colonies of algae. About four feet behind the gills I passed a gash in the skin, marked by small ribbons of torn white flesh which wavered in the current. It was the place where the 'jumper' had driven in the hook. Later I learned that this spot was critical. The 'jumper' had to strike the hook precisely here, in the side of the animal, so that when the whale shark dived, the pull of the heavy rope attached to the boat on the surface turned the whale shark on its side, so it could not swim with maximum efficiency. If the hook was placed too far back in the body, or in the upper curve of the back, the whale shark was not sufficiently impeded and could swim so powerfully that the rope broke, or the thick steel curve of the hook opened out and pulled free, or the boat could be pulled under.

The belly of the whale shark was much lighter in colour. A pair of sucker fish were still sticking there, hitching a ride, unaware that their host was captive. Finally I reached the tall blade of the massive tail. It was waving gently from side to side, and as I swam round it, I again came too close. The tail struck me across the face, and to my pleasant surprise the blow was soft, cushioned by water. Back-pedalling out of range, I looked along the length of the creature, and the baleful image of the ferocious shark was replaced by a totally different vision. Tied there in the warm sea, the whale shark looked like a gigantic, placid cow, but a cow awaiting the slaughter.

When I surfaced, Max Valeroso was already on his way from the shore in a small dugout to inspect the animal. He waved cheerfully at me as he passed, and by the time I got to the beach of

Little Tondo most of the villagers were assembled on the sand, gazing out at the lucky hunt boat with expressions of happy anticipation on their faces. Soon a second boat appeared, this time piled high with styrofoam chests of ice which had been rushed across from Bohol. The chests were carried ashore and stacked on the sand. The shark was untethered and led towards the beach by its rope. Just before the animal parted from the hunt boat, I saw again how immensely strong it was. The huge tail suddenly reared up from the water, curled to one side, and sprang back, releasing a thunderous blow against the outrigger of the hunt boat. The strike was not deliberate. Probably it was just a reflex from the animal. Above the sudden heavy splash of the water, I heard the outrigger bar, a six-inch-thick bamboo, snap.

Small boys, stark naked, flung themselves joyously into the sea as the great bulk of the whale shark slowly approached the beach. The children were beside themselves with excitement. They swam with much splashing and yells of delight towards the huge tail. When the animal reached the shallows and the glistening back was exposed, the children scrambled up on its bulk. There they danced and cavorted like gleeful pygmies attending the funeral rites of an elephant. An adult head, sinister in tight, home-made goggles, bobbed up beside the whale shark. It was the diver who would kill the animal. He leaned across and, two-handed with a long knife, sawed down through the spine and severed the nervous system. Whale sharks lack bones, their skeletons being made of cartilage, but the diver needed his strength to cut through one of the toughest hides in the animal world. The skin on a whale shark's back is made of overlapping tooth-like scales which have been compared to a suit of armour. The most frequent injury for the 'jumpers' was not being struck by a thrashing shark tail, but being severely rasped by the heavy skin.

Now the shark was dead, the villagers sloshed into the water to begin their work. The men carried heavy knives and sharpening stones, and standing chest-deep in the water, they began to carve out cubes of the flesh. The women formed a chain and passed the meat from hand to hand back to the beach or, cradling a block of flesh, waded to land. A quick dip in the water to wash off any sand, and the meat was packed into the boxes until they were full to the brim, and the styrofoam lids pressed on. The flesh was white and rubbery. In the past the meat from whale shark had little value. The flesh was dried and sold for a third the price of manta ray. It was bartered to the poorest villagers in the hinterland of Bohol. Now there were new, much wealthier clients. A dealer from Taiwan had discovered the hunting skills of the Pamilacan jumpers. He had offered to buy the meat of any whale shark they caught, and buy it fresh. The meat would be flown to Taiwan and served in fish restaurants there. The Taiwanese supplied the boxes, ice and cash. The people of Pamilacan provided the meat, the labour, and the poverty which made them willing partners in the commerce. They received 20,000 pesos for each shark, and rumour had it that the Taiwanese dealer sold the meat for 20,000 American dollars. There were thirty-five pesos to one dollar.

Ninety minutes was all the time it took for the gigantic whale shark to disappear into the white styrofoam chests. The fishboxes would be whisked away to the airport on Bohol; the shark skin and fins hung up to dry on Little Tondo's racks. Later they would be cut in strips and sold as ingredients for Chinese soups and stews. The completely unusable body parts like the huge flat head would be towed out to the reef and allowed to sink. Diving earlier that day, I had looked down and seen a skull on the sea floor, the broad mouth grinning up in a gape of death.

It was a shocking waste of a huge and harmless animal, which normally might have had a life-span of over a century. But I understood why the people of Pamilacan looked so happy as they butchered the animal. Virtually every member of the community would profit from that whale shark, not just Max the middleman and the successful hunters, but also the men who helped dismember the shark, the women who packed the boxes, even the teenagers of Pamilacan. There was no secondary school on the island, so in term-time the teenage pupils had to live in a dormitory across the straits on Bohol. When the boxes of shark meat were ferried from Pamilacan, the students came down to the pier on Bohol and carried the boxes to a waiting truck. They were paid a few pesos as porters, and they considered it a privilege.

Before the whale shark disappeared in chunks, en route to Taiwan, two young women arrived from KKP, the Filipino branch of the World Wide Fund for Nature. They had a one-room office beside the Spanish Tower in Chapel Side where they offered advice to the fishermen about the advantages of turning to a whale-watching programme. They also monitored the catch of whale sharks. The two women walked into the water, now darkened with a widening stain of blood. They measured the length of the body and fins — the animal was so large that they needed an architect's field tape for this job — took flesh samples for DNA analysis, and collected external parasites like the sea lice on the skin and the internal parasites clinging to the gills. Their collections would be sent to the local university for a study on the whale sharks of the Philippines. Twenty whale sharks had been taken so far this season, they told me, and all but one were males. By the same month in the previous year, the number of sharks caught had been twice as many. Year on year, the catch was dwindling, and the hunters of Pamilacan were going farther and farther afield to find their prey.

It was a pattern that had repeated itself for one species after another. Traditionally the 'jumpers' of Pamilacan had concentrated on catching the huge manta ray, after which their island was named. The blacksmith family who made the steel hooks was now in its third generation, so that harvest must have continued for over fifty years. Then the big manta ray had become scarce. The reason may have been the introduction of engine boats which made the hunt more effective. So the jumpers had turned to catching Bryde's whales, until they too were difficult to find. Now the prey was whale shark, which do not breed until they are thirty years old, so it seemed all too likely that the stock would be wiped out by the sheer proficiency of their human predators.

Three days after the butchery of the whale shark on the beach, I took another ride on *RJ2*. I asked to be dropped off at the village of Jagna on the Bohol coast where Tonio and his crew stayed overnight on their long-range scouting trips. In Jagna I found a local boat about to head southward, to set nets for devil rays. The skipper agreed to divert from his usual route if I paid his fuel costs, and drop me off on the beach at my destination, Camiguin Island. There I would find a small colony of harpooners. Perhaps they had news of a white whale.

The profile of Camiguin was unmistakable from the north. The island looks like a huge manta ray, spread out on the horizon and swimming directly towards you. Two volcanoes in the centre of the island provided the humps of the manta ray; a low col between them is the forehead; and on each side the land slopes down to sea level in a gentle curve to provide the outstretched manta 'wings'. The fishing boat landed Walen and me on a sandy beach near the tip of the easterly wing.

Ramon was the harpooner I was taken to see. He lives on the south side of the island, and when I arrived, he was sitting on the bamboo bench in front of his house near the beach. The house also served as a small shop selling soft drinks, cigarettes, soap powder and dry biscuits. But Ramon did not look at all like a shopkeeper. He had a calm, self-confident air which translated into the habit of sitting quite still and thinking carefully before he answered any question. Everything he said was spoken quietly and in measured phrases. He did not look directly at you, but seemed to address the middle distance. When he finished his sentence, he would shoot you a sideways glance, full of intelligence. He had a handsome, rather square face, looked fifty years old and was very fit. In fact he was sixty-four, and his vanity was that he dyed his hair black. He had only taken up harpooning, he said, about fifteen years earlier. He owned his own boat, which was drawn up on the beach, ready to go to sea at a moment's notice. Nowadays he relied on a younger man to do the harpooning as it required agility and strength. Agility? Yes, Ramon explained. 'You can throw the harpoon. But it is better if you jump out of the boat with it, on to the animal.'

Ramon got up from the bench and walked round the back of his house. He reappeared, carrying his harpoon. It was a classic pattern. The forged iron shank was tipped with a swivel point that would turn and lock in place once it had struck its target. The shaft was a five-foot length of heavy timber. To me it looked like a copy of a sophisticated hand harpoon of a type used by the American whale ships which operated in the Philippines in the mid- to late nineteenth century. Ramon had no idea where the original design had come from. A local metalworker made up replacements when the harpoons were lost or broken. Not that many copies were needed. Only a handful of men still went fishing with harpoons now that nylon nets were strong enough to take large rays, and there were so few whale sharks left. Word had also spread to Camiguin that the Taiwanese dealers were willing to buy whale shark meat, but it was unusual for a boat to catch more than one animal a year. Less than a dozen Camiguin boats fished for whale sharks, and they did so on a casual basis. The crews did not search out the animals like the Pamilacan jumpers, but waited until a whale shark was seen offshore, then raced out and tried to intercept it. More in hope than expectation, they carried a harpoon onboard when they went out to set their nets in case they met a whale shark.

'What about whales?' I asked. 'Did you ever hunt whales?'

Ramon shook his head. 'Not now. It is too dangerous. There was a time when we hunted whales, because we were hungry, after the war. Only the Pamilacan men hunt whales.'

'But did you ever see whales?'

He paused. 'Of course. Many times, but usually so far off that it was difficult to see how many there were or how big they were.'

'What about sperm whales?'

'I see small ones but not so often. There is one very big one, dark grey, which I see nearly every year. It swims past the beach in the same season, about half a mile out to sea. I think it may be the same one I first saw maybe seven years ago. It was the biggest whale I ever met. More than ten fathoms.' Ramon, like most of the fishermen, always measured his whales in units of six feet.

He went on, 'It was so big that when I first saw it I thought it was a huge log floating in the sea. I was in my boat, and thought to myself, "Maybe this is an enormous tree, which no one owns, and it could be valuable wood." So I went closer, and then the log moved, and I saw it was a whale. So big that I was very afraid, and quickly went away.'

'What about a white whale — have you seen one of those?'

'I've not seen one myself. But Dios Rivera who lives nearby and also has a fishing boat, he saw a white whale, all white. It was about two to three fathoms long, with teeth, and it was robbing his net. The local name is Ugis.'

This was no Moby Dick, I thought to myself. It was too small, perhaps an albino, and possibly a pygmy sperm whale or a pilot whale. But at least Ramon was the sort of person who was interested in the history of his community. He took me half a mile up the road to where the last of the old-style fishing boats lay, half on the grass verge and half on the sea wall. It was a sad, abandoned spectacle. The keel was broken, and weeds sprouted through holes in the hull. Many of the older boats had been made of bamboo mesh, not planks. The mesh was so tightly woven that a thick coat of paint or varnish made it watertight. I had seen one-man boats on Pamilacan still constructed in this way, their hulls like slender needles. They looked like Eskimo kayaks, but cunningly curved up at the stern so that the boat turned like a weathercock into the wind when not paddled, and the occupant could sit facing the waves, fishing with a handline.

The owner of the discarded fishing boat was an 84-year-old, gaptoothed and wrinkled. He hobbled across the road to greet Ramon. The old man had given up the sea long ago and had turned to farming coconut groves. He pointed out the shattered stump of the little platform where the harpooner had once stood, while his companions paddled close up to the prey. Crews of as many as ten men, all crammed together and seated on wooden slats, had to paddle for five or six hours to get to their hunting grounds. They had taken whales occasionally, he told me. But sperm whales were too aggressive, and the meat did not taste good. The only time he had tried to harpoon a small sperm whale, the harpoon had simply bounced off. Baleen whales were fair game, if they were small enough. If they were too big, the harpoon boat might be towed helplessly for one or two days, out of sight of land. On one fishing trip they were dragged so far that it took them four days to paddle back to Camiguin. The men were so hungry that they had cut meat from the animal they were towing.

A white whale 'which stole from fishing nets' had also been seen on Mantigue, a tiny islet less than a mile offshore. Like Pamilacan, Mantigue has no fresh water, and supplies are carried from the main island to the little community of fishermen settled there. Like Pamilacan, too, Mantigue is ideally situated for the local fishing grounds. At certain seasons the hunt boats from Pamilacan base themselves there or bring their catch to butcher on the beach. Mantigue is pristine compared to Little Tondo. Formerly there had been drying racks on the beach for shark and manta flesh. Now the racks had been dismantled, or moved to another location upwind. 'Tourists don't like the smell' I was told. My informant was Theodoro 'Pagung' Portias, a 35-year-old fisherman who looked so oriental with his high cheekbones, narrow eyes and yellow skin that he could have been a model for

Melville's 'tiger yellow' Manila men. Tourism was the islet's future, and its two guesthuts rented to the visitors brought more cash income than fish. In the summer of 1981 a small white whale, three fathoms long, had been trapped in a fishnet, killed, and the flesh sold for 3,000 pesos. Pagung claimed that he often saw a big white whale offshore close by Ramon's house. It was 'about eight fathoms long' and seen usually at sunrise or sunset. But the word he used to describe it, 'balyena', did not necessarily mean a sperm whale, and as he could give no further details, I let the matter drop.

When I returned to Pamilacan, I found the community in a state of shock. A hunting boat had been destroyed the previous day. It had been dragged underwater by a very large whale shark. No lives had been lost, but it was a catastrophe for its owner. A local man, he could not afford to replace the vessel, and he and his crew had seen their livelihood pulled down beneath the waves. Less than a week before the same owner had allowed me to use his boat to film how a jumper leaped into the sea with the 'ganso' or steel hook. Now I did not feel justified in asking him for details of the calamity. The loss of the boat was far too grievous for him to be able to tell me about the incident. Instead, I asked to meet one of the other survivors.

I was directed to a humble thatch-and-plank cabin, painted bright yellow, which stood on the crest of the slope leading down to the brackish wells. There, with the help of Walen, my constant companion and interpreter, I enquired of the woman of the house if she knew someone called Marlon Talaboc, whom I had been told had survived the previous day's disaster.

'Yes,' she answered, 'he is my son.'

Shyly, Marlon came out of the cabin, and I was taken aback to see that he was only fifteen years old. The lad was lightly built and frail. He looked so boyish that it was difficult to believe that he had undergone the terrifying experience he was describing. Yet he did not look shocked. While his mother hovered protectively in the background, he sat on the wooden steps and recounted his story, haltingly at first, but then with increasing animation and confidence.

'We were going fishing for whale shark when some of my friends saw the whale shark and said, "Tung! [uncle] there's a whale shark!" We went very close, and the jumper said to the owner, "Oh! This is very big. How about it? Do you want me to jump it?" The owner said, "Why not? This is why we have come here, to catch shark." And before the jumper jumped, the owner told him, "You must put the hook in the proper place."

'After the jumper hooked the fish and the whale shark is gone down, he got back on board, and apologised to the owner and said, "Sorry I did not put the hook into the side of the shark, but near the gills." Then the owner of the boat said, "Okay, all of you crew move to the right side of the boat because the rope is on the left side." Then when the boat starts to be pulled down by the shark, Eman, who was the jumper, said, "Okay! Cut the rope!" But the owner says, "No, no, no, because the boat is not yet underwater." And the second time he said, "Cut the rope!"

'One, two, three times he tried to cut the rope, and on the fourth time when he cut at the rope, the knife broke. I don't know what happened then. I was the first to jump out of the boat, because the boat is beginning to go under. The last man to jump in is Rupo. And after that I looked for something floating. It was a piece of wood that covers the engine. We stay in the water for more than one and a half hours.'

'Who picked you up?' asked Walen.

'It was another fishing boat. They were looking for someone, too. We asked them, "Please can you take us to land?" And they did.'

Marlon leaned down and plucked at one of his bare toes. He seemed unconcerned, almost cheerful. Life on Pamilacan was too harsh to allow the islanders to brood on misfortune. They had to get on with the daily business of living. Other fishing boats from Pamilacan went searching for the hulk, hoping to salvage it for their friend, or even to locate pieces from the wreckage. But even with their phenomenal eyesight, they found nothing. The hunting boat had vanished entire. It must have been towed far away by the whale shark, and dragged into the ocean deep. Boat and beast, linked by the heavy rope, perished together.

The life of the Pamilacan fishermen was bound up just as inextricably with the fate of the creatures in the seas around them. If they and their families were to survive, the fishermen had to utilise every resource. Every morning when the tidal current was right, two fishermen would make their way past Nita's hut where I stayed. They carried simple spear guns, powered by rubber bands. They spent an hour or two on the reef, patiently stalking small reef fish that would provide a meal, but which neither net nor hook and line would catch. Fifty yards in the opposite direction, Nita's cousin entered the water with his brothers and older children. They carried a fine mesh net, and when they were chest-high among the waves, they threw and dragged the net to catch a few fingerlings. And when the moon was full and the tide was low, a bobbing lantern appeared on the tide line. It was carried between three men whom I recognised as crew from one of the most successful hunt boats. They moved as if in slow motion, stepping carefully through the shallows. One man held the lamp high, his companions on each side bent over like stalking herons. Each carried a cutlass, and scanned the clear shallow water. They were hunting for hermit crabs and small sea creatures. When they saw a slight movement in the water, they would freeze, then pace forward with infinite care. A sudden slash with the cutlass, a hand reached forward cautiously into the shallows to pinch a tiny animal, then snapped shut. They were like children on a holiday, laughing and joking, and jumping back in mock alarm at a scuttling shrimp, though I knew that, in other circumstances, they would boldly throw themselves on the back of a ten-ton whale shark. Their miniature catch was placed gently in a plastic bucket and carried back to the families in their cabins. And when the same men were away hunting, I saw a family group, two mothers and their daughters, silhouetted on the beach against the evening sun. The second youngest child minded a baby, while all the others paced up and down the glistening sand with softest footfalls, lest they alert the clams and other burrowing creatures on which they pounced.

When I talked about whales with the Pamilacan fishermen, their stories often had a familiar ring. I had read many of the same details in Melville's *Moby Dick*, where they were already twice-told because I had also located the same material in the books Melville had plagiarised. The best was written by a sea-going surgeon, and Melville bought himself a copy for $3.38, so that he could mark up the passages that he would weave into the fabric of his masterpiece. Almost nothing is known about Thomas Beale, surgeon, who described himself on the title page of his book as 'Demonstrator of Anatomy to the Eclectic Society of London'. Clearly whales fascinated him. English whaleships heading for the

Pacific, South Seamen as they were called, were required to carry a doctor, and Beale took advantage of this regulation to indulge his curiosity about sperm whales. He found a berth as ship's surgeon aboard the English whaleship *Kent* and sailed to the South Seas in October 1830. Three years and four months later he arrived back with enough material to publish the first comprehensive study of sperm whales. *The Natural History of the Sperm Whale* is a treasure hoard of first-hand information about whale anatomy, whale behaviour, whale sociology, and whale capture. Beale had gathered the data from his own observations, and from talking with the professional whale catchers. Melville judged that 'there are only two books in being, which at all pretend to put the living whale before you, and at the same time, in the remotest degree succeed in the attempt. These books are Beale's and Bennett's; both in their time surgeons to English South-Sea whale-ships, and both exact and reliable men.' The second of Melville's main source books, F. D. Bennett's *Narrative of a Whaling Voyage Around the World, 1833–1836* contained rather more travelogue and less natural history[*] than Beale's volume, though — interestingly from the point of view of the Pamilacan hook jumpers — Bennett did describe whale sharks. He calls them 'bone sharks' and says that the

[*] It also provided the artist J. M. Turner with the images for three whaling paintings.

sperm whale hunters avoided tackling the huge fish. 'They have been occasionally mistaken for whales, and harpooned by inexperienced whalers, when taking away the line with irresistible impetuosity, they have disappeared in the ocean's depths, and left their assailants to watch in vain for their return to the surface.'

Naturally, Melville had to assert his own claims to possessing whaling knowledge superior to his sources by adding condescendingly that 'the original matter touching the sperm whale to be found in their volumes is necessarily small; but so far as it goes it is, of excellent quality, though mostly confined to scientific description'. It was Melville dissembling as usual — in fact he plundered Beale's work shamelessly, sometimes almost copying phrase by phrase, and pirated Bennett with almost equal aplomb.

'The females [sperm whales],' Beale observed, 'are very remarkable for attachment to their young, which they may be frequently seen urging and assisting to escape from danger with the most unceasing care and fondness.' Victor Bano, a veteran Pamilacan fisherman, unwittingly confirmed Beale's remark when he told me how he had foolishly put his steel hook into a sperm whale calf. Victor was a lugubrious-looking man in his fifties, very thin, who puffed nervously at a cigarette as he spoke. He was so gaunt and grey that I wondered whether the cigarettes or his meagre diet were the reason for his haggard look. 'Once when we were on the

119

sea fishing for manta ray and were far from the island,' he told me, 'I saw something like spray from the sea — so we went closer. It was a baby sperm whale. All the crew of my boat said, "Maybe we should try to catch it because it is small enough." I jumped the whale with the hook, and it dived; and all my crew were laughing because I had succeeded in hooking it. Then we pulled the whale to the surface.

'When we had the whale to the surface, and it was close to the boat, I cut it with my knife, and the blood began to flow. Then there was a noise under the sea, and when I looked there were many sperm whale under the boat, who seemed to be coming to help the baby whale. When we saw the big sperm whales, the crew became frightened because we thought the whales would strike the boat and break it. One man shouted, "Get the hook out of the baby whale!" I was able to do this easily, and I loosed the rope which we had tied around the tail, and the baby whale got free. Then we started our engine and made for the island. The other people on the island asked why we had let the sperm whale go, as it was worth money. But I replied no, maybe my life is gone if I do not release the baby sperm whale, because the other whales are coming to help.'

Victor had been fishing for twenty-seven years. It was the only time he ever tried to catch a whale, and he would never do it again, whatever the species. He would stick to jumping manta ray, even though he had been injured many

120

times by contact with their skin, which was almost as rough as the whale shark's. He had suffered injuries on almost every part of his body. The only manta ray he had ever refrained from jumping was the white manta ray which he had seen just once, as it swam towards Jagna from the island of Siquijor. It was a giant: 'When I go very close, I see it was all white. I only looked at it, and did not try to catch it because the white manta ray is much stronger than the ordinary manta ray. And after that the ray went under the sea, very slowly.'

This was the fourth time that I had heard about the giant white manta ray — Max Valeroso had mentioned it, so had the two retired fishermen Francolino Operio and Amadeo Valeroso. So I checked the story with Nita, my landlady. 'Oh yes, the fishermen believe that the giant white manta ray must not be harmed,' she said. 'It is too big and strong, but it is also the leader of all the manta rays and the smaller rays too, the devil rays and eagle rays. If the white manta ray is attacked, it will tell the other rays, and all of them will swim away, and never come back. Pamilacan will lose its fishing.'

Then she added, 'They say the same thing about whale sharks. They believe there is a great white whale shark.'

With that, I realised that I had been overlooking a vital link in my search for Moby Dick.

Pamilacan was a place where the supernatural took many forms. Sometimes it was pagan. A magician or shaman was invited to the island at the start of the manta ray season. He came from Siquijor, an island famous for the skills of its sorcerers. His expenses were paid for by the Pamilacan fishermen who also supplied him with the pigs and other materials he needed for his ceremonies on the beach. There he would make sacrifices and intercede with the spirits of the sea, asking them for good catches for the coming year. The intervention of the shaman, I was assured, produced immediate results. The proof was that he was rewarded with a proportion of the first, always excellent, catch. Only when the shaman died about a decade earlier, and no one from his family inherited his mystic powers, did the annual ritual cease. And, said the fishermen, the catch of big manta had been in decline ever since.

Now, more often, the supernatural takes a Christian guise. The carved wooden cross in the Church of San Isidoro at Chapel Side had washed ashore on the beach as flotsam. The day it arrived, I was told, the bell in the chapel in the centre of the island began to toll on its own, without any human hand to ring it. Alerted, the villagers had searched the shoreline and found the cross. No one had any idea where the splendid cross had come from. The most likely explanation was that it came from a shipwreck. The villagers salvaged the cross, and decided that they should place it in the central chapel, and enlarge the building into a church, even though there was no resident priest on the island. When they tried to carry the cross inland, they could not move it. Miraculously it had grown heavy. Even ten men together, Nita told me, were not strong enough to lift it. Yet when it had been picked up from the beach, it had been light enough for two men to lift. This was taken as a sign that the new church had to be built near the beach where the cross had come ashore, and so Chapel Side came into being.

There was still no resident priest on the island, though the hunters of whale shark were very devout. At the start of every hunting voyage the boats, including those from Little Tondo, would make a short layover in the small cove below the Spanish Tower before the fishermen set out on their dangerous work. The youngest crew member was sent ahead to buy candles. Then the crew walked in single file up from the shore, through the palm trees, to the church. As they entered the church, each man took a candle, lit it, and placed it before the cross. Then he would pray, kiss the shaft of the cross, and set out on a circuit of all the small effigies of saints, half a dozen of them, which were ranged around the back of the altar. Before each shrine he crossed himself, bowed, and prayed.

Nor would the fishermen go to sea on a fishing trip if a church ceremony was in progress. Once a month a priest would come across from Bohol and conduct a service in San Isidoro. At the end of the service, the villagers of Chapel Side took the cross out of the church and carried it around their houses. It was believed that if anyone set out on a journey while the cross was in procession, no good would come of that trip. Even the priest and his staff were not exempt. Nita described an occasion when one of the priest's assistants had wanted to hurry back to Bohol. 'To go to a cockfight,' Nita said. He had been warned to wait until the procession of the cross was ended, but he ignored the advice and set out. Half an hour later he was back on shore in Pamilacan, soaking wet and repentant. His boat had been mysteriously capsized less than half a mile from shore, even though the sea was calm.

It was into this category of strange supernatural powers that I was prepared to place the islanders' belief in the Great White Manta Ray and the Great White Whale Shark. Both animals had the same character. They were huge, far larger in size than the other members of their species. They were both leaders, in some mysterious way, of all their tribe. They communicated with their followers, and held sway over them. They were the 'kings' of their race. And the king manta ray and the great whale shark were all-white. The colour white denoted a mystic power. This was a theme that Melville himself had developed at great length. He had devoted an entire chapter to it, 'The Whiteness of the Whale', and he cited instance after instance of awe-inspiring whiteness, from the White Dog of the Iroquois Indians, sacrificed at midwinter, to the sacred White Elephant as symbol of the royal house of Siam, and in due course included the whiteness of Moby Dick.

But one thing did not fit: the islanders of Pamilacan referred to the white manta ray as being a real animal. The descriptions of the huge pale creature provided by Victor Bano, by Max Valeroso and the old men, Amadeo Valeroso and Francolino Operio, had been respectful, but matter-of-fact. They described seeing a gigantic white manta ray, some seven or eight metres broad. These eyewitnesses were not braggarts. They did not boast, and they did not spin yarns. In common with the other fishermen of Pamilacan I had talked to, they were remarkably low-key in how they described their experiences, which — if they were hook jumpers wrestling with whale sharks and manta rays underwater — were remarkable enough. Nor, as far as I could tell, did the Pamilacan hunters embellish truth. They gave plausible measurements for the size of the animals they took, which were in the range of figures being collected by the representatives of KKP. In short, I had not detected 'fishermen's tales' and, on balance, I believed that they really had encountered an outsized white manta ray swimming in the seas off Pamilacan, perhaps even more than one. But I had never met anyone who claimed to have seen the Great White Whale Shark.

Until I met Miguel Areno.

I had been waiting to meet him since I had first

come to the island. But getting that chance had been difficult. Miguel was the local hero, the ace 'hook jumper'. Everyone, including Walen, who was a good judge of people, considered Miguel to be the most skilled, most daring, and most successful jumper. He had his own boat, and like a semi-nomadic forest hunter, he ranged around the seas of the Southern Philippines looking for his prey. He fished off Jagna, off Camiguin, off Floridel. No one knew when he would return to Pamilacan. He came and went as he pleased. The best chance to meet him, Walen had told me, would be just before a major Sunday cock-fight. Then 'Igue' as they called him might show for a day or so, before heading off again on a hunting trip. He was, Walen said, the finest exponent of the technique of 'flying' down to a manta ray. This meant spotting a manta ray swimming so deep that the jumper had to use a heavy weight to carry him down fast enough to meet and hook the animal. The weight was shaped so it acted like an underwater steering wing, and the successful jumper had to calculate the angle and speed of his descent, anticipate the direction and speed of the manta, and take account of the underwater currents, all in order to arrive on top of the moving target at precisely the right moment. Miguel could do this at depths of seventy to eighty feet. It was said that no one else, except perhaps his uncle, Max Valeroso, had caught so many Bryde's whales in their lifetimes, and Miguel had successfully jumped two whales in a single day. There was no animal too big for Miguel to tackle. He was credited with being the first man courageous enough to try jumping a Bryde's whale at the moment when it was breaching. It was a technique that Miguel had worked out from observing the huge animals as they threw themselves clear of the water. Both Miguel and Max were crazy enough to jump whales when they were drunk, and Miguel was sufficiently swashbuckling — so it was murmured in a low voice — to take a Bryde's whale after the government had banned the catching of whales. The animal had been seen off the west side of Pamilacan, and Miguel simply could not resist the challenge. He and his crew had set out in a boat, and he was so skilful that he had herded the whale out into open water, and out of sight of the cliffs. Then he had jumped and taken it. It was too risky to haul the carcass into Pamilacan for fear that someone would report the kill to the authorities. So under cover of darkness, Miguel towed the whale towards a small, quiet landing place on Bohol. En route he had been intercepted by another boat which he thought was a police patrol craft. He was just about to cut the towline when the approaching boat identified itself as another fishing boat, curious to know what was happening with a night-time tow. Miguel bought the crew's silence by offering them a piece of the carcass, and then beached the whale, cut it up, and distributed it to the markets on Bohol before it could be traced. It was the last Bryde's whale to be taken by the fishermen of Pamilacan.

Miguel did appear for the Sunday cockfight, as Walen had predicted. I arranged to meet with him next morning down at Little Tondo, where Miguel's hunt boat was drawn up on the beach for maintenance. The condition of the boat told me something about the man: the vessel was in first-class order, trim and smart, but not in the least flamboyant. Every item of equipment — the ropes, steel hook, nets — was in its proper place and in good condition, not patched or spliced, and ready to go to sea at a moment's notice. Miguel himself gave much the same impression. He was in his early thirties, a wiry, energetic man who obviously enjoyed his work. He loved the sea, and as long as he was fit and strong enough to do so, he would continue to be a hunter.

'The happiest time of my lifetime was when I was twenty years old. Because in that one year I caught twenty Bryde's whales.' We were sitting on the sand in the shadow of his hunt boat, and I had bought him his favourite drink, a half-bottle of rum mixed with a small Coca-Cola, which he was drinking from a purple plastic jug.

'I began to go fishing with the jumping hook when I was fourteen years old. In my lifetime I estimate that I have caught more than a hundred Bryde's whales, and seventy whale shark.'

I asked him whether he had ever tried to tackle a sperm whale. His reply was straightforward.

'I've often seen sperm whales, close to the island. In groups of up to twenty, and on the surface. But I didn't try to catch them, because I know that when you touch one sperm whale, the other sperm whale will come to its help, and they will hurt you.'

'What about a white manta ray? Have you ever seen one?'

Miguel shook his head. 'No, I've never seen a white manta ray. But Max Valeroso has seen one, and maybe some others.'

'What about a white whale shark?'

'I've seen it,' Miguel answered quietly. Then added, 'And tried to catch it. But could not.'

Walen had been translating Miguel's words, and I asked him to repeat them in case I had not heard correctly. Yes, Walen assured me, Miguel said that he had seen the white whale shark, and he tried to jump it. I asked for more details.

Miguel was again matter-of-fact. 'It was in 1990, before I owned my own boat, and we were on the sea looking for whale shark. I saw something astern of the boat, and told the helmsman to turn back. When we came closer, I said to myself, "Oh, what is this! This is a white whale shark!"

' "Can I jump it?" I asked the owner of the boat, and he answered, "Why not! That's what we need." Then the whale shark comes near the surface and I get the hook, and I jump the whale shark, and it is done. Then the whale shark swims off very, very strongly. The shark does not dive, but swims close to the surface as if he is going out to sea. The shark is so strong that the boat is out of balance. It is rocking from side to side, and the boat is about to get into trouble. The rope is all gone, and at that moment I am scared because the whale shark is so strong. After the shark travels on a little, the hook pulls out. The strength of the whale shark has broken it.

'When we finish pulling back the rope into the boat, I say to the owner that maybe we can skip this day, and go back to the land. I am scared of the sea. When we get back on shore, I told the story to the old men that I had tried to catch the white whale shark, and the old men said, "What the hell! You, Miguel, why did you try to catch the white whale shark? Don't you know that the white whale shark must be left alone — it is the leader of the ordinary whale sharks. If it is taken or hurt, all the other whale sharks will leave and never return!" '

Miguel's story was unvarnished. There was no artifice. I believed him.

'How big do you think the white whale shark was?' I asked.

Miguel thought a moment, then answered, 'I calculate that the mouth was about two fathoms across, and the body was longer than this boat of mine.'

I was impressed. The largest whale shark ever recorded and measured accurately, according to reference books, was just under forty feet long. It had been taken by fishermen off the coast of India. I had no idea of quite how that whale shark had been measured — from tip of nose to end of the tail, I imagined. But that was not much bigger than the largest whale shark already caught that year on Pamilacan. It had measured thirty-seven feet long, and it had not attracted much comment from the fishermen as being anything out of the ordinary. The size of the white whale shark that Miguel had tangled with would have been of an entirely different order. That monster must have been over fifty feet long, perhaps as much as sixty feet. It was the size of animal which marine biologists guess at when they theorise that whale sharks are capable of growing to sixty feet in length. But no such animal has ever been seen . . . except perhaps by Miguel Areno. And the animal he had seen had been all white. I had made another step along the path to understanding how the legend of Moby Dick might have arisen.

Part Three

TONGA

'Queequeg in his wild sort of way jumped upon the bulwarks, from thence into the bows of one of the whale boats hanging to the side; and then bracing his left knee, and poising his harpoon, cried out in some such way as this: "Cap'ain, you see him small drop tar on water dere? You see him? Well, spose him one whale eye, well, den!" and taking sharp aim at it, he darted the iron right over old Bildad's broad brim, clean across the ship's deck, and struck the glistening tar spot out of sight.'

HERMAN MELVILLE, *Moby Dick*

How Kea rode home on the back of Big Whale is a pan-Pacific folktale. Familiar to Fijians, the Maori of New Zealand also know it. In Tonga, line drawings illustrate the story in schoolchildren's primers. On the shelves of Mayor Kemitite's municipal library in Nuku Hiva I came across a scholarly rendition recorded by anthropologists while they were collecting the oral traditions of the vanishing Marquesan culture. The Marquesans believed that Kea had set out from their islands and travelled to the Land of the Long White Cloud, New Zealand, and then returned on the back of Tunua nui, Big Whale. The Maori claim that the journey was the other way round. But in its main elements the story is the same, and the whale is essential.

Kea crosses the ocean with the help of sea animals. In the Marquesan version Kea lives on the island of Hiva Oa, and travels far away to the land of Vanoi, riding in the belly of a shark. On arrival he slices his way out of the shark's stomach with the shark's tooth implement he normally uses for cutting his hair. He finds that

135

he is in a country of women. Lacking husbands, they go down to the beach and impregnate themselves with pandanus roots. Kea hides by the shore, and reveals himself to the chieftainess, Hina i Vanoi. They become lovers, and Hina takes Kea back to her house and conceals him there. Soon her companions notice that their chieftainess is no longer joining them on the beach, and suspect that she has found a man. But Hina denies this. Then on the day when one of the women is due to give birth, Hina tells Kea that two minor gods, Pohihia and Pohahaa, will be summoned from the bush. They will cut open the woman, extract the baby, and the woman will die. Kea explains in detail how birthing can be accomplished without the death of the mother, and how to look after the newborn infant. Hina intervenes at the crucial moment, the birth is successful, and Pohihia and Pohahaa vanish for ever into the bush. From thenceforth the women of Vanoi practise normal childbirth.

Kea and Hina live happily together until Kea notices a single white strand growing among Hina's hair. She points out that Kea's hair is also turning white, and takes him to the beach and asks him to surf the waves. He does so, but it makes no difference. When Hina has ridden three waves, she comes ashore looking young 'and as fresh as a newly peeled shrimp'. Kea realises that his stay in Vanoi must come to an end, because Hina can remain youthful for ever, but he will not. Hina summons her brother Tunua nui, Big Whale. The whale approaches the beach, and Hina instructs him to take Kea on his back and carry him to Hiva Oa. She gives strict instructions to Kea that as Big Whale carries him, Kea must reach out and kick certain islands as they pass. If that is done, Tunua nui will know when to turn around and how to find his way home to Vanoi.

Kea forgets his instructions, and fails to kick the islands. So when Big Whale reaches Hiva Oa, he blunders up on the beach head-first, and is stranded. The people living near the landing place seize him, cut him up, and eat Big Whale. Far away in Vanoi, Hina knows what has happened, and weeps for the death of her brother.

In due course Hina bears Kea's son and names him Te hina tu o Kea. When the lad comes of age, he insists on going to find his father. This time Hina calls up her younger brother Tunua iti, Small Whale, and asks him to carry his nephew to the Marquesas. Once again, Hina tells the passenger to be sure to kick the islands as he passes so the whale knows how to return. This time the instructions are obeyed. Te hina tu o Kea kicks the islands in the correct sequence, Little Whale brings him to land at the right spot, and turns around so that the whale beaches tail-first. The lad steps ashore, and the local people, seeing the whale's tail at the water's edge, rush down to pull it ashore so they can butcher the animal as they did Tunua nui. But they have miscalculated. They grab the tail, and

Tunua iti swims powerfully away, dragging the villagers after him, and drowning them in revenge for the death of Tunua nui.

Kea's story is a glimpse of how the Pacific peoples regarded whales in the days before European contact. The folktale emerges from the era of the seaborne migrations of the Polynesians. The land of Vanoi is in New Zealand, and to get there from the Marquesas Kea would have to have crossed 3,000 miles of ocean. The Polynesians navigated these immense distances by watching the sun and stars, the patterns of waves and ocean swells, the flight paths of birds, the signs of seaweed, fish and flotsam. They were magnificent observers of the natural world, and knew the ocean intimately. They were also animist, attributing living souls to inanimate objects and to natural phenomena. So it is puzzling how seldom whales appear in their art and mythology. Kea's adventure is only one of a handful of whale stories. Sharks occur in these stories much more often than whales. To this day there are islands which recognise shark gods and have shark totems; and everywhere in Polynesia the shark's tooth is a commonplace motif, on necklaces, earrings and bracelets. The traditional tattoo patterns of the Marquesas represent turtles, sharks, fish, octopus — but seldom whales or even dolphins. The omission is perplexing. And when whales do appear in the folklore, often there is an attendant pitiless streak. The murderers of Big Whale meet their just deserts, but in a Maori version of the story, Kea is a powerful *tuhunga* or shaman. When he reaches his home shore, he says his spells, and deliberately holds down Big Whale so that he can block his blow hole with sand. 'The Big Gamboller' suffocates.

This dearth of information about whales was all the more baffling because sperm whales provided Polynesians with an object they prized above all else — the *tabua*.

Some of the finest *tabua* are on display in the National Museum of Fiji: sperm whale teeth, they are stained a rich reddish brown, the colour of prime mahogany newly oiled. A loop of sennit, coconut-fibre cord plaited as cunningly as heavy silk, passes through a hole drilled in each end of the whale's tooth. The loop was held in one hand, and the tooth in the other, when the *tabua* were offered during ceremonies. These are 'presentation *tabua*'. They were so full of spiritual power that when offered to a chief and accompanied by a request, that chief was honour-bound to grant the request if he accepted the *tabua*. In Fiji, Samoa, and Tonga many *tabua* were also the shrines of ancestor spirits. They were also marriage tokens, gifts of the highest value, given as a mark of esteem, and — in a gruesome twist among the war-loving Fijians — awarded to a killer who had successfully finished off a rival chieftain. The grave goods buried with a Fijian chieftain included a musket or a club for his protection against demons, and a *tabua*. The ghost of the chief was expected to throw the *tabua* at a spirit tree in the Otherworld. If he hit the tree, then his wives would be strangled and buried with him so that they might serve their master in the afterlife. It is not known how the *tuhunga* established whether the dead man had hit his mark, but the *tabua* was irrecoverable, so they sometimes buried a copy made of wood.[*]

Several of the museum's *tabua* are surprisingly large; they must have come from the jaws of sperm whales considerably bigger than is usual today. Their size backs up claims by early whalemen that they occasionally took bull sperm whales as much as eighty, even ninety feet in length. Such giants are not seen in modern times, so perhaps there once were sperm whales as huge as Moby Dick. If so, the Polynesians would have been extremely reluctant to tackle such leviathans. They relied instead on removing the teeth from sperm whales which had stranded, and a Fijian folktale traces this practice back to the time of the First Man. He had three daughters and no sons, runs the story. When a half-dead castaway drifted ashore from another island, the daughters rescued him, and fell in love with him. Their father refused to let them marry unless the stranger provided a miracle. The castaway was disconsolate for some

[*] A *tabua* still appears as a symbol on the Fijian twenty-cent coin. To ethnographers, Fiji has a blend of Melanesian and Polynesian cultures.

time, until he remembered seeing a dead whale on the beach. He went back and began to tug out the teeth. One of them was very difficult to pull. When it suddenly came free, his arm flew back and he accidentally knocked out four of his own teeth. He burned the remains of the whale, and went back to the First Man claiming that the whale teeth he carried were his own teeth which he had extracted, planted in the ground, and had changed to whale teeth. This was accepted as a miracle, the castaway married, and First Man ordained that future wedding gifts must always include whale's teeth.

Some whales' teeth in the museum are so big that they had been split in slices, steamed flat, and riveted together to form magnificent breastplates. These were mostly ornamental, but early Western visitors to the islands saw native warriors wearing corselets of body armour made from plates of whale teeth to protect them from arrows and spears in battle. And in the museum those spears were on display — vicious-looking weapons, up to four metres long and tipped with bony stingray barbs. The Fijians were particularly adept with the javelin. An American sailor in 1831 described how a chief he called Santa Beeta gave a demonstration of his throwing accuracy. A coconut was placed on top of the anchor windlass in the bow of the ship. The chief stood at the taffrail in the stern, sixty feet away. Bending back 'at a fearful angle with the deck, and firmly grasping the spear by its centre, he drove it, after careful aim, directly through the centre of the nut'. His aim was known to be so true that another crew member insisted on standing within two feet of the target coconut. It was little wonder, I reflected, that given such ability at throwing war javelins and aiming fish spears, the Pacific islanders made first-class harpooners on the Western whaleships. Melville's tattooed Queequeg was Polynesian, of course, and in the streets of New Bedford Ishmael saw 'Feegeeans, Tongatabooarrs, Erromanggoans, Pannangians, and Brighggians' — presumably all Pacific islanders recruited for whaling.

I was on my way, via Fiji, to track down a 'Tongatabooarr'. This was Melville's flamboyant spelling for a native of Tongatapu, largest island in the kingdom of Tonga. Tongan craftsmen had carved most of the whale-tooth inlays on the war clubs in the Fiji Museum, riveted together the breastplates, and fashioned many of the whale tooth earrings and pendants. Tongan craftsmen had also been the specialists in staining the sacred *tabua*. They would polish the tooth smooth, soak it in coconut oil, then smoke it slowly over a fire of sugar cane. This gave the surface its rich red patina, so highly prized that *tabua* were kept carefully wrapped in a bark cloth so the colour did not fade in daylight, and they were only displayed on special occasions. Tonga, too, was where the sperm whales seem to have stranded most frequently, and Tonga — by coincidence — was the last place in modern times where Polynesians hunted great whales with hand harpoons from open boats. Their techniques would have been familiar on Melville's *Pequod*. If there was a modern heir to Queequeg, my best chance to find him would be in Tonga.

An intimate portrait of Tongan life was written a full generation before Melville wrote *Moby Dick*. This is thanks to another castaway, William Mariner. His story reads like a boy's adventure story, because that is precisely what it was. He was fourteen years old when, in 1805, he shipped out from London as clerk aboard the *Port au Prince*, under the delightfully named Captain Duck. The 500-ton *Port au Prince* was setting off for the South Pacific to raid the Spanish colonies in Peru and Chile, and intercept colonial shipping. Only if pickings were slim would her master seek to recoup the expenses of the voyage by heading for the South Sea whaling grounds. So the *Port au Prince* made a very strange whaling ship. With ninety men aboard, she had three times the usual number of a whaleship's crew, the extra hands being needed for shore raids and boarding parties; and as well as harpoons she was armed with twenty-four nine- and twelve-pound cannon, and eight twelve-pound carronades on the quarterdeck. She was, in other words, a legalised pirate ship.

Her guns helped change Tongan history. The *Port au Prince* cruised the coasts of Chile and Peru — Mariner notes passing Mocha Island where five years later 'Mocha Dick' would put in his first appearance — but failed to capture any rich prizes. In August Captain Duck died, and command passed to the whaling master, Mr Brown. He had had his fill of privateering and, judging the vessel to be dangerously leaky, set off for the whaling grounds to find an island where he could make repairs. In due course *Port au Prince* came to anchor off a small island called Lifuka in the Ha'apai archipelago in central Tonga. By then the crew was openly mutinous, and refused to begin work on careening and repairing the ship until they were given shore leave. Distracted by these difficulties, the unfortunate Mr Brown failed to see the warning signs when a number of Tongan warriors began visiting the ship and lounging around on board, ostensibly to inspect the new arrival.

Soon Brown was lured ashore, unarmed, and then clubbed to death on the beach. By then there were something like three hundred Tongans aboard the *Port au Prince*, and they promptly turned on the hapless crew and massacred them. Mariner surrendered to a couple of the war chiefs, expecting to die. Instead they brought him up on deck, where sat a Tongan warrior described as 'a short, squat, naked figure, about fifty years of age . . . with a seaman's jacket soaked in blood thrown over one shoulder; on the other rested his iron-wood club, spattered with blood and brains; while the frightfulness of his appearance was increased by a constant blinking with one of his eyes, and a convulsive motion on one side of his mouth'. Behind the man lay a row of twenty-two bodies, the corpses of crew members, 'perfectly naked and arranged side by side in regular order, but so dreadfully bruised and battered about the head that only two or three of them could be recognised'. A Tongan who had been counting the kill was reporting the score to his chief, 'immediately after which they began to throw them overboard'.

Mariner, the ship's cooper, and a number of the shore party were spared, and Mariner spent the next four years as an involuntary guest of the Tongan king, whom he called 'Finow'. This was King Finau Ulukalala, a warlord who liked to wear in his belt a whaler's cutlass, the blade of which was two feet long and three inches wide. The carronades he salvaged from *Port au Prince* quickly helped make him supreme over Ha'apai and the neighbouring Vava'u island group. He spared the lives of several other members of the privateer's crew so they could be kept on as gunners. But Mariner became his personal favourite as 'Finow' was under the impression that the lad came from a royal, or at least an aristocratic, family in England. Social status was all-important in Tonga. When Finow went aboard the *Port au Prince* to inspect his prize, he noticed that one of his men, a commoner, had climbed to the top of a mast and was prising out bits of valuable iron. His presumption irritated Finow, and he beckoned to one of his warriors who had a musket. The man took aim, fired, and shot the looter out of the mast-top. The victim plummeted to his death, the impact on to the deck breaking both thighs and fracturing his skull. Much later, when Mariner had learned enough Tongan, he ventured to ask Finow 'how he could be so cruel as to kill the poor man for so trifling a fault. His majesty replied that he was only a low, vulgar fellow — a cook — and that neither his life nor death was of any consequence to society.' In the Tongan social scale a cook was considered the most base, while a canoe carpenter 'esteemed the most respectable.'

Canoe carpenters were also the practitioners of the decorative art of whale-tooth ivory. Their craft had a special name, Fono Le, and was done 'with extraordinary neatness, considering the rude tool they employ, which is generally a *togi* (or small adze) made out of a European chisel, a piece of an old saw, or even a flattened nail to which a handle is affixed'. Only the very best clubs were decorated, either because they had a particularly beautiful shape, or because the wood was exceptional, or if the club had 'done much execution'. In which case, besides receiving its whale-tooth inlay, the club was honoured with its own name. When a canoe arrived from one of the outlying islets with a report that a large, dead sperm whale had drifted up on to a reef, 'Immediately all the chiefs ordered their canoes to be launched,' Mariner writes, and recounts how he went along to see what would happen. They found the stranded whale 'in a very bad state, half decayed, and sending forth a disagreeable odour'. This was no deterrent to 'the lower orders' who managed to make a meal of it. But their chief object was to extract the teeth, which were collected and made into necklaces 'which form an agreeable ornament upon their brown skins . . . much prized by them on account of its scarcity as well as beauty'.

Finow later described to Mariner an episode when a big sperm whale carcass had washed up on an islet so small that only two people lived on it, a man and his wife. Finow had promptly gone there to claim the whale's teeth, only to find that the teeth had already been extracted. The occupier of the island was questioned, and went immediately to his hut, dug into the thatch, and produced a basket. But the basket contained only two teeth. The man suspected that his wife had taken and hidden the rest, but when he questioned her, she denied doing so. In his defence the man pleaded to Finow that it was impossible for him to have concealed the teeth because, as a commoner, he had no right to keep them. If he tried to sell them they were so valuable that he would have been asked where they came from, and the first chief who saw them would have confiscated them. Tiring of the interrogation, Finow encouraged the wife's memory by signalling his retainers to beat in her husband's brains in front of her. This they did, but it was not until they had their clubs raised over her head as well that she had a change of mind. Leading the way to another hiding-place, she produced one more tooth. This was *lèse majesté,* so Finow ordered the woman to be clubbed to death on the spot. Some years later, the missing teeth were discovered by the intervention of a *tuhunga* who divined the spot where they were buried. Mariner by then was sufficiently attuned to Tongan customs to point out that Finow had been acting to the dictates of the society in which he lived. Whale teeth were the exclusive property of the aristocracy; for a commoner to retain them was therefore theft; and in Tonga, theft was punishable by death. 'In the Fiji islands, whale teeth are held if possible, in still greater estimation,' the young Englishman added, 'for it would be dangerous there for a man, unless he be a great chief, and even then, if he were a foreigner, to be known to have a whale's tooth about him. The personal possession of such valuable property would endanger his life.'

Mariner was returning from a fishing trip by canoe when, by chance, he saw the sails of a passing European vessel. Paddling out to intercept, he scrambled aboard and was nearly knocked straight back into the water by a sentry who mistook him for a marauding native. By then the eighteen-year-old Englishman was sunburned dark brown and wore his hair long and tied up in a knot under a turban. His only garment was an apron of leaves.[*]

This was how, according to Melville, his fictional Queequeg had joined the whaling fraternity as a very tenacious volunteer. Queequeg was son of the 'King of Kokovoko', and wanted to see the world beyond the confines of his small island. When the captain of a visiting Yankee whaling ship refused to sign him on, Queequeg paddled out in his canoe to a strait where he knew the vessel would pass. He grabbed hold of the foreign ship, kicked off his canoe so that it capsized and sank, and scrambled up on deck where he clung on to a ring bolt on the deck until the captain agreed to take him. 'Kokovoko', Melville indicated, was imaginary — 'an island far away to the South and West. It is not down in any map; true places never are.' But that does not stop speculation about whether Melville's own travels had provided an original for Queequeg. Mehevi, the 'King of the Typees', is one candidate. Another, much more likely, is the Maori harpooner on the Sydney barque '*Julia*', which picked up Melville from Nuku Hiva between 1 August and 15 August 1842 at the end of his adventure in the valley of the Typees. The '*Julia*' was, in reality, the Australian whaling barque *Lucy Ann* under a Captain Vinton. She was short of crew, and Vinton was looking for replacements. Melville's book *Omoo* describes

[*] He subsequently became an unsuccessful London stockbroker.

149

the subsequent voyage in such detail that it is clearly based on his own observation. The only harpooner left aboard was a 'wild New Zealander or *Mowree* as his countrymen are more commonly called'. The Maori's name was Bembo, and he kept to himself most of the time, 'out on the bowsprit, fishing for albicores with a bone hook'. He was a very competent seaman and for a short while he even held temporary command of the '*Julia*' when Captain Vinton was sick. 'In truth a better seaman never swore,' was how Melville put it. But Bembo was moody, and treated with caution, even fear, by the rest of the crew. He was a hard man, liable to get carried away when his blood was up. There was a story that in one close engagement with a whale, Bembo had thrown both his harpoons, and missed. The whaleboat had closed with the same whale a second time, and again Bembo, the ace harpooner, had missed with both harpoons. The boat crew had jeered, and Bembo was so stung by their taunts that on the third attempt he 'bounded upon the whale's back, and for one dizzy second was seen there. The next, all was foam and fury, and both were out of sight.' The boatmen sheered off, flinging out the whale line as fast as they could, until it suddenly went taut, and the boat surged through the water, towed by the whale. 'Where was the Mowree?' asked Melville rhetorically. 'His brown hand was on the boat's gunwale; and he was hauled aboard in the very midst of the mad bubbles that burst under the bows. Such a man, or devil if you will, was Bembo.'

Melville did not claim himself to have seen a man leap, harpoon in hand, on the back of a sperm whale. It was another 'wild yarn' of the whale fishery, and it seemed a tall story. Later I was to learn differently.

For the moment I was interested that Bembo joined the '*Julia*' when she called by the Bay of Islands in New Zealand at the start of her whaling voyage. This was the place where many of the Maori harpooners signed on, and then spread among the islands of Polynesia during the mid- to late nineteenth century. It was precisely by this route that a young part-Maori harpooner named Albert Edward Cook had come to Tonga in 1890, and established the Tongan whale fishery which lasted almost a century, until it was banned by Finow's descendant, Taufa'ahau Tupou IV, the current King of Tonga. And it was Albert Edward Cook's grandson that I wanted to meet. He was Tonga's 'last harpooner'.

The first thing I noticed about Samson Cook was his almost stone-faced expression. He had lean, regular features, a strong nose, and pronounced cheekbones. Two deep furrows ran from the side of his nose down to the corners of a wide, straight and close mouth, giving him a slightly patrician expression. His skin was the colour of milky coffee, the product of his mixed descent, part Maori, part Tongan, part European. At sixty-seven years of age, his grizzled hair was almost all gone, and when he tilted his head back slightly and looked at you through his narrowed brown eyes, he seemed almost stern. He had what in the theatre is called 'presence'. He also had large, square hands with strong fingers, and although only about five feet seven inches tall, he gave the impression of being a much bigger, more dominant man. He was barrel-chested; he had not an ounce of surplus flesh on him, and he walked on thick strong legs with a slight limp. He had the quick, active paces of a man who seems to have no doubts in his mind and is in a hurry to get on with the next job. He was also, when I first saw him, dressed in a very old-fashioned long black frock-coat, black shoes, and black trousers. And carrying a black bible in his hand. Samson Cook, retired harpooner, had become a lay preacher in the Tongan Wesleyan church.

Father Mapple of the Whaleman's Chapel in New Bedford immediately sprang to mind. Father Mapple is Melville's wonderful creation, the nautical priest who preaches to the whalemen and their families in a chapel decorated with wall tablets commemorating whalemen lost at sea. He delivers his sermons from a pulpit shaped like a boat's prow, and he climbs up into it by a ship's rope ladder, which he hauls up after him. Father Mapple's language is larded with sea-going expression and similes, and he is probably modelled on a real cleric,

Father Edward Taylor, who was a famous preacher in Boston at the time. Samson Cook dressed in a manner reminiscent of Father Mapple, but there the resemblance ended. Instead of a fire-and-brimstone delivery, Samson Cook spoke in a gentle, alert voice, and in a rich Tongan accent where 'Jesus' was pronounced 'Zizuss'.

Samson lived in a tiny house, little more than a shack, on the seafront in Nuku'alofa, the capital of Tonga. The house was midway between the new commercial harbour and the splendid Victorian confection of an edifice which is the royal palace, originally imported piece by piece, pre-fabricated, from New Zealand. On the pavement outside Samson's house was a large portable wooden rack. On it were displayed three tiers of giant white clam-shells. Samson made a very small, very irregular, income by selling seashells to tourists who might perhaps walk so far along the seafront. Turning in past the low picket fence, and pushing open a plain plywood door painted blue, one came into a front room no more than six feet by eight. Here were stacks of clam-shells, helmet conchs, another display rack, and, on a rickety table, a scatter of smaller decorative shells. A second door led through to Samson's living quarters where a low bed served as a sofa. There was a plain wood table, another bed with some old magazines on it, and a wooden chair. A curtain closed off the tiny back room where Samson kept his priest's garb hung on a nail, a few spare clothes and his private possessions in two or three cardboard boxes. He was a widower, and though a daughter brought him supplies from the market, he looked after himself. Everything was neat, clean and shipshape — a dresser with a stack of assorted plates, two mugs hug up on hooks, and a washing-up bowl. There was no running water, but a tap near the back door, and a pair of dangerous-looking electric wires led to the socket where Samson plugged in his kettle.

Slung in rope loops under the single window were the tools of his former calling. There were at least a dozen of them — harpoons and whale lances. Their shafts had been newly replaced in a heavy, reddish wood. And Samson had been overhauling his equipment, for the swivel heads and the leaf-shaped lance blades gleamed with the bright shine of sharpened steel.

Samson gestured to me to take a seat on the ancient bed, and settling back in his chair by the table, tilted his head back and gave me one of those characteristic, almost forbidding glances. 'My grandfather was Albert Edward Cook,' he announced, with a slight pause of emphasis between each word, and at once it was clear that he was immensely proud of his grandfather and his family. 'He came here from New Zealand by sailing ship. When the ship went away, he stayed. He stayed on Ha'apai, and he married a local girl. Ilise. She was my grandmother. He was a clever man, was Albert Edward Cook. He taught all the others how to catch whales. Before then, no one knew how to catch whales. He was a very smart man, very smart,' and Samson shook his head admiringly.

The whales that Albert Edward had hunted were mostly humpback whales. They come seasonally to Tonga to breed and to give birth in the warm sheltered waters of the Ha'apai group and the Vava'u archipelago to the north. In the 1880s there had been, briefly, a whale fishery offshore. Foreign vessels had 'humpbacked' off Vava'u in the 1880s, taking the whales for their oil when the supply of sperm whale was depleted, and it was probably this trade which had brought Albert Edward to Tonga for the first time. When the foreign whaleships moved on, Albert had remained. It was said that he was only in his teens, that he was part Welsh or his European ancestors came originally from Devon, even that he was related to the great Captain James Cook. In any event, he was an entrepreneur and natural leader of men. He built his own whaleboat, a smaller copy of the New England whaleboats, and with his family had begun to hunt humpback whales from the shore, using hand harpoons which he made himself, again copied from the Yankee whaleboats. 'He was a very *smaaaart* man,' Samson repeated, shaking his head in admiration again. 'He make the boats, he show his sons what to do, and he watches the whale very close. Pretty

155

soon, he have two boats. One boat to hunt the whale, one boat to standby, in case they need help.'

'Was there ever an accident?' I asked.

'No, never,' said Samson. 'Albert Edward *Cook*,' and now he stressed the last word, 'never make any mistakes. He too careful. He said that a man's life was worth more than a dead whale, and we should always think carefully. Sometimes the tail swept the boat. Sometimes the boat pulled for three, four, even six hours. But no one ever lose their life.'

'When was the season for whales?'

'In June we start to find. In June when the whale come from North Pole or Europe to born a baby' — Samson knew the humpbacks migrated, but in fact they come to Tonga from the Antarctic — 'July to October we get the whales. Then November, finish! Already born the baby.'

Samson was seven years old when he first went whaling with his grandfather. It was pretty much a family affair, six to eight men in the boat, with a member of the Cook family as the harpooner or the boat steerer. They hunted *tofu'a*, the humpback whale; *tofu'a a lei*, the sperm whale; and *punga punga*, the killer whale. But nearly always they hunted *tofu'a*. 'The palangi [the white men],' said Samson, 'they like the tooth of the *tofu'a a lei*.' And I smiled to hear that sperm whale teeth which the white men had brought to trade with the natives were later being sold

156

back by the Tongans.*

'Did you catch many sperm whales?'

Samson shook his head. 'No. Maybe two or three in a year. Only small ones. For the teeth and bone. The meat is no good, too black. Big sperm whale are dangerous.'

In the 1930s Albert Edward Cook handed over much of his business to his sons, Albert and Ned. They moved operations closer to Tongatapu. At first to a small island offshore, and then to the beach itself when they discovered that whale meat was very popular with the townsfolk. Meat was scarce in the Tongan diet, and between ten and thirty whales were taken every year. The oil was used in lamps and for cooking, the meat steamed in the earth ovens called *umu*. The skin was deep-fat fried as 'crackling'. 'You could tell which house used whale-oil for lamps,' Samson recalled. 'You could smell the oil as you walked past in the night. Sometimes you could also smell the whale meat from the oven.'

The Cook family had been traditionalists. They followed the way of the founding father, used the same equipment and kept the same methods.

---

* In the late 1820s the bêche-de-mer merchants, many of them Yankees, travelled from island to island buying dried sea slugs which they later sold for an immense profit to the Chinese market. They paid the islanders with whales' teeth which they bought from whaling captains, or palmed off walrus teeth or replicas carved from elephant ivory as the genuine, oversize article.

In 1937 they did try the innovation that had turned close-quarter harpooning into stand-off whale slaughter when it was applied on a global scale — the harpoon gun. It was a disaster. The gun exploded, crippling the operator, a Maori specialist, in both legs. The example of the Cook family produced imitators — not so much for profit, as for access to the desirable whale meat. They made three or four new whaleboats, copies of the Cook boats, and sometimes they asked members of the Cook family to serve on them as harpooners. I got the impression from Samson that the operations were very amateur. In Vava'u, the local people tried strapping half-sticks of dynamite to the harpoon shaft. The practice required very careful timing. The fuse for the dynamite had to be cut to the right length and lit just before throwing the harpoon. The technique was abandoned after one harpooner threw the charged harpoon into the whale, the whale dived, and the whale line tugged out the harpoon. It floated up, right under the boat, and exploded, destroying the whaleboat. The crew escaped without loss of life but they had been hoisted, quite literally, by their own petard.

As Samson spoke, he relaxed. He grew more and more animated. His powerful hands began to move back and forth, to illustrate the diving and turning of a whale, the action of throwing the whale line overboard in its wake, the hoisting of a sail, the headsman gesturing back to the man at the helm. His eyes lit up and he began to radiate a delight in his reminiscences. Sometimes he turned his entire body and threw up his arms to make a point. The pitch of his voice rose at moments of excitement, fell back in reflective pauses. Occasionally, reaching a natural break in the narrative, he would stop speaking, fold his arms, and lean back in his chair for a quiet moment, adopting a pose of the storyteller. I could see that he was a happy man, proud of his memory, of his family, of the achievements of his lifetime. And like his ancestors, he attributed human characteristics to the whales themselves. Describing the last moments of a whale, he repeated the last words of the animal: 'Oh Mr Kuki! You have killed me!', clasped his hands to his side where the lance had gone in, and slumped back in his chair.

There was no triumph in his voice, no cruelty. He regarded whales as being the same as fish taken from the sea, or pigs slaughtered for a banquet. They were food.

Samson was mindful of the people who had come down to the beach to ask for whale meat. Whale meat was cheap, one shilling for a large piece, and if they were too poor to pay, then the Cook family would give the meat free. 'People must have food,' Samson said. 'We give them the meat. Take it! Take it!' And he waved his hands in a gesture of dispensing. There was no refrigeration so the entire animal had to be disposed of in a single day. Then the bones were towed out to sea and cut loose and allowed to sink. If whaling were ever allowed to resume, Samson knew what he would do. 'I am reverend minister now. Very kind Zizuss likes to help people. Very easy to catch whale. If you catch whale, you tell the people — you give meat to the people. No money. People come and they say, "Mr Cook! I'm hungry." Okay. Free! Bring a basket. Free, free whale. Come and take the basket. Full of whale meat. If a bag, fill the bag. You have a motor truck. Take the meat. Free to the people. That is Zizuss' way.'

The more Samson talked, the more he smiled, the more he revelled in the memories. And then, in a voice breaking with emotion, he was describing the once-in-a-lifetime day when he was in the whaling boat with his father and uncle and his brothers, and his uncle called him forward and asked him to throw the harpoon. 'You know, this time I'm a kid, a little boy. Fifteen years old. Very kid, small boy. Not a big man. The first time to shoot [strike] the whale. First time! First time I hold the harpoon, I am very, very happy. The harpoon is wood, very heavy. I hold the spear. My uncle calls my father, "Row! Pull!" All my brothers row. We come close. My uncle say, "Shoot! Kuki!" The lad Samson threw the harpoon, struck and eventually took the whale. It was not a large one — 'thirty, maybe forty feet' — but Samson's life was changed for ever: 'My father very happy to see the son, the small son hold the spear — I am kid for the last time — my mother very happy. His son, see, he can shoot the whale. Very happy, small boy, like a big man. First time. Very happy. First time . . .' and Samson broke down. His eyes filled with tears, as he remembered his rite of passage into the adult world, and he looked away, choking with emotion.

As this burly, staunch man leaned forward to wipe the tears from his eyes on his sleeve, I grasped how fundamental was the link which bound man the primitive hunter to the great whale. Samson was the same as the young Plains Indian who killed his first buffalo, the Ainu in Hokkaido with the first bear, a young Masai warrior tackling a lion. Their prey held the gift of manhood. Its death validated the interlocking relationship of hunter and hunted. But first the hunter had to take the physical risk, offering his own life in the balance of the hunt. It was utterly removed from the commercial whaling of harpoon gun and factory ship, and had as much to do with the nourishing of the human spirit in hunting societies as with their need for survival.

When Samson had regained his composure, I asked if he would demonstrate his harpoon. He agreed, and as his living quarters were so small, suggested that I should go out into the small backyard. Here I found a lean-to shed with a pile of old timber, the *umu* pit where Samson baked his food, and a patch of wild grass in the middle of which was heaped a pile of giant clam-shells. Whitened by the sun, they reminded me of a pile of skulls.

161

I loitered there while Samson undid the complicated knots which held his stock of harpoons and lances underneath the window. When he appeared, the bright point of a harpoon, held horizontally, first emerged from the back door, followed by Samson. He was holding the harpoon reverentially, and walking with a strange, almost ceremonial gait. He was still dressed in his nineteenth-century black frock-coat and it reminded me of a priest carrying the Host. He walked past me, stopped beside the tall pile of shells, and putting the butt of the heavy wood shaft on the ground, carefully propped the long harpoon against the shell pile. Then, to my surprise, he turned without a word and walked back into his house. Two or three minutes later he reappeared, carrying a second harpoon in the same formal manner, and propped it beside the first one. As I grew more puzzled, he went back inside the house once more, still without a word, and produced another harpoon. Then another, and another, and then the first of the killing lances. All of them were propped against the clam-shell pile until it reminded me of an *obo*, the piles of sacred rocks into which Mongols and Tibetans thrust prayer flags. Only this time the prayer flags were a dozen ten-foot long harpoons, their barbs and blades pointed skyward. As he carried out the final lance, Samson paused in his stride and looked straight at me. His expression had changed to something I had not seen before. It was as if he had withdrawn into some formal stance, like a master of a martial art preparing for a bout. The look lasted for only a second, then Samson placed the final lance against the shells, more like an *obo* than ever, and showed me how the first section of the whale line was tied to the harpoon with special knots.

Taking the harpoon in both hands, he stepped back on to the open space of grass, crouched down with his knees half bent, took a half step forward, and — in a slow instant — changed. The same withdrawal, the sense of removing into some other world, came over him. It was so unexpected that I felt my skin tingle. Samson glared to left, then right, took another half pace, and straightened up. He was searching for whales and had seen one. He turned his head, and called out to an imaginary boat crew, 'Pull! Pull!' He looked forward again, swayed his body from left to right, took a half step to one side, hefted his harpoon, then swayed it up so that the sharp head pointed to the sky. 'Pull! Pull! Up, up, up!' He was screaming now. I noted that he held the heavy weapon in the classic pose, right hand on the heavy butt, the left hand on the shaft to guide it, not to throw it like a spear, as wrongly shown in many contemporary illustrations of whaling. The heavy harpoon is tossed upward like a caber so that it topples over in its trajectory. 'Pull! Pull! That's right!' Samson was shouting again to his imaginary crew. He was no longer on the grass behind his house. He was out at sea, in close pursuit of the whale. With a loud cry he heaved the harpoon into the sky, it made its arc, and thudded into the grass in front of me. Samson whirled and flung his arms out, the skirt of his black coat flying. 'Back! Back! Back!' he yelled, waving his arms to the phantom crew. He could see them, I could not.

He ran to a lance, snatched it from the pile, and was again shouting to his crew. They must have responded in his dream world, for suddenly Samson turned and threw the lance, the killing weapon, low and flat across the sward. It skittered past in front of me. Samson leaped and gathered in the rope, hauling back the lance for the second throw, and a third and a fourth. Samson was sweating. An old man, he was still strong enough to hurl thirty-pound harpoons and lances with a strength that was almost demonic. He was transported, there was no other way to describe it. He was pouring with sweat, and his chest was heaving with exertion. He retrieved the lance a fourth and last time, flung it, and again spun round, his arms held wide, with a loud, final cry. Then, abruptly as if a fever had broken, he stopped, took a deep breath, and his shoulders dropped. He was exhausted, and what others might have seen as the raving of an old man, I realised was something more profound: I had witnessed the hunting dance, the imitative battle, of the shaman. For perhaps ten minutes Samson Cook had not been a reverend minister of the Tongan Wesleyan church. He had been a *tohunga*.

So it was with a rather awed view of native whaling that I went north to Vava'u. I wanted to see humpback whales, and follow up a description of 'humpbacking' written when Samson's grandfather had begun work in Tonga. *The Cruise of the Cachalot, 'Round the World after Sperm Whales'* was by an English adventurer and rover, Frank Bullen. Like Melville sixty years earlier, Bullen had been swayed by the lure of the sea, the excitement of the chase, the danger, and the exotic locations. In the preface to his book he says he is setting out to give 'for the first time . . . an account of the cruise of a South Sea whaler from the seaman's standpoint'. Apparently he had never read *Moby Dick*, because he continues, 'Pending the advent of some great writer who shall see the wonderful possibilities for literature contained in the world-wide wanderings of the South Sea whale fishers, the author has endeavoured to summarise his experiences.' But whaling with hand harpoons from sailing ships was on its last legs by the time Bullen joined the decrepit *Imperial*, a rickety old whaleship which he disguised under the name *Cachalot*.

Bullen's tale often repeats episodes similar to what Melville wrote about life on board a whaleship, about the habits of whales, the risks and accidents. There is no White Whale in Bullen's account, but there are several encounters with 'fighting whales'. In the Indian Ocean the lookouts on the *Cachalot* sight a 'solitary', a bull sperm whale leisurely puffing his way along, oblivious to the whaleship which lowers two boats, expecting an easy target. But when the harpooner struck, Bullen recalls, 'a surprise awaited us. As we sheered up into the wind away from him, Louis [the harpooner] cried, "Fighting whale, sir; look out for the rush!" . . . he [the whale] turned on us, and had it not been that he caught sight of the second mate's boat, which had just arrived, and turned his attentions to her, there would have been scant chance of any escape for us. Leaping out of the water, he made direct for our comrades with a vigour and ferocity marvellous to see . . .' A tremendous battle ensues between the angry whale and the two boats, which ends when the second mate uses a shoulder-held 'bomb gun' to fire a grenade down the animal's throat. By then a thrashing blow from the whale's tail had splintered one of the boats and killed an oarsman outright.

This 'fighting whale' had a malformed lower jaw. It turned out at right angles a short distance from the throat, the break thickly covered with barnacles and limpets, and was the result of an old injury. Perhaps this is what made the whale so irascible. Surgeon Beale had noted broken jaws in otherwise healthy sperm whales nearly a century earlier. Bullen had studied Beale's *Natural History of the Sperm Whale* as well as his fellow whaling surgeon Bennett, just as Melville

166

had done. Bullen's was a straightforward 'manly' account. Almost every chapter produces its hair's-breadth adventure — narrow escapes from great sharks, storms, quarrels aboard ship, and so on — and some of them stretch the reader's credulity. On one occasion after their whaleboat is sunk, Bullen and his crew finish up sitting like a row of seagulls on the corpse of a floating dead whale. While they await rescue, they eat chunks of raw whale meat and drink rainwater which collects in the cavities in the body. But Bullen was a good observer, too. He is watching a school of sperm whale, when 'as if instigated by one common impulse they all elevated their massive heads above the surface of the sea, and remained for some time in that position, solemnly bobbing up and down among the glittering wavelets like movable boulders of black rock. Then, all suddenly reversed themselves, and, elevating their broad flukes in the air, commenced to beat them slowly and rhythmically upon the water, like so many machines.' It is a perfect description of what marine biologists now call spy-hopping and lobtailing.

Bullen was a great admirer of the Polynesian sailors. He had made his promotion to fourth mate by the time the *Imperial* called at Honolulu, and took on a number of Hawaiian volunteers. The captain assigned two of the 'Kanakas', as Bullen called them, to his boat crew. Samuela and Polly were natural whale hunters, and Samuela became the lead harpooner. At Futuna

Island more Polynesians were recruited, and Bullen remarks how they were 'willing, biddable, and cheerful learners. Another amiable trait in their characters was especially noticeable: they always held everything in common. No matter how small the portion received by any one, it was scrupulously shared with the others who lacked.' When the cruise ended in New Zealand and his Kanakas set off homeward, Bullen declared that saying goodbye to them was the worst part of his whole experience. 'No man could have wished for smarter, better, or more faithful helpers than they were.' He also waxed lyrical about the beauty of the Vava'u archipelago. The *Imperial* lay at anchor while her four whaleboats cruised between the islands looking for whales. Here was 'every variety of landscape, every shape of strait, bay, or estuary, reefs awash, reefs over which we could sail, ablaze with loveliness inexpressible; a steady caressing breeze, and overhead one unvarying canopy of deepest blue . . . when at sunset we returned to the ship, not having seen anything like a spout, I felt like one who had been in a dream . . .'

For once, reality matched the rhapsody of physical description. Vava'u is enchantingly beautiful. The scatter of fifty or so islands are forested in luxuriant green; the sea channels between them glow with the turquoise and aquamarine promised by tourist brochures; and each morning the trade winds bring a pleasant breeze. The only town, Neiafu, lies on the edge of an anchorage reputed to be the finest between California and New Zealand, and when long-distance yachts come to replenish, their crews still find it difficult to get away. One of William Mariner's fellow captives from the *Port au Prince* had felt the same. A European ship offered to take him back to England. The man replied that he was old, and would far prefer to live out his time in the comfort of Vava'u. The Vava'u group is voluptuous and seductive.

I stayed on Mounu, a tiny gem of an island — you could walk around it in ten minutes — because it was among the whales. From time to time the breeze would bring a strange sound, a dull, regular thumping. There might be a dozen blows, then silence, then again a dozen thuds. Occasionally the thumping sounds would be repeated over and over again, lasting for twenty minutes or half an hour. They were the sounds of humpback whales lifting their huge tails out of the water and repeatedly beating them on the sea. Or they were rolling over and over like children showing off in a swimming pool, flailing their fifteen-foot-long pectoral fins and smacking them down in a burst of spray. Or they were sending shock waves of sound through the ocean by leaping at a steep angle from the water, and falling back with a gigantic splashing thunder. No one is quite sure of the reason for these antics. Is it sheer playfulness? Are competing bulls sending warning signals? Are the whales merely advertising their presence as suitors? Or are they trying to shake off skin parasites? The species are such spectacular acrobats, the water is clear, and the whales stay conveniently in the shallows, so whale scientists come to Vava'u to study the humpbacks' behaviour, and film crews to film.

Nosa is their preferred guide. Over six feet tall, handsome and with a superb physique, Nosa was the very image of the splendid South Sea islander. He tended to wear a loose singlet which showed off his well-muscled brown chest against which bounced a pendant in the shape of a traditional Polynesian fish hook of carved bone. There was a small earring in his left ear-lobe, and he also had a gold tooth in his mouth which gleamed when he laughed, which was often. He was in his twenties, and after leaving school had started work as a bartender, then as an assistant for a tour diving company. He switched to his present job four years earlier when whale-watching in Vava'u began. Now he operated a boat based on Mounu, and took tourists and scientists to observe the whales in the same locations where his uncles had once tried to harpoon the animals with half-sticks of dynamite. Nosa had learned his whale-watching skills from his boss, a New Zealander, and excelled at the work. Once again, the Pacific islander was adapting to the habits of the foreigners.

The relationship between islander and great whale was still ambivalent. When I told Nosa about Samson Cook and the whale-hunting

170

days, Nosa's eyes gleamed. He slapped the steering wheel of the whale-watch boat and chortled, 'Oh, the meat must be good!' He took fishermen out to sea to catch big fish — mahi mahi and tuna — and I had the impression that to Nosa a caught whale would not be any different from any other edible creature of the sea. Yet Nosa had a highly developed understanding of the local whales. He knew when and where to look for them, and he was uncanny in his ability to anticipate their movements. The whales often moved in groups of three — a mother, a calf, and an escort. If Nosa's clients wanted to swim with the whales, he would abruptly spin the steering-wheel of his boat and head off in a completely different direction, stop the engine, and tell his clients to jump in the water and wait. Five minutes later the whales would turn round and pass the spot that Nosa had anticipated. The 'hunchbacks', as they were sometimes called, were not hunted very much in the nineteenth century. They were too swift through the water — Bennett's ship, the *Tuscan*, mistook humpback whales for sperm whales off the coast of California and tried chasing them, but had to give up when outpaced. Also the humpbacks produce little oil compared to sperm whales, and their bodies are not as buoyant. Harpooned humpbacks often sank and were lost or, if the sea was shallow enough, the hunters had to wait until the gases in the rotting flesh brought the bloated carcass back to the surface. Yet the

171

whalemen knew of the 'songs' of the humpbacks long before they were first recorded by scientists in the 1970s. A Yankee whaling captain wrote of their 'doleful groans', and humpback 'talk' is how the Tongans put it. Nosa himself had seen humpbacks singing when lying comfortably on their backs underwater, or when travelling — indeed in almost any activity. His observations at that time contradicted scientific theory, which held that humpback whales only sing when hanging vertically in the ocean and stationary. Later the scientists changed their minds in the light of such eyewitness evidence, and this had left Nosa with a slightly sceptical view of the scientists. 'How come they say they know about whales, when they spend so much of their time in school or at conferences? If they want to know whales, then they must come and swim with them. Here!' And he twirled on his helmsman's seat, shaking his head from side to side and roaring with laughter.

Watching the whales with Nosa was to add moving pictures in bright colours to what I had read in Beale and Bennett's whale books. The humpback mothers and calves kept to warm, sheltered waters in the bays and channels. Their pale underbodies showed up in the water so their paths could be traced as racing spectres in the blue sea. Their long fins often looked like the wings of underwater aircraft. When they were loitering, Nosa, who swam alongside them, described them as 'just like airships'. The calves had small lungs, so mother and child would frequently surface to breathe. They appeared with the characteristic first, strong, exhalation, a sound so distinctive that experienced whalers claimed that even in pitch darkness they could identify any particular species by the sound of that first breath. Mother and calf would then swim along close to the surface, dipping and bobbing for perhaps half a dozen breaths, before sliding beneath the water with that arching of the spine that gives them their name. When it was the prelude to a deeper dive, there came the slow, high, controlled flourish of the broad tail, a gesture which the baby would try to imitate but sometimes fail at, flopping sideways with an endearing splash. In a playful mood, the calves were as curious as human children, and left their mother's side to come over to inspect the boat. Medieval Norwegian sailors claimed that humpback whales — the 'merry whale' — were so curious that they deliberately put themselves in the path of a boat to take a closer look — then became angry if the boat ran into them. Nosa pointed out that multi-hulled yachts were particularly attractive to the animals. On one occasion an adult humpback had once surfaced right beneath Nosa's boat, briefly lifting the hull off its waterline until the animal, unharmed, swam away. 'It make your heart beat a little faster,' Nosa grinned, pounding his own massive chest. 'Everybody a little afraid, I think.'

The present generation of adult whales

around Vava'u appeared surprisingly relaxed. Often they allowed the watch boats to come within a few yards, and even when skittish, the whales rarely fled as if frightened. Watching the calves coming so close to the boats, I wondered whether these younger whales would grow to accept the presence of the boats as part of their normal environment. Nosa hoped so. 'They are like us. They are mammals. After four, nearly five, years working with whales I think people shouldn't kill the whale. People in Tonga thinking they should kill the whale because most people in Tonga never see whale. If they see how beautiful it is, they will never want to kill whale.'

He paused, searching for the right phrase. 'I don't know how to explain this: it's so marvellous. I think the whale is so beautiful.' He waved his huge hand, shrugged amiably, and gave a gentle, self-conscious smile.

'I must confess,' Bullen wrote at the end of his stay, 'that I felt far greater sorrow at leaving Vau Vau than ever I did at leaving England.' He was still enraptured by the beauty of the islands and the friendliness of the people. When the *Splendid* weighed anchor and left, the people of Vava'u helped to man the windlass. They had asked the visiting whaleship if they could have the meat from the humpbacks after the blubber was removed, and it was given to them. But on the whole, *Splendid*'s campaign had been a failure. Bullen could not understand why so few whales had been caught, although the Tongan whaling grounds had been left alone for many years by foreign whaleships. Samson Cook, the native harpooner, could have told him. 'When whale born, only one born the baby,' he had said to me. The recovery rate of the whale population was very, very slow. The stocks of humpback whale were already badly depleted in Bullen's time, and would come close to extinction when the factory ships appeared in the southern ocean twenty years later. Those vessels slaughtered thousands of humpback whales, and a very minor casualty was the livelihood of men like Samson Cook. His geography was inexact but he was aware of what had happened. 'In Germany, Russia, England, America, Japan — too much kill the whale, bye-bye the whale, finish the whale.' And he realised that whale stocks had to be protected. 'Let the whale grow up. Maybe next time, plenty whale. We don't know. Now we stop. Now plenty whale. Plenty.'

But what of Moby Dick? Samson had seen sperm whales with white patches on their bodies. Nosa could identify individual humpbacks by the white markings on their flukes and flippers and undersides. But neither Nosa nor Samson had ever encountered an animal remotely like Moby Dick, nor even heard of one. Yet I left Tonga satisfied with what I had learned. Nosa had shown me how close observation brings a sympathetic understanding for the living animal, and Samson had revealed a quite different context for the myth of Moby Dick in the Pacific.

Melville's book has a highly charged scene when the three pagan harpooners — Tashtego the Gayhead Indian, Daggoo the huge African, and Queequeg the tattooed Pacific islander — pledge themselves to the pursuit and death of the White Whale. They drink a toast from the hollow sockets of their harpoons, as Ahab looks on. Melville intended the scene to be full of drama and symbolism. But he had touched upon the more intimate relation between native peoples and the great whale. For some Pacific peoples a 'fighting whale' was not a remote adversary to be hunted down for revenge or profit. It was a creature, Samson's memories had shown, which met the spiritual needs of the hunters, even as the great animals could supply some of their material wants. If the whales vanished, man would be diminished.

Part Four

LAMALERA

'Was it not so, O Timor Tom! Thou famed leviathan, scarred like an iceberg, who so long dids't lurk in the Oriental straits of that name, whose spout was oft seen from the palmy beach of Ombay?'

HERMAN MELVILLE, *Moby Dick*

'Call me Ishmael.' I read again the opening words of Melville's story, sitting high above the volcanic sand beach. It was an hour past dawn, and the sound of cocks still crowing came up from below me. A large banyan tree arched over the cliff edge where I sat, and looking down beneath its branches I could see dogs playing on the crescent of foreshore. Their paws left tracks where the retreating tide had smoothed the sand and left it damp. The horizon was indistinct in the morning light. The sea had a calm dark purple sheen except where random currents stirred a few patches into ripples. Lighter streaks were the reflections of high clouds carried by the first winds of the south-east monsoon. Opposite me the sun had just climbed above the mountain peak of Pantar Island, and it would be another very hot day. Already I could feel the sweat beginning to gather. Last night had been warm and sultry. Two or three times I had been awakened by heavy rain showers suddenly drumming on the corrugated-iron roof of the schoolmaster's little house.

I was in the village of Lamalera, the last community on earth where men still regularly hunt sperm whales by hand. Below me I could see the thatch roofs of the sheds where the hunters kept their boats. The tropical sun had bleached the thatch a soft iron-grey. Patches of yellow straw marked where recent repairs had been made. From the open end of each boatshed poked what looked like a crude step-ladder. It was the harpooner's platform which projected from the prow of the hunting boat, the place where the harpooner stood with his fifteen-foot lance at the moment of attack. From where I sat, I could count eleven boatsheds. There were as many again, I knew, out of my line of sight beneath the edge of the cliff. There was no one on the beach for the moment, only the dogs. What looked like whorls of light mist drifted over the ridges of the boatsheds. They were wisps of smoke oozing from the cooking fires where the families of the sea hunters were preparing their meals. In an hour, the men would come down to the beach and assemble. Crew by crew they would muster by the boats, and get ready to go to sea to hunt the whale. I planned to join them.

Lamalera lies almost at the end of the long trailing arc of southern Indonesia. Here the sweeping archipelago, which begins at the Malay peninsula, tapers away a few hundred miles from the huge continental block of Australia. With the exception of Timor, the islands give the impression of becoming smaller and smaller the further you go along the arc. Geographically this is not actually the case, but in terms of travel it is an understandable sensation. Reaching Lamalera requires patience. Foreign visitors usually set out from a major gateway airport, Jakarta perhaps, or Denpasar in Bali. From there a local propeller-driven aircraft takes you to Maumere on the island of Flores. The plane only makes the journey twice or three times a week. Booking ahead is unreliable, and if the *haj* to Mecca is in progress, impossible. I had found myself on a plane filled to the brim with returning pilgrims. In the airport waiting-room before departure, they all opened suitcases and gleefully pulled out white Arab robes which they donned, complete with head-dresses and imitation gold head-bands. As the plane then began its descent into Maumere, there was a second flurry of activity as mirrors were produced, men turned round in their seats to check with one another whether head-dresses were straight and gowns properly adjusted, before making a grand swirling exit down the aircraft steps, beaming with pride. Lining the airport perimeter were hundreds of friends and family members, clapping the returning *hajis*.

My own journey still had another two days to go. From Maumere there was a choice of using a hire car or a public bus to reach Larantuka at the far end of Flores. It was four hours by jeep and six hours in the very cramped public bus. I took a jeep. It brought me to Larantuka, a town which could only be described as an end-of-the-world settlement. It had two streets. The first ran parallel to the waterfront. The central section had about thirty small shops of the hole-in-the-wall type. They sold ironmongery, a small selection of groceries, cheap clothing, and shoes. There was one stationery shop with a dusty display of pens and schoolbooks and the inevitable photocopier required for duplicating government forms, for Larantuka is a very minor outpost of local government. There was also a single shabby restaurant, inappropriately named the Nirvana. But it was so well camouflaged among the down-at-heel shops that you would have walked straight past it without stopping. If you had done so, you would have gone hungry, because the three hotels in town are really guesthouses and very basic. They are reluctant to supply meals, and the street vendors sell only uncooked provisions — dusty vegetables, damaged fruit, and some putrescent-looking fish. The second road, which parallels the first, is set fifty yards back from the shopping street, and has no shops on it at all. There is a technical school, then a sequence of drab houses, and about a quarter of a mile further on, the road swerves and joins the first. From that point onward Larantuka is a single-road town. To make the place even less inviting on the day I arrived, there were smears of dried blood on the road surface. A rabid dog had started a rabies outbreak a week earlier. The provincial government had sent an emergency response team, not with medicines to vaccinate the population — three of whom died — but with guns to shoot all the dogs. Unfortunately the gunners had not been very expert, and several badly wounded animals had been hunted down in the open, and finished off.

To the people of the outer islands, by contrast, Larantuka is a thriving metropolis. It is the jumping-off place for their ferries. The scruffy harbour is the focal point for a flotilla of rag-tag vessels which scurry off along the channels leading to nearby islands with exotic names like Solor, Adonara and Lembata. On some routes the boats operate daily, or even twice a day. However, to get to Lamalera direct, you could only travel once a week. There were two small vessels on the Lamalera run. But both skippers wanted to catch the Friday market trade, so they chose to operate the service on the same day each week. And when you wanted to return, both boats chugged back on a Wednesday, no other day.

Like other small ferry towns, Larantuka had good Samaritans who helped the traveller. My own Samaritan in Larantuka was Camillus. He lived with his family of three daughters and three sons in a small house set back from the road about a mile out of town. A small signboard, almost hidden in the bushes, announced that it was the office of Lamaholot Tour and Tourism. The single-storey building in front comprised a large open room furnished with three plastic garden chairs, a low plastic garden table, and a cheap wooden desk. The top of the desk was bare, and the drawers empty. There was also a large school blackboard on which was written several lines of Japanese grammar. Camillus was teaching himself Japanese because he believed that from Japan would come his customers. For the moment he had no clients. He was in his mid-fifties, and had the worried air of a branch bank manager whose books are about to be audited by suspicious accountants. Five feet four inches tall, Camillus wore thick glasses behind which his eyes had a mournful beagle look. He was lucky in his wife. She was part Dutch, part Javanese, and clucked over him with real affection and concern. She lived in the little house behind the front office, and cooked him large, excellent meals which failed to fill out his gaunt frame, and watched over him because Camillus was absent-minded. She would locate the pens he had dropped, remind him to take along his reading glasses, and when Camillus and I set off for Lamalera together, she provided a packed lunch for the ferry.

Camillus was a native of Lamalera. He spoke Lamaholot, the local language, and English, and could be my interpeter. Just as important, he was familiar with the complicated social structure of Lamalera, which is based on a potentially explosive mixture of clans. Camillus's father had belonged to one of the most senior clans, though

184

Camillus himself had spent all his working life away from the village. He had been a government employee in the national tourism office. I never found out why Camillus had given up his job and decided to set up in private business. Now his ambition was to promote his native village and to develop its tourist potential. It was, I soon observed, a difficult task, but Camillus was genuinely committed. He was one of the kindest-hearted people imaginable, and so sincere and honest that when he spoke of a subject close to his heart, his eyes would fill with tears.

He was also a very devout Christian, his father having taught catechism in Lamalera. Sharing a room at the schoolmaster's house in Lamalera, Camillus would sometimes wake me by talking in his sleep. His dream talk often involved snatches of prayer, and more than once he woke me with a start by suddenly sitting up his bed and crying out 'Santa Maria!' then falling back, sound asleep.

Camillus advised that we take the second of the two ferries on Friday, as it would be less crowded. The first ferry must have been a sight to see, because the small wooden boat we took had not a square metre of deck free of passengers. They sat under a blue plastic sheet spread to offer shade, mothers and children, returning students, nondescript travellers who were going home to Lamalera after visiting relatives on Flores or after a shopping trip in Larantuka. The captain knew Camillus, so the two of us were allowed inside the wheelhouse. This was a box-like structure with an old-fashioned ship's wheel of many spokes, and sliding windows of ordinary household glass, most of them cracked. When steering, the captain sat perched high up on an ingenious long-legged, wooden chair like a child's high chair scaled up. But it was still not tall enough for the captain to look forward through the high window, so someone had nailed wooden slats across the arms of the chair, adding an extra storey. The captain sat unsteadily on this structure, gripping the huge steering-wheel and with his bare feet tucked up on the normal seat. To pass orders to the engineer, the captain would reach forward and tug on what looked like a bishop from a chess set. It was the wooden toggle attached to a length of cord which led through a hole in the deck. From the bowels of the vessel came the ting of a bell, the numbers of strokes denoting the desired speed of the engine, or whether it should be in reverse, ahead or neutral. The arrangement was so slack, the response so slow and the captain's chair so unsteady on its legs that I guessed that the Lamalera ferry habitually sailed on calm seas. The slightest swell would have sent the captain's chair toppling.

With a series of sharp tings on the bell, we set out from Larantuka. I was surprised that the diesel engine ran as quietly as it did. Then some adjustment was needed, and the engineer's assistant appeared. A lad about sixteen years old, he threw back a hatch in the wheelhouse floor, and the roar and thunder of the clattering old motor came straight up into the cabin, along with an extra dose of diesel smoke. Refuelling was done by the simple means of opening a large drum of fuel loosely tied to the open deck, and using an old-fashioned winding pump to squirt the fuel down a plastic pipe somewhere into the bowels of the vessel.

We chugged along, first down the narrow channel between the islands of Flores and Adonara, and then east, along the Solor channel. It was a typical day for early May, the beginning of the dry season. There was bright sunshine, a mild breeze from the south-east, and a few scattered clouds. On our right the slopes of Solor had once been forested with sandalwood trees until clear-felled for profit. Scrub and bush had replaced the forest. Normally the hillsides of Solor would have been green with vegetation, but not this year. It was a year of severe drought, an El Niño year, and there had been no rain. The slopes were scorched and barren, and the hills of Adonara to our left had the same bleak aspect. Camillus told me that the crops had failed. In remote villages the people were already starving. They were reduced to eating the bark from trees, and digging for roots that normally the wild pigs would forage.

Our ferry trundled along for three hours and made a brief stop-over to pick up and discharge passengers at the little port of Waiwerung. It was an interesting manoeuvre. The captain spun the wheel this way and that, from time to time skipping down from his high chair, and running first to one side-door of the wheelhouse, and then the other, to glance out and see his position. Then at the crucial moment he shouted to a sailor to throw over a stern anchor to bring the vessel to a halt. 'Leggo!' he shouted, and ting-ting went the bell.

We were turning the corner of Lembata Island, two hours later, when the steering broke. One moment the captain was adjusting the course, the next instant the huge wheel was spinning uselessly in either direction, its spokes a blur. Our boat began to go in wide slow circles, out of control. Had the accident occurred twenty minutes earlier, we would have run up on the rocks. The captain abandoned his high chair, and called on the ubiquitous grease monkey. The two of them began to clear the deck space behind the wheelhouse. It was covered with passengers, piles of suitcases, sacks, baggage of all sorts, and several clusters of live chickens, their legs tied together. The team exposed the deck planks, levered them up, and revealed a huge iron quadrant, the steering mechanism attached to the rudder. It was swinging back and forth dangerously. The grease monkey had to capture it, then hold it steady, while the captain retrieved two broken ends of the rope which led to the steering-wheel. The rope was knotted together, and replaced. Before the planks were put down again, I noted there were at least four more temporary knots in the frayed steering-rope, from previous emergencies.

It should have taken only another two hours to reach Lamalera. But we stopped twice more along the coast. Each time it was to take off passengers and cargo from coastal hamlets. The passengers were sitting on boulders lapped by the sea, waiting for us. They looked like cormorants. Their friends then brought them out in dugout canoes while the ferry idled offshore, its engine in neutral. The cargo was varied. Once it was a large, cheap plywood wardrobe, precariously balanced across the wobbly dugout, then manhandled up on the ferry's wheelhouse roof as there was no other space for it. The second consignment of cargo was a pile of five sacks of what I guessed was copra, dried coconut, which the coastal hamlet was exporting. The sacks were loaded on to the most primitive dugout I had ever seen. It was a single log, crudely hollowed out. Unfortunately the log was not deep enough, so the builder had extended the sides upward by sewing on two strips of woven palm-thatch four inches broad. They failed to keep out the water as the dugout was badly overloaded. So the top-heavy canoe rolled over halfway out to meet the ferry. Three of the copra sacks floated, and were retrieved by a second canoe which hastily put out to help. Our obliging captain reached back in the wheelhouse, and unhooked a pair of home-made goggles which he loaned to the two new passengers. The ferry then waited for another half-hour while the pair of them swam around face downward in the sea until they had located the missing copra sacks, hauled them up, and brought them, dripping wet, to be hoisted aboard.

At Lamalera a flotilla of small boats shaped like bean pods came racing out, rocking wildly from side to side. Two young men paddled each leaky craft. These Charons were paddling maniacally, hoping to be fast enough to make a double journey to the beach and back, and earn twice the landing fee. We were expected to commit ourselves and our bags to them. Lamalera had neither harbour nor jetty, and all arrivals and departures were made through the waves and on to the volcanic beach. Behind the crescent beach, the land rose in a steep, rocky mountainside. Here and there immense boulders had tumbled down the slope, and lay tilted against one another. The rocks were mostly charcoal grey, a few were dark lava red. In the narrow space between the beach and the foot of the mountain was crammed a double row of small houses, set behind the boatsheds. Two paths led away to left and right. The path to the right sloped up gently, around the flank of the mountain. Below it were the thatch or metal roofs of a few more dwellings. The path to the left climbed much more steeply. It mounted a flight of steps cut in the face of a small cliff. On the top of the cliff were the first few houses of an upper settlement perched on a small plateau. The site reminded me, unexpectedly, of a classic Greek coastal village below its rocky headland, only here in Indonesia the boulders were drab and sombre, not limestone white and yellow. There was no flat land, no sign of cultivation, no road. The entire focus of Lamalera was the half-moon of volcanic sand, about six hundred yards across. Here, as Camillus and I landed, a group of five men were using wooden levers to roll a large, black, rather awkward shape to the edge of the beach and out of the way. It was the severed head of a small sperm whale.

The house of Guru Ben the schoolmaster, where we were to stay, was perched on the lip of the small cliff. To reach it, we climbed the flight of steps, and turned off the path to scramble up between huge boulders, following the grooves worn by feet before us and the occasional red spatter of betel-nut juice. We passed two or three black pigs, tethered by cords threaded through holes in their ears. Each animal occupied a small niche between the rocks, and was apparently happy in a situation more suited to be a seagull's roost than a pigsty. Behind Guru Ben's house was a small clearing with a banyan tree and a platform of bamboo slats, on which I could sit and watch the activity on the beach beneath me. Our young boatmen had told us that two whales had been taken just two days previously. They said this was a good sign because the traditional whaling season had not yet begun. The two whales had already been cut up, and from the high vantage point I could see what looked like a big white necklace swashing back and forth in the shallows. It was the spinal column of one of the whales, the meat removed. The ebb tide would soon pull the spine out to sea. The men rolling the whale's head had finished their work by now, and all that remained was the smell. It was overpowering. Chunks of whale meat were hung up to dry throughout Lamalera, and the tropical heat was at work. The stench that wafted up to the schoolmaster's house was of decay and death. I hoped that I would get used to it. The smell was sometimes so strong that it made my nostrils twitch.

Camillus insisted that we pay a courtesy visit as soon as possible to the village headman, the *kapala desa*, of Lamalera B. This was the official name for the settlement down by the beach, Lamalera Bawa, meaning Lower Lamalera. The name for the twin settlement on the plateau was Lamalera A, for Atas, Upper Lamalera. The two villages had separate headmen, separate water supplies, separate censuses, and — to a large extent — separate attitudes. They even paid heed to separate shamans. Some days later I was to observe at an extraordinary public meeting of all the fishermen from the two communities. The meeting was to discuss the new whaling season — which boats could participate, how the catch should be divided, and so forth. The fishermen — there were no women present — sat down on the beach, arranging themselves in the form of a giant horseshoe. The men from Lamalera A were all on the western arm of the horseshoe; the men of Lamalera B on the eastern arm. Several of them glared across the space. At the closed end of the horseshoe, a little apart and sitting side by side, were the two village headmen. They were obviously trying to remain neutral. With them were the two shamans. The debate grew so heated as speakers hurled their opinions across the horseshoe that the translation outpaced Camillus. When everyone had exhausted their spleen, the two headmen spoke in turn, apparently soothing the crowd. To my surprise, they then stood up and walked down to the water's edge. The two shamans accompanied them. Each carried what looked like a white drum. They were the largest vertebrae from a sperm whale's backbone. These bones were carefully placed on the sand, and the four men put their heads together in a huddle.

'What are they doing?' I whispered to Camillus.

'They are praying to the ancestors that the results of the meeting will be accepted by everybody, and that there will be no more anger.'

'What about the whale bones? Why have they got them?'

'That is to seal the agreement, to link them with our ancestors. With the whales.'

Camillus was out of date in his politics. The *kapala desa* of Lamalera had changed since

Camillus was last in the village. The man he took me to see was now retired after twenty-three years in the job. He and his elderly friend, who dropped in for a chat, were gloomy about Lamalera's future. Lamalera was slowly draining to death. Young people were leaving. Soon there would not be enough men to provide crews for the whaleboats or the skilled craftsmen to keep them in repair. Men had emigrated from Lamalera in the past. They were well known for being well educated by the mission school and industrious. They became carpenters and plumbers in the cities or, like Camillus, trained as schoolteachers and civil servants. But now the young men were leaving because there were no reasons for staying at home. Lamalera was a backwater. The village had been promised a road, but it had never been built. They had been promised a new water supply, as the springs were drying up. But nothing had been done. They had been promised an electricity supply, but there was no generator. 'No electricity, no water, no road — promises, promises, promises,' said the ex-*kapala desa* and shrugged. The only ray of hope was tourism.

'Tourism?' Tourists came every season to look at the whaleboats. About forty or fifty tourists each year. Recently the fishermen had begun charging a fee to take them out as spectators on whale-hunting trips. The cash meant that several of the whaling boats had been refurbished. Two years ago there had been only seventeen boats operational and maybe six boats in decay. Now three of the old boats had been repaired and were back in work whenever there were sufficient crews to man them.

The two old men cheered up when they talked about whaling. Their memories were extraordinarily precise. They remembered the exact day when this whale or that whale was taken by the hunters. They recited the names of the successful boats that had been involved. The boat names were unusual and, to a stranger, often confusing. The two old men rattled them off like the names of their own children — *Dolu Tena, Holo Sapang, Teti Heri, Kebako Puka, Soge Tena, Praso Sapang*. The elderly friend recalled the day when he had been tangled in a whale line and dragged overboard. 'Down, down,' he said. 'I took off my clothes underwater, to get clear of the rope, and came to the surface, naked. *Soge Tena* picked me up and gave me some clothes to wear. A man called Larga was with me, an old man. He was underwater for half an hour, and drowned.'

'When was that?' I asked.

'In June of 1978. The whale was pregnant. *Baka Tena* and *Soge Tena* shared the whale.'

In March 1993 an epic calamity had been narrowly avoided. A sperm whale of exceptional strength and stamina had towed away four boats, thirty-four fishermen in all, and that was nearly the last the village saw of them.

'*Kebako Puka* first harpooned the whale, then

Teti Heri,' the old man recalled. 'But they could not manage the whale. So *Kelulus* and *Kena Puka* came up to help. They also harpooned the whale. But the whale was so strong, it pulled all four boats far out to sea. After some time, *Teti Heri* realised the danger and cut their line. Two days and two nights later, *Teti Heri* came back to Lamalera, by herself. But the other boats could not get free and were gone. The whale kept swimming until *Kebako Puka* and *Kelulus* were both swamped. Their crews cut the lines and swam across to *Kena Puka*, who picked them up. Now there were three boat crews on one boat, and still the whale was pulling them.'

'At last *Kena Puka* cut the line, and the whale went free. Luckily a cruise ship saw *Kena Puka* on the sea and took her in tow to Kupang in Timor. The men on board had been four days and nights on the sea, and were without water or food. They were chewing their clothes.'

'What about the two boats that had been swamped?' I asked.

'They had to be abandoned. Later the government sent us money to build replacements.'

'Could *Kena Puka* have sailed home on her own from Timor?'

'Maybe. But the crew were in such bad condition that a ferry brought the boat and her crew to Larantuka, and she sailed home from there. During all that time the women had been camping on the beach, day and night, crying and praying and waiting for news. No one was killed, and on the first of May each year when we hold the ceremony to open the whale season we give thanks to God for their rescue.'

Camillus and I walked back towards Guru Ben's house along the coastal track, and I heard the clang of hammering, metal on metal. We came upon two men. They were beating a lump of glowing metal with sledgehammers. A dozen or so elderly men were seated on makeshift benches, watching. There was a festive atmosphere, and I was offered a glass of *tuak,* palm toddy. Someone courteously passed a plate of knobbly reddish-pink lumps, and gestured that I might like a snack. I took the smallest piece and popped it into my mouth. It was raw squid tentacle, soaked in palm wine vinegar. The flesh was so tough that I could only chew off the raised suckers. They tasted like bits of acrid tyre rubber. As discreetly as possible, I removed the remainder from my mouth and tossed it into a convenient bush. Every few minutes one of the old men would jump to his feet and take the place of a colleague standing beside two large bamboo tubes planted upright on the ground. A thin bamboo cane emerged from the open end of each tube. The old man grabbed the sticks, and began pumping them up and down vigorously. They were the handles to a primitive air pump. Clusters of rags or chicken feathers at the ends of the bamboo sticks formed pistons, and as they slid up and down the bamboo tubes, they forced air out through a nozzle and into a charcoal fire.

For a moment, as he worked the handles up and down enthusiastically, the operator resembled a very active cross-country skier with his ski poles.

A tall, very sinewy and gaunt man with close-cropped white hair was stooped over the fire. He was heating up a leaf of metal. I recognised the shape of the leaf. The gaunt man was making a harpoon-head.

His name was Rufinus Keraf. He was a renowned harpooner, now retired. Only a man who knew how to wield a harpoon knew how to forge a good one. The process was part-ritual, part-smithcraft. The raw material was a section cut from an old car spring. The two stalwarts with the sledgehammers were doing the rough work. The metal was heated and beaten, heated and beaten, folded over, heated and beaten out again until Rufinus was satisfied. He fixed the little slab, now about the size of the blade of a garden trowel, into the tree root as a handle. With a smaller hammer he began tapping the glowing metal into shape, thinning it, tapering it, splitting off an ear of metal which he turned into the single barb of the harpoon head, and finally giving a cutting edge. There were frequent breaks to reheat the metal in the charcoal. The old men, fuelled by *tuak*, pumped away energetically on the bellows. A younger man, fierce-looking, wordless and naked to the waist, took over when Rufinus needed a break. It was his nephew, who was learning the blacksmith's skill, and he was an active harpooner. After an hour's intensive work, the harpoon head was ready for its final treatment. Rufinus smeared on a green paste of mashed leaves and thrust it back into the crucible. The wet paste hissed and turned into liquid trickles; momentarily the metal was iridescent, then turned black.

'The paste will make the harpoon strong,' explained one of the old men. 'It is for *Dolu Tena*. On the day the two whales were taken, the harpooner of *Dolu Tena* lost four harpoons, and then he lost four harpoons belonging to *Nara Tena*. They were all taken by a young whale. It was very brave because it had a white mother.'

'White?' I asked, my interest suddenly aroused.

'Well, part black and part white,' he replied. 'If you want to know what happened, ask Nadu.'

Nadu was Bernardus Bataona, and he was a modest young man. Honest too, because he said that the old man had been mistaken. The whale that had taken their precious harpoons had been a female whale, accompanied by her calf. But there had been a 'speckled' whale alongside as well. Everybody had seen it.

Nadu told me that he had been on the beach getting his small one-man boat ready to go out fishing, when he heard the call 'Baleo! Baleo!' It was the signal which alerted the community to the unexpected arrival of a school of sperm whale, close enough to the beach to attack. A baleo was a rare event. Some fishermen could spend their entire lives without participating in one. Normally the village fleet patrolled for whales offshore, and very occasionally a school of sperm whale ventured into the bay. The 22nd of April was just such a day.

'Whales were appearing everywhere,' said Nadu. 'So many that their backs were like boulders exposed when the tide goes down. There were whales coming from the west, and whales coming from the east. Our boat, *Dolu Tena*, was not in the water, but we pushed her afloat as quickly as we could. *Nara Tena*, *Praso Sapang*, *Holo Sapang* and *Demo Sapang* were already afloat. We came close to a whale and our harpooner struck it, and the whale turned back and came along our right-hand side, very close. It was very dangerous. Then the whale disappeared down and our harpooner saw a whale on the right-hand side, and thinking it was the same whale, he put the second harpoon into it. But he made a big mistake. The first whale was on the left-hand side, and the whale on the right-hand side was a different one. So we had harpoons in two whales. One wanted to go to the east, the other to the west, and our boat will be broken.

'We shouted to *Praso Sapang*, and they come close and we give them the rope for the second whale, and they go away with that whale. Our whale is very strong and we have much trouble. So we call on *Nara Tena* to help, but the whale is pulling us so fast that *Nara Tena* cannot come close enough to harpoon the whale. So they pass us their harpoons, and leave us. The whale is the mother, and she has her child swimming with her. The mother whale pull us towards the headland, but then turns back, and we see that she is getting tired. So we again call *Nara Tena* to help us. But when *Nara Tena* comes close, the whale hits with its tail, and breaks the bows of *Nara Tena*, and now they cannot help us. So they cast off their rope. We have no more harpoons so we lash a knife to a pole and try to stab the whale. But the whale keeps her tail towards the boat, and it is difficult to cut properly. Then the tail of the whale comes underneath our boat, and damages it also. Water is coming in, much water. *Nara Tena* comes close to us, and they tell us to cut the rope, as there are some men who have the same problem in 1993 — towed away by the whale. Some of our crew want to cut the rope, others say no. The whale is lying on the surface now, very tired. So all our crew decided that maybe something was wrong. That we did not do correctly, and that we must pray, asking for the blessing of God. After we pray, we decide to pull in the rope — and the harpooner jumps in the water and goes hand over hand along the rope, to kill the whale. But when he comes close to the whale, the whale begins to move again. There are eight harpoons in the whale, with their ropes. Now we think it is very expensive, that whale. So the harpooner goes hand over hand along the biggest rope. It is the most costly. And he cuts the rope. We lose the harpoon but we save the rope. Then we pull the boat closer to the whale, and cut all the other ropes, and the whale swims away.'

'What about a white whale?' I asked. 'I was told there was a white whale.'

'No,' he replied. 'The mother and the child whale were normal colour. But all the time there was a whale with white spots keeping nearby. We think it is the husband whale, the father of the baby, and that is why the whales fight so bravely. It was a big whale, fifteen metres long, longer than our boat. There was white around its mouth, and some white spots on the top of its head, and white around the ears. The rest of the whale was the normal black. All the other boats saw it, too.'

Dolu Tena had not encountered a pure white whale, but something else: an 'emperor' or grizzled bull whale, watching over its family.

And if the Lamalera people believed that even a part-white whale denoted courage, there could not have been a more apt place for the encounter. The waters where Nadu and his comrades had fought and lost their whale lay south of Lamalera, between Lembata and Timor. It is part of the Gulf of Ombay. In *Moby Dick* Melville mentions three famous 'fighting whales'. He had read about them in his 'whale Bibles', the books written by surgeons Beale and Bennett. They listed three sperm whales whose pugnacious exploits were famed among whalemen, and were considered near-impossible to catch. The first was 'Mocha Dick'.

The second was 'New Zealand Tom', a belligerent animal often encountered in the whaling grounds off New Zealand. The third was the much-feared Timor Jack, whose name Melville changed to 'Timor Tom' for alliterative effect. Timor Jack's domain, the place which he had met and sunk several whaleboats, was the Gulf of Ombay.

The whale hunters prayed. They stood on each side of their boat as it lay in the thatched shed. There were nine of them, men of all ages, and they faced towards the open sea. Two could not have been more than fifteen years of age. The serious-faced harpooner and his assistant were probably in their early thirties. The rest were old men, and in Lamalera a man was considered old when he had reached his fiftieth birthday. They shared one feature: all of them were thin. In Lamalera I never saw a person who was fat or overweight. Life was marked by scarcity and toil.

The harpooner led the prayer. First he plucked the sheath from the stem-post of the boat, and hung it carefully to one side. The sheath was a tube of plaited leaf, a faded golden brown, about twelve inches long. It seemed to have no practical function, for it did not protect the bow of the boat. It was a token, but important, because every boat in all the other sheds wore a similar plain cover which was handled in the same, almost ritualistic, way. Next, the harpooner reached into the boat and brought out a glass bottle which had once held a soft drink, but was now resealed with a cork. He drew the cork and sprinkled holy water on the boat and crew. He crossed himself, recited a prayer, and made the sign of the cross again. Behind him, the crew repeated the words of the prayer, and also crossed themselves. They turned inward, towards the boat, and removed the slanting wooden props which held it level. Then all nine bent their shoulders to the hull. They crouched like runners in the starting block, one shoulder against the hull, one arm straight down, hand pressed against the sand for balance. With a deep double grunt one of the older men gave the signal. The team strained against the dead-weight of the boat. It did not shift. The crew alternated their efforts, heaving against one side then the next, to rock the boat and break the inertia. Grudgingly, the boat began to slide forward on the worn branches which had been laid down to prevent the keel sinking into the soft sand. With a rush the boat advanced ten paces, and then came to a halt. The crew paused, straightened up to rest their backs, and glanced to left and right.

From one boatshed to the next, the prows of whaleboats were emerging, their ladder-like harpooner platforms like the horns of prehistoric beasts. Each boat was different. To the professional eye there were subtle changes in design: a lower bow, a distinct curve to the hull, some peculiar feature of the boatbuilder's craft. To the casual onlooker there were more obvious distinctions: each boat was decorated to the taste and tradition of the owners. Some were plain. There were unpainted wooden hulls with just a stylised eye, the oculus, drawn on the bows, or the upper plank a single colour — usually white — and the name of the boat picked out in red on a yellow background. *Kelulus* sported this plain white upper plank, and her hull was a sober buff. Her oculus was tastefully set within a well-executed painting of some sort of yellow and green fruit, and the boat had a festive air. Short pink and white ribbons dangled from her plank seams. *Teti Heri* looked battered and knocked about. Her paintwork was scuffed and streaked. *Kopo Paker* was crisp and smart with a freshly painted green hull, a brown crocodile behind the oculus, and across her prow someone had sketched a small mouth, with a set of sharp, white-painted teeth. Ocean monsters featured on two boats: the fanged head of a sea dragon about to swallow the moon; and a double-ended sea snake which emerged from the blue ocean and twined around the volcano which rose behind Lamalera. They were clan signs, whimsies, or pictures of local legends.

Now the whaleboats, fourteen of them that day, were slithering down the gentle slope of the beach. They converged on the water's edge, and lined up to queue for the best launching spots. Children too young to participate in the hunt and very old men picked up the wooden skids from behind the boats, carried them forward, and threw them down in the boats' path. Again the crew bent down to put their shoulders to the vessel. They strained and heaved. Bare feet dug into the black sand. It was back-breaking labour, and would be even worse when the boats returned that evening and would have to be pushed up-slope, back into their sheds, by crews with depleted strength. I wondered why they did not rig a winding winch on the beach, run a cable to each vessel, and ease the drudgery. Or why no one had taken dynamite charges and blown sky-high the nasty outcrops of rocks which partially blocked the launching sites. But this was not how the Lamalera men worked. For time out of mind they had manhandled their boats, each six or seven tons deadweight, down the beach each day in the whaling season, and manhandled them back to the shed on their return. Perhaps there was symbolic value to this effort. Maybe without the input of toil, there would not be a harvest from the sea.

The boats were nuzzling the water. The regular surge and suck of the waves required careful timing. The leading crew was up to their knees in the sea, holding the boat at right-angles to the crests, allowing it to rise and fall on each wave. The harpooner had scrambled aboard, and taken his place in the bows, a long bamboo pole in his hand. He placed the butt against the sand, and struggled to hold the bow straight. Behind him the crew saw their chance. A gap between two smaller waves, and they thrust forward their boat and were scrambling into it before it bucked and reared. They snatched their paddles and began to dip them in the sea. The *lama uri*, the steersman, was last to jump aboard. He put his steering paddle over the stern and took control. The paddlers urged the boat through the line of waves and out on the calm sea beyond. The harpooner laid down his quant pole. He too picked up a paddle. There were five miles to go to the fishing ground.

The crew of *Sili Tena* of the Bataona clan insisted that Camillus and I climb aboard early, before the water's edge. I sat there, feeling a useless extra burden, as the crew laboured for our departure. But it was better to let them get on with their work, and not hinder by trying to help. For them this launch was a routine repeated day after day after day. There was no guarantee that they would catch anything at all, despite their effort. The launch, the patrol, and the beach retrieve was the treadmill of their working lives.

I looked around the boat. It was a relic of another age, the Stone Age at a guess. It had no deck. Short lengths of plank made up the wide shallow hull. Twine rolled from palm fibre or old fishing line held the planks in place. These lashings locked one plank against the next, or to a series of roughly shaped ribs and internal wooden struts which were themselves held in tension by further lashings. The boat was some thirty feet long and seven feet in the beam, and there was no attempt at finesse. The planking was rough and battered. No shipwright had bothered to smooth the crossbeams on which we now sat uncomfortably. Everything seemed crude and unsophisticated. Yet this was a false impression. Closer inspection revealed that the entire hull was very cunningly made. The engineering was sound, though no two pieces were identical in shape and form. This was a boat built to be strong and flexible enough to survive head-to-head conflicts with the biggest of big game in the world. The Lamalera whaleboats were not the delicate attack craft of the Western whalemen. The Western boats had relied on speed and agility; the slightest tap from a sperm whale's tail stove in their half-inch cedarwood planks. The Lamalera boats were also vulnerable — no wooden boat ever made could withstand a direct blow from a sperm whale — but they relied on a different principle: the Lamalera whaleboat was a survivor. It could take tremendous punishment from an angry whale, be shaken to the core, lose pieces from the hull, and yet, by emergency repairs while at sea, return to the fray, and come home afloat. In the Indonesian language the boat was a *peledeng*, but speakers of Lamaholot called it a *tena*.

The gunnel plank beside me had strange marks on its upper edge. They were chips and dents as if it had been attacked with a giant rasp. The crew member in front of me saw my glance, leaned forward and with pantomime gestures explained why the plank was so badly chewed. It had been bitten by the lower jaw of a sperm whale.

'Hoollaybeh! Hoollaybeh! Hoollaybeh!' chanted the crew. With every stroke they leaned their entire body forward, using their paddles with a short chopping motion. As the blade came past the man, he drew back his elbow and tapped the handle against the hull. It was the beat of a giant metronome. 'Hoollaybeh! Hoollaybeh! Hoollaybeh!' There was the chopping stroke, then a pause as the paddler sat upright and the boat glided forward, then the action was repeated with another chop, the thump of the handle, the draw of the blade, and the pause. The rhythm of the strokes was not regular. Every twenty strokes or so, the lead singer repeated the refrain quickly, 'Hoollaybeh! — Hoollaybeh! — Hoollaybeh!', and the crew took several rapid strokes without any pause in between. Picking up a paddle I joined them. Within ten minutes my arm was tired. But the Lamalera men, accustomed since childhood to the swing and sway and chop of the paddling, could maintain the pace for hour after hour after hour.

Hoollaybeh! Hoollaybeh! Hoollaybeh! The refrain came across the water. Thirteen other *tena* were fanning out, using the same rhythm and stroke, the same work chant as they headed out to sea. For half an hour we paddled, until we felt the first slight whisper of breeze. The men put down their paddles. The younger members of the crew got to their feet, and began untying the ropes which secured the lowered mast and its sail in a stowage crutch to the starboard side. The sail was not made of cloth, but of palm-leaf mats, woven in rectangles a foot square and sewn together like a giant quilt. At the moment it was rolled around its bamboo spars. The legs of the bipod mast were two long strong bamboo poles, and the crew spread the legs across the boat so they fitted over the end of a crossbeam. 'Satu, dua, tiga!', one two three, and the mast was swung upward, pivoting on its legs until it stood V-shaped above the deck. The harpooner made fast the forward stay, the steersman tied down the aft stay, and now the bipod stood on its own. 'Satu, dua, tiga!' and the sailors were hoisting up the matting sail. As the sail rose, it unfurled like a roller-blind. A few wisps of broken palm leaf blew away in the light breeze, floated downwind and settled gently on the water. The sail hung almost flat, just the slightest belly in the matting to show that we had a breath of wind. Someone made fast the halyard. The men returned to their seats, the paddles were stowed, and all sat quietly, facing forward, their heads bowed. An old man intoned a paternoster. The crew responded 'Amen'. Then everyone sat up and relaxed. They turned to one another and formally wished one another 'good day'. The old man on the thwart behind me began to roll a cigarette. He passed his tobacco canister forward to a friend. The helmsman, sitting right in the stern, crouched with his knees high so he could look aft and to the side. One of the older men stood up, his hand gripping a mast stay, and gazed across the sea, adopting a lookout's stance. The harpooner checked his rack of harpoons and stood, his back against one of the mast legs, looking forward. His eyes were the most acute on the boat. *Sili Tena* glided onward. The hunters were in position. All that lacked was the prey.

It was a scene repeated on every boat in the fleet. They covered an arc at least a mile wide. Each harpooner usually acted as captain. He decided when the boat should change course, or turn around, or roll up the sail and begin paddling when the wind died completely. His was not a formal command. It was just that the entire purpose of the day was to bring the harpooner close enough to his prey to strike. It took years to become a harpooner. I had seen the small boys on the beach, six and seven years of age, playing with bamboo sticks. They would climb a boulder, and stand there on the crest, imitating the stance of *lama fa,* the harpooner. They would fling the stick, follow through with the harpooner's jump, and land on the sand, retrieve the stick, climb the rock, and repeat the process, again and again and again. They played by themselves, each child in the solitary role of the harpooner, the hero, in an imaginary world. Maybe, twenty years later they would be the real hero.

By then they would have gone to sea as lads charged with the task of using the bamboo scoop to empty out the leaky bilge. From there, they might be allowed to start handling the ropes which controlled the sail. Another five or six years, and one morning, perhaps, the *lama uri*, the helmsman, was sick and did not show up on the beach at launch time, and the young man took the steering paddle. A few more years and he could have graduated to be the harpooner's assistant, responsible for relaying the harpooner's commands to the helmsman during the chase, for maintaining the harpoon shafts, handing the right harpoon head to the harpooner, managing the line as it rattled out over the gunnel in the wake of a fleeing sperm whale. Finally, the day might come when the owners of the boat invited him to take the harpoon itself. Then, at last, he would have his chance to strike the whale, using the same throw and jump that he had first begun to practise as a child on a rock on the beach.

Beside me on *Sili Tena*, the old man produced a light fishing line and small hook. He tied a wisp of leaf fibre to the hook and threw it into the water. A few minutes later he hauled in a flying fish that had taken the lure. Carefully removing the hook from the fish, he used the fish to bait a larger hook on a heavier line, and again flipped the line to trail in the water behind us. He was hoping to catch a dorado or perhaps a tuna. But this was a minor diversion. *Sili Tena* was hoping for much larger prey. The man settled back, to wait.

I had expected silence. Fourteen *tena* were spread out across the slick skin of the sea, and almost motionless. I anticipated the same nearly breathless hush when, in a forest, hunters wait in silence for their prey to appear. But just as the forest hunters translate the noises of the forest, so the crews of the *tena* were listening to the messages from the sea. Across water, as well as in water, sound travels more clearly and farther than on land. In the background, I heard the slow thud of an engine. Puzzled, I asked which whaleboat had a motor. But none had. The sound, I was told, came from a big foreign oil tanker, *'minyak kapal'*. It was out of sight, well over the horizon, perhaps twenty miles away. Yet the fishermen knew it was there and that it was on the regular run between Australia and Japan.

Close to hand came the random skitter and flip of flying fish. They sprang into the air, sometimes bursting out singly from the mirror surface of the water, but more usually in twos and threes. Each animal fluttered away each on its own trajectory, its 'wings' trembling, and a trail of drops in its wake. A gentle splash as it landed.

Watching them, the pattern of their flights was made plain when there was a sudden swirl underneath, a deeper vortex of water. It was the heavier rush of their predator, a hunting dorado. The sound of its hungry lunge carried clearly.

Abruptly, there was a hollow, plump explosion a hundred yards away. A devil ray, three feet across, had come hurtling out of the water like a confused flying blanket, and flopped back into the sea. Two minutes later, there came a deeper splash, even louder, clearer and crisp . 'Pari' — manta ray — muttered a crew member with a note of satisfaction in his voice. Manta ray, after sperm whale, is the preferred target of the harpooners. Every sound of the sea animals was as distinct to the experienced crew as bird calls are to an ornithologist.

A sudden, panicked flurry of flying fish. A shoal of twenty or more sped from the water and — there! — hurtling out on their trail and soaring a good four feet into the air was the tightly muscled silver lozenge of an albacore, its tall thin dorsal fin and sharp tail like knife blades. The big fish flung itself far clear of the water, arched over, and disappeared with a mighty fifty-kilogram splash.

The sea was alive. Long tendrils of plankton, as fat as tree pythons, slowly undulated a foot beneath the surface. The water was a thin brown soup of organisms. The tip of a fin wriggled past, and disappeared in an aimless swirl: a small shark.

Now came a loud sound like a troop of horses splashing across a ford. It is a sound so continuous and so sure that I wonder what animal is confident enough to advertise its presence in that way. 'Lumba, lumba' is the explanation.

Dolphin, a hunting school of at least fifty animals, churning and splashing, and breathing out quick grunts like a herd of wild boar in the undergrowth. The sound continues for perhaps two minutes as the animals sweep back and forth, then — in an instant — they have gone.

'Uuummmmph' — deep and massive, a distinct expulsion of air, and a tall column of spray rises from the sea not fifty yards away. It is followed by the long, slow, slab-sided emergence of a sixty-foot-long body. 'Kelaru,' explains the old man next to me. Baleen whale. It is a fin whale, or maybe even a blue whale. At first sight it is hard to tell. The animal is feeding on the plankton soup. With a succession of massive breaths the great whale cruises carelessly on the surface, ignoring the hunter boats. The crews don't give it a second glance. They do not hunt baleen whales. They take only the toothed whales — sperm whale, pilot whale, killer whale. Camillus has earlier explained to me that one of the Lamalera clans believes that their forebears arrived in Lamalera riding on the back of a baleen whale. This clan was forbidden to hunt baleen whales, and in solidarity the other clans obey the same taboo. The big baleen whale, which I now identify as a blue whale, takes half a dozen distinct breaths, and then slowly dives, arching its thick tail as it slips beneath the water. Ten minutes later it reappears in almost the same spot, circling and diving, and calmly grazing on the krill. It stays in the area for almost three-quarters of an hour, apparently on its own.

Suddenly, the harpooner gives a low call. He has seen something. The crew of the boat come alert. The harpooner is standing bolt upright, looking fixedly at a spot on the calm sea about thirty yards away, to the starboard side. The crew are fully vigilant now, reaching for their paddles. But the harpooner holds up a warning hand, cautioning them to wait, to be still. They will not have to paddle him to within striking distance. The prey, whatever it is, is swimming towards the boat. 'Io' — shark — says the harpooner quietly. His assistant reaches down and selects the correct size of harpoon head. He fits it to the proper weight and length of bamboo shaft, and quietly passes it to the harpooner. He has moved forward along the harpooning platform. Not to the end, because the shark will pass close to the boat. The harpooner raises the harpoon high, holding it nearly vertical. He takes into account the refraction of the image through the water.

The man stabs down. There is a powerful flurry and churning in the water. The line attached to the harpoon head makes a drumming sound as it runs out over the gunnel. The harpooner still has the bamboo shaft in his hand. The metal harpoon head has pulled clear, as it is meant to do. It has been an easy strike.

The shark gives up quickly. Within a few minutes it reappears close to the bow of the boat. The harpooner is ready. He waits a moment, again stabs down with a fresh harpoon head, and secures the animal with a second line. Now the shark has virtually no chance of escape. It thrashes back and forth, diving a few feet until brought back up to the surface by the pull of the tethering ropes. The crew of the whaleboat have left their seats on the thwarts and are standing by to assist. The head, and then the tail, of the shark burst out of the water as the animal fights back. I see what the rest of the crew have already known from the very first minute: it is a hammerhead shark, quite a large one, maybe nine feet long. The animal is very active, and still dangerous. The harpooner and his assistant guide the struggling creature aft along the side of the boat. The thrashing tail throws up sheets of solid water. The crew do not hurry or panic. A well-aimed lance thrust reduces the animal's strength still further. When it is amidships, the shark is drawn closer by the harpoon lines, and two of the boat crew lean outward. The whaleboat heels over, and I see the real function of the stout length of bamboo which is lashed parallel to the hull at the end of three projecting crossbeams. Technically it is an outrigger bar which will reduce the chance of capsize. But its main purpose, I now see, is to act as a fender to prevent the struggling shark, or manta ray, or whale from smashing in the vulnerable side of the boat. At this moment it is also useful for hauling the hammerhead shark aboard. As the boat takes on an angle, two men lean out and grab the shark by the head. Their timing must be precise, or they could lose a hand to the snapping jaws. They use the projecting sides of the hammerhead as handles, and drag the shark halfway over the outrigger and up into the boat. The harpooner takes a long, thin-bladed knife and cuts through the spinal column. The shark goes limp, and is heaved inboard. It flops into the bilge, so big that its body cannot fit between the struts of the hull. The crew of *Sili Tena* look thoroughly pleased with themselves. This is food for their families.

'Are there many sharks?' I asked the assistant harpooner. He shook his head.

'Even when you take a whale? Don't they come to the blood in the water?'

'We used to see very many shark when the whale was cut,' intervened one of the older men. 'But not now. We don't see sharks even when the sea is full of blood. Not since the foreign fishing boats came. They work offshore, fishing with long lines, and now the sharks have gone.'

'What about whale sharks?'

'Sometimes, and they are easy to catch. We call them *io bodo*, the stupid shark, because they don't run away.'

'And sperm whales? Are there more or less of them than before?'

'Last year the whole village only caught nine sperm whale, and of those we caught six on a single day. It was not a good year. But we saw many sperm whales; we just did not catch them. We were unlucky.'

'When speaking about the sperm whales,' Camillus explained for my benefit, 'the crew don't like to call them whales. That brings bad luck. Either you do not talk about the whales directly, or if you have to do so, then you use another word. Sometimes the fishermen just say "fish" or call them "our ancestors", or something like that. There are many other words they must not use in a boat. They never talk about sailing towards the land or the village, they say "towards the church, or away from the church". And to paddle is "to eat with the spoon". The fishermen believe they must speak in this way if they want to catch whales. When they speak incorrectly — or if there is some quarrel or bad feeling among the boat crew — then the whales know this, and stay away.'

The hammerhead was the only catch of the entire fleet that day, apart from the flying fish. Two or three times there were false alarms. A nearby boat crew took up their paddles, responding to a call from their harpooner, and urged their boat in the direction he was pointing. But the prey dived down before the boat could come within striking range. The older crew members on *Sili Tena* identified their intended prey as manta ray.

We turned for home at about one o'clock. Every *tena* in the fleet tacked and set course for the long haul back to the landing beach, as if to the orders of a single commodore. There had been a gentle breeze since nine o'clock, and the fleet looked superb with their sails glowing butter yellow in the tropical sun. But luck was against them, and the breeze was treacherous. It failed when the fleet was three miles from home. Worse, the tide had turned, and the fourteen boats were left to paddle home against the current. On *Sili Tena* the crew lowered the now useless sail, brought down and secured the mast, and produced their paddles. They had not had anything to eat or drink for nearly eight hours, and were faced with at least an hour of grinding physical work. But they were unperturbed and stoic. The paddling chant began. First one old man, then another, led a long plaintive song, setting the rhythm for the paddlers. Every person aboard the *tena* steadily attacked the water with the fervent chopping blows of his paddle, and did not relax until we were within a stone's throw of the land. Here, to the west of the village, a headland offered protection from the worst of the head current, and we crept along, at times alarmingly close to the huge boulders. The waves surged and rebounded among the rocks. Occasionally I thought we would come to grief. But our *lama uri* knew his business. Wrinkled as a walnut, he was as tough and weatherbeaten as his worn leather bush hat which he must have scavenged from a passing tourist. Each time a wave nearly flung *Sili Tena* against the rocks, I glanced back at him and raised a quizzical eyebrow. He grinned conspiratorially back at me, smiling his gap-toothed smile, twisted his steering paddle and deftly sheered away from the next impending collision. Half a mile from home I was amused when he brought the boat to a halt, and kept her bobbing up and down at the same precarious spot while we paddled at half pressure. The harpooner and his assistant had decided to swim ashore. They had seen some children near the strand, retrieving the little containers which are tied to the toddy palms for collecting their sap for *tuak*. The two men plunged into the waves, bought two jugs of the alcohol, and swam back, holding their prize above their heads. The *tuak* was shared among the crew, the paddling chant began again, and half an hour later we brought *Sili Tena* back to Lamalera beach.

Volunteers hurried down to the water's edge to help us retrieve the boat. A dozen extra helpers struggled with the vessel and slowly pushed *Sili Tena* up the incline back into her boatshed. Then they turned, ran back down the beach, and helped the next vessel to come ashore. It was the morning's laborious scene repeated, but now each boat required three times as many human drudges to overcome the slope. Watching this grinding effort, I tried to estimate the reward. *Sili Tena*'s hammerhead shark had been quickly cut up and distributed among the crew. Not a morsel was wasted. A small girl walked homeward along the beach, a tin tray balanced on her head. In it lay the severed head of the shark. The other boats brought home only the flying fish they had caught and trailed as bait. These mangled and limp fish were carefully removed from their hooks and taken home to eat. My guess was that the fleet had caught perhaps sixty flying fish in total. This was all that they had to show after eight hours at sea, and the labour of more than a hundred men.

The man who had forged the harpoon head receives a portion of the catch. This is the custom. Today it was Rufinus Keraf, the retired harpooner whom I had seen the previous day at his smithy. Outside his door Rufinus had planted two whale ribs to formed a bleached white arch. Inside, wooden models of manta dangled from the rafters, and the sun-dried head of a large shark, jaws gaping.

Rufinus was even more gaunt at close range than when I had seen him at the smithy. His cheeks and temples were hollow, and he was more stooped than I had first assumed. When he spoke or turned his head, he moved slowly and looked exhausted. I suspected that he was suffering from malaria, a common affliction in the village. His nephew Vincensius brought us glasses of *tuak* as we sat beside the two whale ribs and Rufinus told me about his life. He was now sixty years old, and had first gone on the whale-boats when he was ten. At that time his father had been the harpooner for *Kebako Puka*. When Rufinus was twenty he had already graduated to be harpooner's assistant, and five or six years after that, the owners of *Tene Ana* had invited him to be their harpooner. He kept that post until his father had retired, and Rufinus felt obliged to fill his father's vacated position as harpooner aboard *Kebako Puka*. It meant that he had been harpooner on two vessels, and his active career had spanned close on thirty years. It was a remarkable achievement, and made Rufinus one of the most experienced of all the Lamalera whale-hunters.

I put the question that I had been waiting to ask: 'In all your time as a harpooner, did you ever see a white sperm whale?'

Rufinus was a little deaf, and for a moment I thought he had not heard the question. In fact he was thinking it over.

'I myself have seen the white sperm whale only one time, when I was with *Kebako Puka*,' he replied. 'The white whale was with another group of whales. It came after we had harpooned an ordinary whale, a black one, and the white whale watched. The white whale followed us when we took the dead whale towards the land. It stayed with us until we were close to the village. Then the white whale swam away.'

I asked, 'How big was this white whale?'

'Very big. This kind of animal we do not have the courage to harpoon. It was more than fifteen metres long. It was bigger than the biggest whale I ever took, and that was about sixteen metres long and three metres high when we brought it to the beach. Its teeth were as big as a beer mug. We needed a ladder to climb on it, and three days to cut up and divide the meat among the people. Even then, there was meat left on the beach. The white whale was bigger than that.'

Rufinus was talking as if he knew much more about the white whale than he could have gleaned from one single encounter.

'How does the white whale usually behave?' I asked. 'What does it do?'

Rufinus was on sure ground, and replied at once.

'It swims with the other whales, to look after them. Normally the white whale is under the water and we do not see him. Sometimes he will come to the surface, but he prefers to stay deep. He never comes first, but always later. All the other black sperm whales arrive, and then, after-wards, the white whale comes. If a whale is har-pooned, then the white whale comes to inspect.'

'Why do you think he is doing that?'

'He is looking, and maybe he is talking to the other whales. I think that they are sea animals, and they talk. Maybe they are talking about something, perhaps to destroy the boat, who knows?'

'Is the white whale dangerous?'

Here again, Rufinus did not hesitate. 'Only sometimes,' he replied. 'The other whales they can be dangerous. They can make trouble or an accident. But the white whale, he prefers to con-trol. He is the leader of the normal whales. He will attack only when it is necessary.'

Here was my first eyewitness report of an

all-white sperm whale, and from a man I judged to be a reliable source. But there was something else. Rufinus accepted the existence of the white whale as being a perfectly normal fact. It was as if the white whale were common knowledge, and no one had bothered to ask about it before. I had the feeling that Rufinus was wondering what all the fuss was about. The great white whale was there, it behaved in a certain manner, and Rufinus was almost apologetic that he had not seen the animal more often.

'You're quite sure that there is a white whale, only one, and that there are no others?' I asked Rufinus a final time, hoping not to offend him by appearing sceptical.

'Yes. A white whale. It is the same one, a big one,' he answered. Vincensius, his nephew, had been listening politely and respectfully all this time. He shifted nervously and said something in a helpful tone.

'What did he say?' I asked Camillus.

'Vincensius says he also saw the white whale, less than three weeks ago. He is an ordinary crew member on *Sika Tena*. It was when *Dolu Tena* harpooned a black sperm whale, but then had to cut the line. The white whale came and escorted the injured black whale away, out to sea.'

Was Vincensius's white whale the same as the whale with white spots which Nadu had told me about? Or was it a different animal, one that was all white, like the one Rufinus had seen? I would have to enquire among the other whale hunters.

But I knew I was getting closer. The white sperm whale was within reach.

The shaman wore a smart red polyester shirt with a tasteful pattern of white ciphers. The colours went well with his neat black trousers, and the short sleeves showed off his glossy brown skin. With his trim moustache and youthful figure he looked more like a spruce young bridegroom than the mystic and venerable figure that I had expected. Yet he was heir to the occult powers which allowed him 'to call the whales', as Camillus put it. Camillus also assured me that the young man's whale calling was very effective. The previous year a television crew had come from Japan to film whale hunting. The Japanese had stayed for weeks, but had seen no whales. In frustration, they asked the shaman to go to the mountains and 'call the whales'. He had done so, and the next day a large school of sperm whales appeared in the bay. Unfortunately the Japanese film crew had not anticipated his success, and gone off to film inland.

In late April, at the start of each whaling season, the shaman climbed to a high place on the mountain. He wore a ceremonial woven belt. It was a copy of the belt he had inherited from his family, though it was now so tattered it would disintegrate if he used it. He showed me the original, kept in a tin trunk in his 'temple', little more than a shed, beside his house. With it were

226

a small elephant tusk, also inherited, and three or four flat stones in a wicker basket. The stones he described as 'leaning stones'. Formerly the clans had met in assembly to settle their grievances. If a clan member kept his foot on one of the stones, he would be successful in his argument. The other main items in the shaman's collection were two gongs. The larger one hung outside the temple on special occasions, and the smaller one he carried when he climbed the mountain. With him went representatives of three senior whale-hunting clans. On the heights the shaman recited prayers to the ancestor whales, made a sacrifice of food, and sounded the small gong. Then he and his escort descended the mountain. They did not use the normal footpath, but travelled almost in a direct line down the steep slope. Seven times they would halt, and perform a brief ceremony. Each time they would beat the gong, and the larger gong at the shrine house would respond. One stop would be at the Whale Rock. A boulder six feet high and twenty feet long, it was by a freak of nature a close replica of a sperm whale, half awash in the sea. It was once a real whale, said the shaman. Whales breathed fresh air so they were 'an ancient sort of cow which has gone to live in the ocean'. The whale of Whale Rock had been on its journey down from the mountain when the sun rose, and the animal turned to stone.

The shaman's role derived from the time, its

date now lost, when a boat called *Kebako Puka* had arrived at Lamalera from far away, carrying the refugees from a great natural disaster. The new arrivals were a fisher people who used harpoons, and their leader was a man called Korohama. They asked the original inhabitants of the land if they might settle on the promontory overlooking the bay. They paid for the site with five brass bracelets and a gold necklace, and in due course Korohama's three sons became the founders of the three leading clans of Lamalera. One of the sons moved down to live near the beach, and because the gold necklace which Korohama had given in payment for the land had a magical tendency to return to its previous owner, the settlers agreed to substitute for it a boat. They built this boat and gave to the original 'lords of the land', and the boat came to be called *Baka Tena*.

This, in essence, is the foundation legend of the first Lamalera whale hunters. Two whale-boats still carry the names *Kebako Puka* and *Baka Tena*, and to this day the whale hunters seek the permission of the shaman of the mountain, and the shaman of the beach, for approval to begin the fishing season.

Several other clans arrived in due course and added their own myths. One clan came with the special equipment for catching sharks. The forefather of another clan, the Eba Ona, rode in on the back of a friendly baleen whale. This man carried a bamboo tube of water, and had fixed a

228

ladder in the whale's spout hole so that whenever the whale dived, he climbed up the ladder to stay out of the water. As he stepped ashore, he accidentally dropped the bamboo water tube on the rocks. Where it shattered is now a spring of fresh water.

In 1979 and 1982 an ethnographer, Bob Barnes,[*] lived in Lamalera and succeeded in untangling this skein of traditions and beliefs. He revealed how membership of a descent group or clan affected almost every aspect of a person's life, whether it was where a family lived in the village, with whom they inter-married, or on which boat the men went to sea. With meticulous and scholarly detail Barnes examined every aspect of the village, from its economy to how the whaleboats were built and used. He laid bare a society so conscious of its roots that a shipwright would claim precedence over his colleagues if he traced his descent from the master boatbuilder who constructed the first *Kebako Puka* many centuries before.

The power of the ancestors and shamanism was a challenge to Father Bernardus Bode of the German Divine Word Society, whose statue

---

[*] Later appointed Professor of Social Anthropology at Oxford University, he published his findings under the title *Sea Hunters of Lamalera*. He was accompanied on visits to Lamalera by his wife and children, and Ruth Barnes became the acknowledged authority on Lamalera's textiles.

stands outside Lamalera's large church. Depicted in his clerical garb, he is posed on the prow of a concrete *tena*, Bible in one hand, the other held up to give a blessing like a latter-day St Peter. As a missionary Father Bode was unbending and extraordinarily effective. Arriving in 1920, he spent the rest of his working life persuading the people of Lamalera to be devout Catholics. Today no boat goes to sea on a Sunday even if sperm whales appear in the bay; the angelus is rung every noon from a bell hanging from the branch of a tree outside the house of the *kapala desa;* and in the evening it is not unusual for a small procession to walk between the houses, with the leader holding up a picture of the Virgin Mary while an entourage of small children carry candles and sing hymns. Father Bode fought a long, strict campaign against the old pagan ways. The larger 'leaning stones', like those the shaman held, were ripped up and immured in the foundations of the new church. The skulls of the ancestors were buried instead of being used in ceremonies. Idolatry of any sort was condemned on pain of being banned from church services. Shaman rites were given a Christian gloss with Christian prayers and formulas.

But the old ways still keep leaking through, even with someone as devout as Camillus. He described his traumatic experience when, as tourist chief, he tried to arrange the first visit to Lamalera by a small cruise ship. The event took months to organise. There had been meeting

230

after meeting to win the co-operation of the fishermen. On the appointed day the whaleboat crews did not go fishing but assembled on the beach and waited for the cruise ship to appear. The plan was that the boats would put to sea, circle the cruise ship, and make a display of whale hunting. The hours went by, no cruise ship came over the horizon, and the fishermen, a hundred men or more, grew bored and angry. They rounded on poor Camillus, and accused him of wasting their time. They swore never to co-operate with him again. Then, just as the day seemed a complete disaster, a pod of sperm whales surfaced in the bay. Thanks to the tourist scheme, all the boats and crews were ready and waiting on the beach. To the cry of 'Baleo! Baleo!' the entire fleet launched and set off in hot pursuit of the whales. They disappeared round the headland, and Camillus was left on the beach. He prayed that the chase would be successful, that at least one whale would be caught, and his reputation restored in the village. So it happened. The cruise ship never showed up, but the fleet returned with two whales taken.

'My prayers were answered,' Camillus told me. His voice was shaking with emotion, and he pulled out a handkerchief and began to dab his eyes. 'I had to say thank you, thank you. Thank you for hearing for my prayers.' And Camillus, the man who called upon Santa Maria in his sleep, lifted his face from his handkerchief and added, 'The whales had heard me. My ancestors had helped me.'

From my vantage point at the schoolteacher's house on the cliff top, I was becoming familiar each day with the sights and sounds of the village. Soon after 3 A.M. a big gecko usually woke me. The lizard began by clearing its throat loudly with the ratcheting noise of a badly oiled grandfather clock about to strike. Then it gave six or eight shatteringly loud calls before falling silent. This would wake Guru Ben's youngest child, sleeping in the next room, who would whimper until shushed by his mother. A dog might bark in the village below. On a few mornings I heard rain on the leaves of the big banyan tree outside the window. When the shower ended, the air was momentarily cleared of the stench of whale meat and blubber on the drying racks. Then the smell re-established itself, almost palpably wafting through the village, a miasma carried upward by the steamy air rising off the warm earth.

At 5.30 the bell outside the *kapala desa*'s house began to wake the villagers and remind the faithful to pray. Half an hour later I joined the boat crews as they trailed along the path leading down to the boatsheds. They walked with the resignation of men on their way to hard physical work. They brought no food for their day at sea. The most they carried was a little box of tightly woven lontar palm leaf or a plastic pill bottle dangling from a string. These contained a

232

cigarette lighter, a ball of tobacco grown in the hill villages, and a dried strip of leaf that they used as cigarette paper. The men were dressed in an assortment of ragged clothes. There were always several yellow T-shirts printed with the tree symbol of Golkar, the ruling political party of Indonesia, and issued as propaganda. Other men wore singlets or patched cotton shirts. A few had shorts. By far the most common garments were sarongs, worn around the waist or thrown casually over the shoulder like a toga. Feet were bare, and nearly everyone wore some sort of hat as a precaution against the glare of the sun at sea. The local design of hat resembled the top storey of a Chinese pagoda and was made of varnished palm leaf. It could only be worn perched high on the crown of the head, and had to be held in place with a length of fishing line fastened under the chin. The hat was such a frivolous shape that it would not have looked out of place on the head of a pert model on a fashion-house catwalk. The rest of the headgear came from an extraordinary variety of sources. There were panama hats, felt hats, trilbies, yellow Golkar baseball caps, knitted hats, and the type of long-peaked caps with oak leaf decoration favoured by Indonesian and American army generals. One assistant harpooner had somehow obtained a hood which must have become detached from a winter anorak. The hood was made of a grey, synthetic furry material and must have been uncomfortably hot in the tropics. So he wore it loose, and the weird impression as he peered from within the hood was enhanced by a pair of dark glasses which in one corner bore the tiny white rabbit insignia of the Playboy Club. His dress sense belied the fact that he was one of the most competent whale hunters in the community.

Eight men was considered the minimum needed to operate a *tena;* thirteen or even fifteen men the optimum, though it was rare that so many were available for a single boat. Sometimes not enough men showed up to work a boat — or the harpooner was missing. The others would loiter in the boatshed, lend a hand to launch the other *tena,* then join the idlers and longshoremen who spent the entire day on the beach, waiting for the fleet's return. There was something sad about the oldest men at this time, a wistful look in their eyes, as they watched the fleet depart. They knew they would never again have the strength and stamina to share in the fishery. After the boats left, they turned and walked slowly to find a place to sit beside one of the sail-makers. These men stayed behind, sitting or kneeling on the sand in front of the boat-sheds, working at the small weaving frames which stretched out the squares of matting for the sails. Beside them the little cluster of old-timers smoked, gossiped and gazed out to sea. Children and dogs played. Teenagers sprawled on the sand, turning their bodies restlessly. Women sat with bundles of goods tied up in cloth, metal basins on the sand beside them. They were waiting for a boat with an engine to take them a few miles to market along the coast. The bundles contained their trade goods, and the basins were their shopping baskets.

Everyone faced towards the sea, never towards the land. Once again, the keenness of their eyesight was astonishing. From the beach, virtually at sea level, the observers could identify each *tena* at six or seven miles distance. To an untutored eye they were little more than rectangular specks. But each boat had its distinguishing feature — a patch on its sail, the angle the sail was set, some distinguishing mark. From the beach people watched them knowingly. From years of experience they guessed what was happening. When a boat lowered its sail entirely, it was in pursuit of a whale. If it merely brailed up the sail, perhaps it was chasing a manta ray. If the boat stayed stationary, then maybe it had harpooned the ray, but the animal had dived. The old men commented to one another on the possibilities, and waited for the fleet to return with confirmation of their guesses.

For several days I went out with the fleet as a guest aboard a *tena,* to experience the daily routine and see how the boat crew worked. On several days the fleet caught nothing at all. Usually the catch totalled less than three or four sharks or rays. And the chances of my being on the boat that made the catch, one out of twelve or thirteen vessels, were slim.

So I unpacked the bundles that the boys who rowed the little beach boats had eyed with such curiosity when they brought Camillus and me ashore. The packages contained a twelve-foot inflatable rubber dinghy, bright yellow, with a mast and sail and sculls, and a five-horsepower outboard motor. There were also four plastic cans of petrol which, I calculated, would last me a month if I used the dinghy under sail as often as possible. With this equipment I hoped to be able to monitor the fleet even when it was seven miles offshore, though this was farther than normally prudent for a very small rubber boat.

Camillus was no sailor, so I recruited Bernardus. He was a grizzled veteran in his early fifties, and why he never sailed with the fleet I did not know. Perhaps it was because he had spent so much time away from the village that he had lost contact with a regular crew. In any event, Bernardus quickly learned how to operate the little outboard engine, and his knowledge of whale lore and whaling was invaluable. The next day, 15 May, when the fleet went out to sea, it was preceded by a tiny vessel that bore some resemblance to a bright yellow banana. A mile ahead of the fleet, Bernardus shut off the outboard, and we sat and waited.

The grand view of the approaching Lamalera whaling fleet was unforgettable. The boats were gliding across a royal blue sea, dwarfed by a dramatic and mountainous backdrop. From the dinghy I could now appreciate how Lamalera was built at the foot of an extinct volcano. The slope of the mountain swept upward, the first section green with scrub and small bushes, and then a broad band of bare rock leading to the ragged crest. In foreground, on the bow of each boat stood the harpooner. He held his fourteen-foot harpoon shaft, butt down against his foot and vertical. Where the land curved to the east under the rising sun, the *tena* were advancing into silhouette on a sea of bright silver. The outline of each boat was black and crisp. Now, from a much greater distance, when the harpooner and the bodies of the paddlers had diminished in size, the row of figures reminded me of the stick-like outlines of hunters drawn by prehistoric artists on the walls of caves. I half-expected to see the figures of bison and mammoth rising from the sea.

At 7.30, when the fleet was about three miles offshore, a harpooner suddenly bent forward and pointed with his arm. He had spotted an entire shoal of giant manta ray swimming like a squadron of aircraft underwater. Other harpooners had seen the same phenomenon, and at once there was frenetic activity. Men snatched up their paddles, and began hacking at the water. Half a dozen boats altered course to converge on the spot where the manta ray had been seen. Harpooners pranced on their platforms, dancing from one foot to the other in excitement, calling out and urging on their men. Their lances rose and wavered like pikemen going into battle or horse-riding knights swaying in the saddle at a tourney. Boats criss-crossed and swerved as they sought to follow the track of the manta ray. Bernardus and I could hear the grunts of effort from the paddlers, the cries of encouragement, and the thump of the paddle handles against the sides of the boat. The hunters were thin and hungry, exerting every nerve and muscle. Boats churned through the water, splashes of foam dashed up from the paddle blades.

Abruptly, the shoal of giant manta ray turned, banked, and dived into the depths. They were out of range, gone, and all the excitement drained away in an instant.

Few had noticed the two boats *Praso Sapang* and *Kelulus*. They had peeled off from the manta chase. Their lookouts had spotted even bigger game — sperm whale.

There were three whales, all bulls. Later the fishermen told me that these three whales were following in the wake of a large school of sperm whale. This school had swum past Lamalera earlier that morning, moving westward with the current. The three bull whales were travelling in the same direction, lagging some distance behind the school. One animal was a quarter-mile in advance of his companions when they were spotted by the hunters. This whale was already clear of any pursuit. But to my astonishment one of the two remaining bulls appeared to be lying stationary on the surface. He was calmly wallowing on the same spot, the slight swell sluicing his back so he looked like a shiny blunt-ended black log. This bull whale was showing no sign of alarm as *Praso Sapang* thrashed down in attack. It was puzzling. The whale must have detected the boat's presence. The *tena*'s maximum speed was perhaps six knots, with a dozen paddlers working flat-out. So there was ample time for the whale to dive and escape. Or it had only to swim in the opposite direction at a leisurely pace and it would quickly leave behind the hunters. The harpooner was balancing like an acrobat halfway along his platform. Gazing at the whale, he was empty-handed and leaning forward from the waist, knees slightly bent, and swinging his arms back and forth in rhythm to urge on the men behind him. The whale lay directly in the path of the onrushing boat. The huge animal filled its lungs with air, rhythmically inhaling and exhaling as if it had all the time in the world. Everything seemed to be happening in slow motion — why didn't the whale flee, or dive? It dawdled in the same spot, as *Praso Sapang* closed the gap.

I saw the assistant harpooner pass forward the long bamboo lance. From the rack of bamboo poles he had selected the stout, heavier pole that is kept for whale attack, and had fitted the big whale harpoon head. The harpooner took the lance, raised it high, and moved to the end of the projecting harpooner's ladder. He held the weapon with his left hand about five feet from the butt of the lance, his right hand close to the end. He brought the tip of the lance forward down in a slow arc until it pointed at the whale, and flexed his knees until he stood in a half-crouch. I could see the slight curve in the bamboo shaft as it drooped under the weight of the metal harpoon head. Behind the harpooner his assistant stood up, gesturing with hand signals to the steersman to keep him on course. The paddlers were howling and roaring and chanting the stroke. For a long moment the scene held. Then the harpooner judged his distance, and struck.

He leaped from the boat. He burst upward from the half-crouch and flung himself forward, still holding the lance. Harpoon head, shaft, and human were all one single projectile, hurtling through the air. The harpoon travelled forward and down, and for one moment the man looked like a flag attached to the long pole and trailing behind it. The harpoon head struck the black target of the whale's back, the forward motion stopped, and the harpooner tumbled into the water right beside the thirty-ton animal. It appeared to be a leap of utter madness.

The bamboo shaft was too light to give impetus to the strike, and the harpooner had used his body weight to drive home the harpoon.

For a few moments nothing happened. The whale simply lay there on the surface, and I saw the head and shoulders of the harpooner, tiny beside the bulk of the animal, as he turned and swam rapidly back towards *Praso Sapang* where the crew hauled him aboard. In that interval *Kelulus,* coming up in support, managed to get close enough on the far side of the whale so that her harpooner could throw his lance almost straight down. The strike was not as effective as the jump and throw of *Praso Sapang*'s attack, but now the whale had two harpoons fast. Belatedly the massive animal lunged into action. There was a tremendous heaving uprush of water, a great surge and swirl, and the whale started off at full speed. Frantically the assistant harpooners on the two boats adjusted the angle of the whale lines. This was the most dangerous moment. The lines had to run forward, flowing smoothly over the bow of the boat. If the line had a snag or a hitch, it would catch and snap, or rip a piece out of the hull. The strength of a bull sperm whale can tow a modern steel whalecatcher backwards, and here the animal was in contest with two Stone Age vessels fastened together with lengths of tree fibre. The shock load could tear *Praso Sapang* and *Kelulus* in pieces. And if the *lama uri,* the helmsman, did not keep his boat true in the whale's wake, or the harpooner's assistant allowed the whale line to slide and pull sideways across the boat, then the vessel would be dragged over, corkscrewing into the sea. The other crew members — boys and old men — dropped their paddles, scrambled to their places, and hung on tight. There was nothing else they could do now.

The wounded bull whale ran out the line. Under my urging, Bernardus had brought the yellow inflatable within thirty metres of the whale. It was close enough for me to see the heavy whale line spring taut, as the animal reached the end of the tether. *Praso Sapang* and *Kelulus* had been lying at different angles in the water. Suddenly both boats swung round, parallel and close together, like twin needles responding to a single, unseen magnetic source. The whale was towing them like an enormous draught-horse. With a surge the two boats accelerated away. I had expected a sudden hurtling rush, but the motion was sedate, unstoppable. The whale was in control of the two *tena*. The animal was keeping close to the surface, so the two boats were not pulled under, but sledged forward across the sea.

Unexpectedly, after a hundred metres the animal doubled back, and swam close enough for the harpooners to plant two more harpoons. Their bamboo shafts broke off, as they were designed to do, and bobbed to the surface. Bernardus and I, skittering around the scene in our little inflatable boat, scooped them up, intending to return them later to their owners. I saw one of two other bull whales turn back, approach within about thirty metres of his stricken comrade, then swim away. Moments later the flukes of both unharmed whales rose into the air as they dived, and got clear to safety.

Meanwhile half a dozen more *tena* had arrived

in the area. They formed a loose, open circle around the two boats that were fast to the whale, and waited. It appeared as if they were standing by to assist. 'Will they also try to harpoon the whale?' I asked Bernardus. He shook his head vehemently. I remembered that Lamalera custom decrees that the boats which strike a whale have an absolute right to take that whale. If they call for help, then the helpers can take a share in the catch. For the moment *Kelulus* and *Praso Sapang* were convinced they could handle the harpooned whale, and did not need assistance. They believed that the harpooned whale was firmly caught and had very little fight.

'Maybe *kea* come,' said Bernardus. The watching whaleboats were keeping a sharp lookout for the sperm whale which arrives full tilt on the scene when another member of the pod is under attack or in difficulties. A *kea* — it is a specialist Lamaholot word — appears from no one knew where, swimming towards the whale in distress. Perhaps it is coming to the rescue, perhaps it arrives just to keep it company in its troubles. The clansmen say that *kea* whales sometimes take one look at the situation, turn, and swim off, never to be seen again. But at other times the *kea* will linger close to its harpooned companion, apparently encouraging it to break free of the harpoon line, or even trying to bite through the whale line with its jaws. And then, say the whale hunters, if the harpooned whale is finally subdued and killed, they have witnessed the loyal *kea* swim up close to the corpse, touch head to head, and 'kiss it goodbye'.

No *kea* appeared. But we were wrong to think the harpooned bull whale was submissive, an animal that would give in easily. Instead it proved to be a 'fighting whale'. At first it charged in short bursts, away from its tormentors. When it felt the tug of the whale lines, the animal plunged head down, raised its tail and thrashed the sea in anger, raising great gouts of water. The beating tail was clearly a weapon of defence. If it had struck a *tena*, the descending flukes would certainly have smashed the boat to matchwood. But the hunters stayed clear. Then the whale turned, and either by accident or design, butted the whaleboats with its head. They were glancing blows, usually delivered as the whale surfaced right alongside a boat. I saw the *tena* shudder with the impact, and tip abruptly. If the blow had been direct it would have stove in the hull. But the boat held together, and the struggle went on and on. The head-butts were repeated, first on *Praso Sapang*, and then on *Kelulus*, as the whale circled and struck, and the whale lines tangled. After half an hour the whale was weakening. Blood was leaking from the wounds and spreading in a great stain. Every time the animal came close enough, the harpooner or assistant stabbed with a pike, trying to find a vital spot. *Kelulus* took such a steady battering that her crew partially withdrew from the contest. Most of her crew clambered out of the boat and scram-

244

bled aboard *Praso Sapang*, and fresh men climbed in from *Praso Sapang* to continue the affray.

It was a duel between pygmies and a giant. The whale was no more than average size, ten metres long, about the same length as one of the boats. It was the bulk and strength of the animal which gave the contrast. The hunters looked tiny in comparison, puny and slight. The great roar of breath which exploded from the whale each time it surfaced accentuated the difference in power. The sound carried clearly. Strangely, each time the whale snorted out its huge burst of air, there came immediately a high, lingering, cheer from the boat crew. They kept up this response all through the battle. It was such a strange sound that at first I thought they cheered to keep up their own spirits in such a perilous situation. Then I wondered if it was bloodlust, a sort of frenzy with the great wounded animal close at hand. But the cheers continued and they grew more hoarse and softer as the whale weakened, and its snorts, too, became more feeble. The two sounds seemed to decline in tandem, to match one another, and I imagined a link held between prey and hunter. The whale was giving itself to the hunters. The crew seemed to communicate with the animal. Their shout mingled thanks, praise, and satisfaction. In that cheer I heard the expression of all the hours and hours of wearisome paddling, the man-hauling of boats up and down the beach, the privation of meagre food, broiling sun, and profitless hours at sea scanning the waves. The men in the boats ranged from teenagers to sixty-year-olds. Most of them would probably never take more than ten or fifteen whales in all their lives. This was a supreme, rare moment. There was no thought of inflicting unnecessary cruelty or pain on their prey. Instead there was a sense of justification and earned reward. The ancestors, the whales themselves, had helped, and the rope-makers, the sail-makers, the shipwrights, the smith who forged the harpoon heads, the shaman, and the clan. The shouting of the whaleboat crew was part triumph, but chiefly, I sensed, it was their expression of reaching a hard and long-sought goal.

As the whale turned and churned, the whale lines wrapped around its body. They criss-crossed in a tangle until I was reminded irresistibly of the death of Fedallah, the leader of the Manila men in *Moby Dick*, whom Melville called the 'Parsee'. Fedallah falls out of his whaleboat when attacking Moby Dick and disappears, only for his corpse to be glimpsed next day entangled in the old and broken whale lines which are wrapped around the white whale. 'Lashed round and round to the fish's back; pinioned in the runs upon turns in which, during the past night, the whale had reeled the involutions of the lines around him, the half-torn body of the Parsee was seen; his sable raiment frayed to shreds; his distended eyes turned full upon old Ahab.' How that could happen I saw when *Praso Sapang*'s bull whale surfaced right alongside the boat, and lay there motionless. The whale had been struggling for more than an hour, and seemed totally spent. Sensing the chance to finish the animal, the crew of *Praso Sapang* hauled in the lines until boat and whale lay side by side, black whale skin touching the faded white upper plank of the boat. There were no harpoons or lances available, so the assistant harpooner leaned out, holding a long-bladed knife. He had the knife raised high, holding it with both hands, and was about to plunge it into the whale's body when the animal suddenly moved. *Praso Sapang* rocked violently, and the assistant harpooner, out of balance and with no free hand to hold himself back, was flung out of the boat. Desperately he gave a leap to try to clear the whale and land in the sea. Instead he sprawled across the whale's back and slithered into the water, arms flailing. In that instant, if his slide had been arrested by one of the whale lines, and his foot or arm had been caught, he would have been pulled under and drowned. The 'fighting whale' was far from surrender. It swam clear of the whaleboat and the struggle lasted for another hour.

The attendant whaleboats had moved off. There were no *kea,* and *Praso Sapang* and *Kelulus* were solidly fast to their whale. The rest of the fleet continued hunting, while the two lucky whaleboats battled it out with their prey. Each surfacing of the whale made the scene more bloody and regrettable. I found myself wishing that the struggle would end quickly, and the exhausted crews must have felt the same. Their harpoons and lances were all used up. There was a bright scarlet gash in the animal's back, and a broad patch of sea was dark with blood. Yet the whale kept making shallow dives, then surfacing with a great whistling gush of air. It was often so close to the boat as it rose that the spray and mist from its spoutings drifted across the hunters, and they ducked or shrank back from the whale's breath. As the animal grew weaker, its movement slowed. There was an air of numb exhaustion. The whale lines shortened as the men reeled in their huge catch. The whale drew closer and closer to the boat. Instead of diving deliberately with a thrust of its tail, the animal now sank horizontally in the water or even tail-first like a doomed ship slipping below the sea. Now it came back up vertically, the huge square head rising right alongside the outrigger of the boat and its scarecrow line of half-exhausted men. Some of the sailors were so tired that they were slumped on the far side of the boat and taking no part in the struggle. I heard a highly pitched creaking. I could not tell whether it was the sound of the whale's skin rubbing against the battered boat, or whether the sound was the rapid clicking squeaks of sperm whale communication. The huge head bobbing from the water looked like an immense black navigation buoy. Then the jaw opened, and the illusion ended.

The long narrow jaw, armed with its row of teeth, looked pathetic rather than menacing, a bird's mandible rather than a predator's bite.

I watched for the final signs: the nineteenth-century whalemen claimed that a dying whale always swam in a circle, turning towards the sun. 'That strange spectacle observable in all sperm whales dying — the turning sunwards of the head, and so expiring' is how Melville expressed it. Sure enough the whale made a slow, tired circle, and to my imagination it seemed to be towards the sun. It had to be the end. The men aboard *Praso Sapang* fell silent. There was no cheering now. They picked up their paddles and eased their boat within arm's length of the whale. Someone leaned out with a length of rope to loop it around the body and begin the tow. As he did so, the whale suddenly revived. With a sudden lunge, it rammed *Praso Sapang* so violently that a crew man was flung into the water with a yell of fright. The whale swam in a circle and came back at the boat, its jaws snapping. The head reared up, and the mouth seized the port outrigger and shook it. The men leaning over the gunnel shrank backwards out of reach. The boat rocked violently, and for a moment it seemed it would be capsized.

It was the whale's last throe. This was the final 'flurry' which surgeon Beale and the other nineteenth-century whalemen had warned of. The last moments of a whale, they said, were marked by a spasm of frantic effort. The whale's jaws released their grip on *Praso Sapang* and the great head slid back underwater. When it next appeared, a little distance away, the whale was lying on its back, and its jaw hung open and slack. It bobbed in the water for perhaps ten seconds, then slid quietly under the widening dye of blood.

A hunter slipped into the water from *Kelulus* and swam over to the corpse. He climbed on the semi-submerged body and began to untangle the whale lines and retrieve the precious harpoon heads. Behind him the two crews started on the complex task of sorting out the ropes and broken bamboo poles. It was half an hour before they were ready to pass a towline between the two boats and lash the whale close alongside *Praso Sapang*. Then the crews settled on their seats and began the long, arduous paddle back home. It would take three hours to haul the ungainly thirty-ton weight of the whale back to Lamalera's beach, battling the currents in the bay.

A speck appeared in the sky to the west of the volcano behind Lamalera as the men began to paddle home. It was a sea eagle flying out from the cliffs. The bird circled over the slow-moving boats, turned, and flew back to land. Two hours later I saw the eagle again. It was flying back and forth, over the beach, patrolling for the scraps it knew would soon be floating in the shallows.

The day they caught the whale was Friday, ferry day. As *Praso Sapang* towed the dead whale

250

into the shallows at Lamalera beach and the crew secured their prize with a long rope to a rock, the little wooden ferry from Larantuka dropped anchor in the bay. Among her passengers was my friend of many years, Trondur Patursson. He had come with his son Brandur from their home in the Faeroe Islands in the North Atlantic. Trondur's uncombed beard and strong features give him the look of a kindly Norse sea god, and he is a talented artist as well as the most skilled traditional sailor I have worked with. He forges his own harpoons and has helped to feed my crew on all of my major boat expeditions, taking shark, barracuda and kingfish with deadly aim. Trondur is also a sensitive and knowledgeable observer of sea life. Whales are a recurrent theme in his drawings, paintings and monumental sculptures in glass and metal, and I had suggested that he join me to see the last sperm whale hunters in the world. The Faeroese still take pilot whale for food in their remote islands, and as Trondur came ashore, he sniffed the odour of whale and grunted, 'Like home, same smell.'

The butchery began next morning. Unexpectedly, it had a balletic quality. The master-builder of *Praso Sapang* acted as ballet-master. He held a thin, long-bladed, long-handled knife which could have been his baton. Walking round the enormous black carcass as it lay in the edge of the surf, he pointed with the blade to the point where each new cut should made, or stepped close up and sliced a gash to indicate the next portion to be carved. His clansmen and their helpers then hacked and cut and sawed, attached short lengths of rope, and pulled away strips of flesh and blubber like peeling the skin of a gigantic orange. Some of the portions were so heavy that it took two men to drag the piece up the beach above the tide line where they let the morsel flop. The Western whalemen called these chunks 'blanket pieces', and rendered them down in boiling pots aboard ship for oil. To me the whale pieces looked more like large squares cut from a thick foam rubber mattress, and in Lamalera they were food. From time to time the master-builder reviewed the growing line of blanket pieces. With the tip of his knife, he delicately scored each with a series of parallel lines like a butcher scoring the surface of a joint of rolled pork. He was following a mental diagram similar to those stylised pictures displayed in a butcher's shop which show the various cuts of meat, drawn on the carcass outline. Strict tradition defines Lamalera's equivalent. The master-builder knew which part of the whale went to which person. The harpooner, for example, receives the meat and blubber from the base of the skull; the smith who made the harpoon head gets the flesh from above the whale's eyes; the tail goes to the clan which owns the boat; and the working crew share out the great mass of meat and blubber from the torso. Even the tips of the fins and tail have special allocations. The head and brain are reserved for the shaman, the 'lord of the land', so that he can include the spirit of the whale in his temple.

By the time dusk fell, most of the whale had disappeared. In a community where food is scarce, there had been no waste. Even the lung mass was salvaged, carried away by three men like a gigantic wet bunch of light purple grapes. Metre by metre, the men also untangled the enormous, slithery, blue-grey intestines, and walked up the beach with lengths of whale gut looped over their shoulders like hawsers. They squeezed out the contents with their bare hands, then split the gut and chopped the mustard yellow lining into morsels. They dropped these bits into bamboo tubes and carefully stoppered each container. Soon the contents would putrefy into a pungent gruel which was popular in the hill villages. Men and women from Lamalera would climb into the mountains and trade the tubes of whale offal for fruit, rice and tobacco. The hill people would use the reeking sauce on their rice as a delicacy.

The spermaceti oil from the 'case', the reservoir in the sperm whale's head, was less valued. This was the bright-burning oil for which Western whalemen had hunted the sperm whale so ruthlessly and efficiently. They took the best oil from the heads of the dead whales, and the second grade oil from their blubber — then threw away the rest. They considered sperm whale meat too dark and rank to be eaten. By contrast, the native whale hunters were carefully allocating every scrap that was edible, and the oil was free to all. Women and girls collected it when the huge backbone and the strange block of a head, standing five feet high, was all that was left on the beach. The women wore their oldest clothes, for this was greasy work. They brought plastic cups, jugs and metal bowls, and stood waiting until a worker cut into the 'case' of oil. Then the women handed up their utensils, and the man reached in and filled them, handed them back, and the women tipped the contents into larger containers. Their daughters clustered against the sperm whale's head, and were scraping the sharp edges of coconut half-shells against the oozing flesh to catch a few spoonfuls of oil. The Lamalera families would use it in their cooking. The oil was the colour and consistency of pale yellow, light Aragon olive oil, and according to surgeon Bennett, had a 'bland and creamy taste, not unlike that of very fresh butter'.

The only discarded item that I could see was the glistening translucent body of a large squid. It lay in the shallows where it had fallen when the whale's stomach was cut open. The squid looked as tasty as on a fishermonger's slab. 'Can't you eat that, too?' I asked one of the workers. He shook his head. 'No, it has been in the whale's stomach and is very salty. It will make you very ill.' Here was one small puzzle: sperm whales swallow their prey almost entire, so perhaps the

254

squid was already saturated with powerful stomach juices that would help the whale digest its food, but give humans acute stomach ache.

Finally the head was severed from the spine. Men came with ropes and passed them around the gigantic trophy, and by hauling and using levers, they slowly rolled the skull away to one side. The head was beyond recognition. What had been a blunt black battering-ram was now a hollow bony cranium, deathly white from the strands of pale fibrous matter which had once held the oil and still clung to the bone. The teeth were long since gone, prised from the jaws, doubtless for sale to tourists. The lower jaw had also been detached. Now the skull bore a macabre resemblance to the head of a monstrous bird, a white egret perhaps which had fallen in the water and decayed. There was the great sharp beak of the upper jaw, sockets for large eyes, and a double dome of the bird's head crest. The hollow brain-pan, where the spermaceti oil had been, was the size and shape of a gigantic armchair.

The schoolmaster's wife served fresh sperm whale meat to Camillus, Brandur, Trondur and me for our evening meal. It tasted of very strong venison, and was coarse and tough. Sperm whales store oxygen in their muscles, so their flesh is saturated with myoglobin that gives the meat a dark red, almost black, colour. For a vegetable our hostess had cooked a dish of tree leaves. The leaves, Camillus explained, came from a small shrub that grew locally. The soil was too rocky to grow vegetables, and these shrub leaves were a substitute. Cooked in whale oil, they became quite palatable. That is why the hill people also liked to buy whale blubber from the village. By putting small pieces of blubber in the pan, they could cook even the bitter leaves of the papaya tree, and have something to eat when times were hard. Papaya leaf, Camillus added, was also a medicine for malaria. But then you had to boil it up on its own, for it was the bitterness which contained the cure.

The drying racks had fresh burdens all over Lamalera the next day. Cuts of whale meat were slowly releasing their moisture to the tropical warmth, shrivelling until the dark flesh came to resemble the twisted roots of ancient vines. Blubber, cut in strips, hung across the drying poles in enormous earlobes. Drop by slow drop, the oil was oozing out and dripping into crude gutters — the spine of a palm leaf or an off-cut of corrugated iron — and trickling to a small bucket which collected the run-off. As it dripped, the blubber turned from white to butter yellow and finally a deep amber.

Twists of dried whale meat make Lamalera's unit of currency. Until recently the villagers seldom used bank notes or coins. Whale meat is still their standard of value, and they say it is 'buying money' if they have to sell whale meat for cash. They prefer to barter for their necessities. Every Saturday groups of Lamalera women set out through the darkness, with basins and cloth bundles and baskets balanced on their heads. They walk the rocky path that leads eastward along the coastline. Dawn finds them halfway to the little hamlet of Wulan Doni. Here the women of the more agricultural villages meet them. The rendezvous is an expanse of bare earth under the market tree. The Lamalera women stay to one side, waiting and watching while their counterparts squat down on the ground and arrange their offerings. They spread out clumps of bananas, displays of vegetables, bottles of *tuak* and palm oil. And sit back and wait. The two groups of women are different. The gardening people wear brighter patterns, small items of costume jewellery, and their clothes are newer. The Lamalera women, by contrast, are sombre in their dress, more workaday and plain. At about ten o'clock the warden of the market appears, a schoolmasterly figure with heavy horn-rimmed glasses and dressed in a vaguely military uniform with red shoulder flashes. He blows a whistle to draw attention. The chattering of perhaps two hundred women momentarily subsides as he reads out the market rules, though no one really listens to him. Then he blows three more blasts on his whistle, and the Lamalera women briskly sally forward from the sidelines. Now they have unwrapped their bundles and baskets, and carry them on their hips. Every container has the same — clusters of dried whale meat, black and rock hard. The

Lamalera women move purposefully through the gathering, looking down at the fruit and vegetable for trade. These foodstuffs are difficult to grow on Lamalera's rocks. Six units of whale meat are held out on offer, and six bananas, six plantains, or six of whatever produce are given back in exchange. The Lamalera women move on. Within ten minutes the containers which once held whale meat now hold mostly fruit and vegetables, and the tempo of the market slackens. The barterers stroll now. They are more leisurely in the final items of exchange. The women who have been squatting, stand up and begin to compare notes on the success of their day. The gossip renews. By noon the Lamalera women are beginning to leave, the baskets and basins again on their heads, for the long walk home. The market closes for another week. No money has changed hands.

Agnes Bataona had heard that I was asking about white whales, and sent her brother to intercept me as I walked past her house on the evening after the market. She had once seen an entire school of white whales, her brother told me.

I found Agnes in the small yard behind her family's house. The Bataonas are among the premier whaling clans — they have five *tenas* — and their main house is close behind the boat-sheds. Agnes was seated on the ground, weaving. She was leaning back to keep the tension on a backstrap loom as she made a double strip of dark red cloth. I recognised the pattern. It showed *tena* in pursuit of sperm whale, a leaping harpooner, and manta ray. It was not a traditional Lamalera pattern, but one which Camillus in his days as tourism chief had suggested as marketable for tourists. The pattern had become so popular with the Lamalera women that they now wove their own sarongs with the same motifs. I guessed that Agnes was about forty years old. She had a round face with a light mahogany brown skin, and her dark eyes were deep-set under a heavy brow, which could have made her look surly except that she smiled a lot and was very animated. She was also graceful. As she slid the weaving lath back and forth, she moved her arms and shoulders with elegance, and when she gestured — which she did frequently — her arms and wrists flowed. Her fingers, as they arranged the threads, could have been caressing the keys of a piano.

"It was seven years ago, after I came back to Lamalera from Surabaya because I was very sick with malaria,' she said. 'I came home, but there was no medicine for here and I got worse. After four months my weight had dropped from sixty-nine kilos to thirty-six kilos. My brothers said that if I did not get to hospital quickly, I would die. It was the bad season for travel, and they arranged for me to go in an engine boat. The waves were very high. I was so frightened and held on tight to the edge of the boat. The boat was lurching from left to right, and my

259

younger sister Lisa, she came with me, she was lying in the bottom of the boat, vomiting and sleeping.'

Camillus was finding it difficult to keep up with the translation. Agnes was talking in Lamaholot, and as her story progressed she became more and more fervent. She was speaking faster and faster, pausing every now and then to wave her arms in emphasis. It was clear by the excitement in her voice, and the way she would suddenly pause and draw a deep breath, that she was reliving events very bright in her memory.

"About eleven in the morning we came near the headland at Ata Dei, and the white whales appeared. They were maybe ten of them, all white. I said, "Be careful!" I was afraid we would drive into them. They came so close that I thought they would strike the boat. They swam beside us. They were as white as paper. My brother Kor told me to lie down and rest, but I was so afraid and could not sleep. Then I recalled what our grandparents had said, that the whales are our ancestors. I thought maybe they had come to help us if we had lived good lives.'

'What sort of whales were they?' I asked. I had never heard of a school of white whales, unless they were beluga or narwhal, and neither species is found off Indonesia.

'I know the killer whale is part-white. But they were not killer whales,' replied Agnes. 'They were big. So big that a sucker fish on the belly of one whale was the same size as a baby shark. I saw it clearly. The heads of the whale were coming up all around us. They were following us, like our ancestors, and they swam forward with us to bring us good luck, just as our grandfathers say. At Cape Ata Dei there is always a bad current, but that day there was no current and we came so quickly to Alor that no one could understand how it happened. I think the whales helped us. We arrive in Alor by four in the afternoon. When I told my sister Lisa about the whales, she said, "Why don't you wake me up so I can see them too?" But I said, "You were so seasick, you could not stand. I have seen our ancestors." '

Agnes finished her tale, and to emphasise the conclusion she thumped the weaving blade solidly through her work. As far as I could tell, she was telling the truth, but only as she saw it. Had she been hallucinating while in the grip of fever? I rather thought so, and her brother Kor was not there to corroborate her story. Yet the folklore of the white whale in Lamalera obviously had gained another episode, and a woman had been the source this time. Men had provided the previous sightings of a white whale, real or imaginary. The men went regularly to sea for their work and stood the best chance of meeting the white whale. Now, among the women of Lamalera, there was a matching tale of white whales in the role of benevolent ancestors ready

261

to help those who had led virtuous lives.

Benedictus Gora had first heard about a white whale when he was still in elementary school, and remembered being told that the animal had appeared on an occasion when no less than four ordinary sperm whale had been successfully harpooned. Benedictus was now fifty years old, and lived a hundred metres from the beach in a small house approached along a rocky path, which he still found difficult to negotiate on his new aluminium crutches. So Camillus took me to meet him. The day Benedictus had seen the white whale for himself was the same day he had lost his leg.

The one-legged villager was no Captain Ahab with his fierce obsession to track down the white whale. Benedictus was an unassuming man of medium height, with a lined face and a heavy-hearted countenance. His head of wiry hair was just beginning to turn grey. When we arrived, he was dressed in a deep pink shirt and chequered sarong and sitting in the shade outside his house. Until recently he had been an ordinary seaman, a paddler, aboard *Kebako Puka*. Now he was tearing the leaves of lontar palm into strips and weaving them into sleeping mats. It was the only paying work that he could find, because he would never go whale hunting again. His left leg stuck straight out in front of him, and ended just below the knee in a bandaged stump. The amputation still hurt him, and Benedictus leaned forward from time to time to massage the wound as

262

he talked in a light, gentle voice about the day of his accident.

'It was beginning to be afternoon, and we were on our way back to the beach in *Kebako Puka* when the people said that there is some breath of the whales. There were three whales coming from the west. Two of the whale spouts were normal, but the spout of the third whale was so big and so powerful. I think it was about more than ten metres long. We took down the sail and turned back our own boat to follow them.

'We gave the harpooner the harpoon and he fixed it on the end of the bamboo pole, and climbed on to the harpoon platform. The harpooner took aim at the whale with the harpoon, and then suddenly shouted that this whale was white. He came scrambling back to tell us to stand up and look because the whale is white, all over, and very big. It was perhaps fifteen metres in length. We all stood up and said, "Hey! don't kill it!"

'This whale is a different whale, like a sea ghost. We all thought, "Please let him go away!" We were so frightened that we yelled aloud at the white whale. There were some other boats sailing alongside us, and we shouted to them about the white whale. It was the first and only time I saw the white whale for myself.'

Soon afterwards, the whaling fleet met a whole pod of sperm whales of the normal black colour. *Kebako Puka* came close enough to harpoon. The whale line rushed out over the gunnel, and a loop of line caught Benedictus round the lower leg. The noose dragged him to the edge of the boat and trapped him there. Tightened by a thirty-ton whale, the noose squeezed down, cutting through flesh and bone. By the time another crew member had cut the line, Benedictus's leg had been crudely severed. The lower limb was held on only by a shred of skin, and Benedictus had fainted with pain. *Kebako Puka* brought him to the beach as quickly as the crew could paddle, but there was no doctor in Lamalera. The nearest hospital was in Larantuka, thirty miles away, and the weekly ferry was not due for several days. The only hope was to transfer the injured man to a boat with an engine and bring him immediately to help. But the community had no emergency transport, and Benedictus was too poor to afford the cost of the fuel. Fortunately the Japanese film crew was visiting; it was the same unlucky day when they had gone to the mountains to film and the whales had arrived. The Japanese immediately offered to pay the cost of transport, and Benedictus reached hospital that evening. But it was too late to save his leg. Now, almost a year after the accident, a well-to-do Lamalera emigrant had sponsored the cost of a artificial leg and it had just arrived. Benedictus's wife, who had been patiently listening to his story while she helped weave an extra mat for sale, went to fetch the limb. It looked as if it had been taken from a display dummy in a shop which sold inexpensive clothes for men. The plastic foot wore a cheap black plastic walking shoe and there was a bright green woollen sock with three horizontal white stripes. It looked awful, and I doubted if Benedictus would ever want, or learn, to use it. As his wife tenderly placed this grotesque object beside her crippled husband, I thought to myself that there could have been no more poignant symbol of the price that the fishermen, in their own need for survival, sometimes paid to hunt the whale.

A story pattern had emerged: the white sperm whale was not a solitary. According to all reports the white whale — or white whales if there was more than one — usually appeared in the company of other, more normal, sperm whales. Yet it was not entirely a sociable animal either. It appeared on the fringe of the school, or showed up when a group of whales was under attack. So my chances of my ever seeing the white whale were exceedingly slim. An entire whaling season might pass without a major encounter with whales. In some years the Lalamera whaling fleet never came close to a large school. Bapak Pol, an elderly widower who lived by himself next to the beach, kept a log of all the whale catches, written up in an old schoolbook. During the previous fifteen years the most whales caught in a single season had been twenty-seven animals, and that was an exceptional year, 1995. Usually the seasonal catch was less than twenty. In 1983 the entire fleet had managed to catch just two.

Nevertheless Bernardus and I kept our little

yellow dinghy pumped up and stored next to the *tena* sheds. Their crews became used to seeing us puttering around the vicinity as they patrolled the bay. Their catch was disappointing. One day the entire fleet caught two small whale sharks and two manta ray. The following day nothing at all.

The day after that, *Teti Heri* was in luck. She was the most work-worn boat in the fleet, with so little paint on her planks that she was positively shabby. But she was well handled. Bernardus and I were fifty metres away when her harpooner saw something flicker below the surface of the sea and pointed. His crew took up their paddles, and began to dig at the water. The harpooner was a veteran, perhaps in his mid-forties. He stood balancing at the end of his ladder, and we could see him gesturing. He was waving his right arm in slow circles, signalling to his steersman which way the prey was swimming. *Teti Heri* turned, and the pursuit lasted for perhaps five minutes before the harpooner struck. He used the thin harpoon pole, six metres long, and this identified the prey to my companion, Bernardus. 'Pari' — giant manta ray — he grunted. We were close enough to pick up the harpoon bamboo as it broke away and came to the surface. The harpooner had already climbed back aboard *Teti Heri*. Then nothing happened. It was as if the entire boat crew had frozen in place. No one spoke or moved. Our little yellow inflatable and the worn *tena* just

266

floated there on the calm sea, as if adrift. There was silence. I looked at Bernardus and he made a downward, diving, gesture with his hand. The manta ray had felt the harpoon, and sought shelter by swimming straight downward. Now it was either lying on the bottom of the sea, or at the full extent of the harpoon line, keeping still. The fishermen were motionless, hoping that the harpoon head would not pull free. A giant manta ray was a valuable catch.

Hauntingly, the crew of *Teti Heri* began to sing. The first line came from an old man, and then the crew followed with a deep, rolling refrain. It was a quavering song, plaintive and patient. It carried clearly across the few yards of water that separated us, and was so melancholy that it could only have been a lament. The song rose and fell, rose and fell. 'They will sing while the manta ray is underwater,' said Bernardus. 'They are singing about their wives and children who wait to be fed.' It was an eerie sound as we sat there, rocking gently on the surface of the sea. And it continued for almost half an hour. No one on *Teti Heri* moved, except for two men near the bow. They took it in turns to lean over the gunnel, and put a hand on the harpoon line which stretched taut, straight up and down. Delicately they felt the line, sensing the strain, the slight quiver of the huge animal far below. The giant manta ray was much too large and powerful for the crew to pull it to the surface. It had to come there of its own will, in response to the dirge sung by the crew, or so they believed. After a long time I saw the third man in the team gather a coil of line into the boat. But then the manta ray pulled away again, and the loop of rope was gently eased out. So the wait continued. There was no hurry, just utter patience, and the singing went on.

The voices only died away when the manta ray began its final move. Slowly, with infinite care, the crew man leaning over the side of the boat, began to take in the line. He did not pull. He merely kept the thin hand-spun cotton rope taut. Gently, the great ray swam upward. Above it hovered the men. Two of them now held heavy harpoon poles, and were peering down into the water, ready to strike. They shuffled from side to side, seeking a defining glimpse of the huge animal, as its shape emerged from the depths. They raised their lances high, and then stood stock-still. Now was the moment for one single, sure, strike. If they missed or if they hit askew, the shocked manta ray would tear itself free. The two harpooners simultaneously jabbed downward. Both were successful, and one blow was so accurate that the animal was killed outright. Normally the huge beast would have been a threat to the boat itself, battering the hull and outrigger with massive slaps from its enormous wings. Instead its strange head with its twin prongs of 'devil horns' rose to the surface as the lucky crew drew the carcass alongside and amidships. There they leaned out and manhandled the leading edge of the giant diamond-shaped animal on to the outrigger. The ray was so heavy that its weight tilted *Teti Heri* until the gunnel was almost underwater. Inch by inch, the crew heaved the enormous carcass on board. At the halfway point, when it was spread-eagled across the gunnel, I guessed that the animal measured at least nine feet from wing tip to wing tip. The ray was not thin and flat like a small flounder. Its sturdy back, a glistening sedge brown, swelled up in an impressive hump just behind the head. I calculated that it must weigh at least half a ton.

The next day, 19 May, everyone's luck came good, including for Bernardus and myself. The day began much as usual. Bernardus and I had followed the fleet out to the fishing ground and were keeping a watchful eye on every boat. The morning was hot and cloudless, with very little wind, and the sea was a dense blue. The fleet was five miles offshore and slightly toward the eastern side of the bay. It was Bernardus who saw the tell-tale. Of all the hundred and more pairs of eyes in the fleet, his was the first to spot the low puff of spray. It rose from the sea in the characteristic forward slant of the sperm whale's blow. It came from about four hundred metres ahead of us. Our little inflatable dinghy was the closest in the fleet. Bernardus gave a low grunt, pull-started the little outboard motor, and we eased forward to get closer to the whale — but not so close as to frighten it. Bernardus and I saw it clearly now. It was a sperm whale, perhaps twelve metres long, and lying just awash. Its back made a low, black line on the ocean. Less than a minute later, another low spurt of spray announced that the animal had taken another breath, and was in the process of ventilating its lungs.

In that same instant a *tena* crew spotted the whale. They scrambled to lower the matting sail, then swing down and secure the tripod mast. It is too dangerous to attack and fight sperm whale encumbered by the top-heavy weight of mast and spars. The *tena* — I could see it was lucky *Teti Heri* again — was ready for action in less than a minute. She turned and bore down on the whale, her crew paddling frantically. From our dinghy we had extraordinary perspective. The whale was between us and the *tena,* and I was looking over the back of the whale at the bows of the onrushing boat as she came directly towards us. The harpooner was already in position on his ladder. He was wearing a yellow shirt, and holding his lance so that it seemed to point directly at us. We could hear the chant of the crew, and the clatter of the paddle handles. The whale again exhaled. The spray rose in the air. Once more I found myself wondering why on earth the animal did not dive. How could it just lie there, breathing deeply and virtually stationary? Where was its instinct for self-preservation? Why was it not alarmed? One part of my mind wished the animal to move and flee; the other part observed with fascination how the harpooner on the bow of *Teti Heri* was flexing his knees, hefting the length of the harpoon in his two hands, and sighting down its length. I could see the assistant harpooner close behind him, standing up at the base of the harpooning ladder and half leaning forward as he peered under the harpooner's arm to keep his gaze on the whale. *Teti Heri* was now travelling as fast as her crew could press her: perhaps five or six knots, enough to produce a small white bow wave. My position foreshortened the perspective so that it seemed as if *Teti Heri* was about to run her bow right up on the whale's back before the harpooner threw his weapon. In fact he must have attacked from ten yards' distance. He leaped forward in the air, and flung his harpoon at the same instant. I saw the splash of the man's body hitting the water, right alongside the whale.

Again, there was a moment when nothing happened. The harpooner must have swum back to his boat and grabbed hold of the outrigger, but I did not see it. Instead, after two or three seconds, *Teti Heri* suddenly spun around, the stern turning to where the bow had been an instant earlier. The boat disappeared from my view for a moment. My eyeline was only a half a metre above sea level, and *Teti Heri* had very little freeboard. There was a low swell running, just enough to conceal *Teti Heri* when she and my dinghy were both in a trough. When *Teti Heri* next appeared in sight, there had been another pause. The *tena* was still pointing in the same

271

direction, and on the same spot. Then, with a spectacular surge, the *tena* shot forward. It was a more dramatic acceleration than anything I had seen previously. This was what the Yankee whalemen had called the 'Nantucket sleigh ride', when a whale boat is towed in the wake of a speeding whale. *Teti Heri* looked as if she had been fitted instantly with a powerful motor. The *tena* lunged forward, her bow angling upward, and the hull rocking from side to side. I could hear the wild cheering of her crew. The boat tore across the surface of the sea, leaving a vivid white wake behind it. Then, equally suddenly, she came to a halt, dropped level in the water, and then abruptly turned back through 180 degrees and shot off in the opposite direction. The sperm whale had dived and reversed course.

The new direction lasted for only a minute. Then the whale and its attached *tena* stopped. I was only fifty metres away, and distinctly saw the blunt snout of the sperm whale come above the water as it reared its head up in the air, and took a look back at what was tormenting it. The animal was clearly taking stock of its situation. Then the whale sank back down, contorted sideways, and the next instant the flukes heaved up from the sea in a cloud of spray and thrashed down in a heavy blow. The strike missed, but solid water drenched the crew of *Teti Heri*.

Bernardus tapped me on the arm and, when I glanced round, he pointed urgently to the south. In that direction five *tena* were moving through the water at attack speed. Their masts and sails were struck down for action. Their harpooners were already standing on their platforms, not with their lances raised, but balancing casually, almost relaxed, their heavy harpoons held at a diagonal while their crews strained every muscle. A hundred metres ahead of the racing *tena* I saw the black bobbing shapes of nine, ten or perhaps eleven sperm whales. *Teti Heri*'s whale had been a straggler. The main pod had surfaced.

The next half-hour was pandemonium. *Tena* are too cumbersome to chase the whales. They cannot paddle or sail fast enough. So the whales have to come to the surface in just the right spot, and dawdle long enough for the boats to get within range. The wind and tide have to be favourable, the whales moving in the right direction, and the encounter can start no later than early afternoon so there is still time for the *tena* to get back ashore. For a boat to be attached to an angry whale in the dark would be folly. For once, all the proper conditions for a battle royal between hunters and the sperm whales were on hand.

The five leading *tena* closed with the whales. In ragged succession the harpooners jumped and threw the heavy shafts. The whales turned to escape or, if struck, went into paroxysms to break free or defend themselves. Sidling up as close as I dared in the little dinghy I could see the rippled skin, with its prune-like wrinkles, as the backs of sperm whales curved up out of the water in the moment before they dived, or the huge tail came curling up to deliver a great enraged blow. If the blow was downward, there was a thunderous crash; if it was sideways, a great sheet of solid water splashed over the surface of the sea. Most shocking of all was the moment that an enraged sperm whale came barrelling up head-first directly under a boat. Then, the *tena* received a massive crunching thump into its hull. The entire boat, six tons or more, was flung up in the air, and came down with a splash. The crew hung on grimly. Sometimes the boat fell directly on top of the whale, and there was a crazy moment as the vessel tilted sideways, then slid off into the water. There was no opportunity for controlled manoeuvres or caution. The hunters simply closed with their prey, and the harpooners leaped on their victims. It was mayhem. Sometimes the harpooner need only topple sideways from his perch because the whale was directly beneath him, the boat virtually aground on the animal's back. At other times the harpooner sprang dramatically outward, clutching the harpoon shaft, intending to use all his body weight to drive home the harpoon head. I saw one man do this, fly through the air, make a direct hit, and the harpoon stopped, standing vertically out of the water as if it had struck a rock. The man lost his grip, swung out of control around the shaft, then slithered down, and sprawled on the animal's back. Another harpooner was about to throw, when a whale different from his target struck the *tena* with its head. The harpooner went tumbling headlong into the water. Many of the home-forged harpoon heads failed to hold, and the whales escaped. But a few harpoons took fast, and at that instant the successful boat was attached to a living tug that exerted several hundred horsepower with the thrust from its broad tail. Boats careered here and there, their crews shouting with mingled fear, excitement and triumph. Foam and white water flew in all directions. Boats surged together and hit one another with shuddering crashes. A whale surfaced beneath one boat, and the small vessel lurched into the air, spilling paddles while its crew grabbed on to the benches to stop themselves from being thrown overboard. I saw a harpooner flat on his stomach, clinging tightly to his platform as his boat was shaken from side to side. Then he lost his grip and fell, all arms and flailing legs, on to the head of a sperm whale.

Even from less than twenty metres away it was impossible to tell which *tena* had harpooned which whale. Doubtless there were two *tena* attached to the same whale, or a single *tena* with harpoons planted in two different whales. And as the whales twisted and turned, and each sought its own escape, so the attached boats were pulled this way and that. The boats clashed together. They sheered off harpoon platforms, collided and tangled with their outriggers. One whale must have decided to flee precipitately. The boat fastened to it swung round, pointed out of the general mêlée, and suddenly shot off, away from all the others. I watched it disappearing into the distance. Its place was taken by other boats, hurrying up to join the tussle. Every vessel in the fleet was now trying to reach the spot, their crews rushing to lash down the loose spars and hurl themselves into the fray. Eight boats converged in a group, the water sometimes boiling underneath them as if from a submarine eruption.

Then, like the petals of a flower opening, the cluster of boats opened up. Two *tena* came shooting out of the formation like speedboats, low in the water, bow waves spreading. It was an eerie sight. In front of each boat, not more than ten metres ahead, was a sperm whale. The animals were swimming at full speed on the surface, undulating their bodies up and down as the creatures powered ahead with tremendous thrusts of their tails. They looked like enormous locomotives. The two whales swam side by side and towed their boats in close parallel, so the ensemble reminded me of some extraordinary circus act when two shire horses canter massively round the ring side by side, and the performers stand on their backs and hold the guiding reins.

I was spellbound at the sight, and trying to film it, when Bernardus knocked my aim askew as he slapped the little outboard engine in gear, opened the throttle and we spiralled off to one side. Looking up from the viewfinder, I saw that the circus act was bearing down on us, and in a few moments would have run us down.

From a safer distance I watched the ebb and flow of the hunt. There were patches of red blood now, staining the sea, and I could see one whale was almost stationary, cautiously surrounded by three *tena* who were hoping to give it the *coup de grâce*. A whale burst upward, creating a great vortex of water, and shook off the harpoon shaft sticking in its back. A boat on the far side of the pack abruptly came in view. It was being pulled clear by its whale, and must have been on a long line because the boat was swaying wildly on the swell. In another second the line must have slipped as the whale changed direction. The speeding boat capsized. One moment it was above the water. The next instant there was a dramatic tumble of men, mast, rolled-up sail, paddles and tackle, and the boat was upside-down. The line broke with the sudden tension, and the *tena* was left as an upturned keel, surrounded by the bobbing heads of her crew as they swam to the safety of the nearest boat.

The hunt moved off now, the action splitting into two groups of boats, and there was yet more blood on the sea. Bernardus and I had drifted perhaps a hundred metres downwind.

Whaarrooompph!! It was a huge sound. Just behind us. I spun round to look. There, on the surface not ten metres away from us was the open blowhole of a large sperm whale. The S-shape of the breathing slot was glistening clear. The animal was moving so fast that it was obliged to let out its breath in an explosive grunt that I could compare only to the imagined bellow of the Minotaur. It was a gargantuan snort, an urgent exhalation of air from a sperm whale travelling on the surface at full speed, surging up and down, 'head out' as the whale-men used to say. The whale was not fleeing the scene. Rather, it was arriving pell-mell. Bernardus let out a shrill whistle to alert the fleet. This was a huge *kea,* one of the rescuing whales which had detected the disturbance from a distance away and come charging in to see if it could help.

The *kea* raced past our dinghy, which rocked in its wake. The animal took not the slightest notice of us. It was heading for the thick of the fray. Just a hundred metres short of the *tenas* I saw the charging whale slow down and almost stop. It turned broadside to the boats, and began to cruise slowly along. It seemed to be inspecting the situation, and was puzzled. It was calculating what to do. But there was nothing to be done. Those whales which had broken free of the har-poons had escaped. Those who had been firmly struck were now in their final throes. The *kea* swam along, irresolute.

I glanced up. A boat had noticed the new arrival. It was *Demo Sapang.* Her harpooner saw his chance to make a splendid kill. He was on his platform, harpoon in hand, and his crew were frantically paddling to get within range of the hesitant *kea*. For me it was a repetition of the moment that had opened the encounter. Once again I was looking over the whale, and straight on to the bows of the attacking boat. I could see both banks of paddles flashing up and down on each side, as *Demo Sapang* came down on her intended prey. I found myself quietly saying to the whale, 'Dive! Get clear! There is nothing you can do.' I had seen enough slaughter. I was deeply touched by the thought that the animal had come to assist its comrades, but was exposing itself to destruction. The *tena* was no more than twenty yards away, just out of harpoon range, when the *kea* appeared to decide that all was lost. The animal arched its back slowly, the great flukes raised up out of the sea, and the creature slid from view and into the safety of the ocean. The oncoming harpooner immediately straightened up and reversed his harpoon, butt down. His crew relaxed. This was a whale which would live.

The sight of those eight men, some of their torsos naked, arms pumping, the paddles moving up and down, the narrow shape of the advancing *tena*, had recalled another image — the picture of a large North American Indian canoe. I recalled the words of the shaman of the mountain who said that the whales were 'a sort of cow which had gone to sea'. With sudden insight I realised that in witnessing the aboriginal ritual, a scene from pre-history, there was a parallel to the sperm whale hunt. On the great plains of North America the native peoples had hunted the great herds of buffalo. Like the sperm whales, the buffalo had moved seasonally, following their established paths. The Indians had waited for them in certain places at certain times of the year, and then charged in and picked off the stragglers with great personal courage. This is exactly what the Lamalera whale hunters still did. Their prey was larger, much more difficult to subdue, and just as essential to their survival.

Bernardus and I stayed with the fleet to see if we could help with the salvage of the capsized *tena*. But our assistance was not necessary. It was a frequent accident, and the remedy was well rehearsed. The crew of the upside-down boat climbed up on the keel and used their weight to spin the hull around. The boat was still nine-tenths underwater, stern down, with the harpooner's ladder protruding from the water like a primitive marker buoy. Another *tena* came alongside, and the bow of the waterlogged hulk was dragged up on its outrigger as if the wreck was an outsized catch. Then the combined crews worked together to rock the waterlogged boat back and forth, sloshing out some of the water. At the crucial moment they pushed it off, and the disabled boat floated clear, level now, with just an inch or so of freeboard. Her crew swam around it, leaning in with baskets to bail out the water and lighten the vessel, until first one and then a second crew man could climb aboard without his weight submerging the vessel again. Finally, all the crew were in place, and an hour later the boat was emptied out, the mast and sodden sail retrieved and stowed, and the *tena* started for home.

Bernardus and I went ahead, and were waiting on the beach as the fleet came home in the early dusk. Again there was the similarity with American Plains Indians, as they returned from the successful buffalo hunt. The catch was superlative, five whales taken. Three of the *tenas* had a carcass lashed alongside; their crews had caught their whale unaided. Four *tenas* shared the capture of two other whales, so they towed their captures jointly. The boats came round the headland, one behind the other, moving very slowly, delayed by the enormous weight of their catch. The crews were ecstatic. As they paddled, they sang in triumph. The men roared out the choruses. They flourished their paddles with each stroke, and there was delight on every face.

Next morning a line of five dead whales was rolling in the surf. They were all the normal black whales, though I noted that abrasion on the sand had rubbed off the black surface during the night, exposing patches of white. Trondur pointed out the disc-shaped pale marks on the whales' heads. The suckers of squid had made them as they wrapped their tentacles around their predator. Three of the whales also had puncture marks in their skin, left by sperm whale teeth, the result of fights. All the animals were between eight and twelve metres in length, a modest size for sperm whale but then, as the village headman had explained, the harpooners struck only the whales they could manage. The very big ones, the monsters, they left alone. It would take almost two full days for the village to cut up and save the meat of the whales. Once again, there would be no waste. Only this time even the widows and distant clan members would receive a share.

Twenty-five years earlier the World Food and Agriculture Organisation had sent a scientific whale hunter to instruct the people of Lamalera in modern techniques. He was a Norwegian, a 'Mr Paul'. He had arrived with a fibreglass whale catcher, twelve metres long and powered with a sixty-horsepower Yanmar diesel. The boat had been purchased in Japan and fitted with a harpoon gun. Mr Paul's remit was to teach the Lamalera people how to catch more whales, how to fish with nets, and how to process the catch in a cannery. He had been first-class at his work. He would disappear over the horizon with his boat and come back soon afterwards with whale after whale in tow. Soon there were so many whale lying on the beach that the villagers could not keep pace with butchering them. The value of whale meat dropped in Wulan Doni market, the villagers began to sell the meat for cash in the neighbouring towns, and worst of all, they left parts of the carcasses on the beach. Mr Paul left after three years, his contract expired. The villagers had liked him, and they were genuinely sorry to see him go. But it was all wrong, said the *kapala desa,* shaking his head. 'The nets tore, and were too expensive to replace. And we did not need so many whales. We did not know what to do with them. They stayed on the beach and smelled bad. It was a waste.'

Nowadays, as the *kapala desa* well knew, the foreign experts from the international organisations came to Lamalera to count the sperm whales, not harpoon them. The new visitors were collecting data to help decide whether the whale hunt should be banned. I could have told the *kapala desa* that the scientists now believe that between 1.5 and 2 million sperm whale swim the world's oceans, a number as great as all the other five great whale species put together, and that Lamalera's catch of fewer than forty whales a year, taken by human-powered boats, is sustainable by any standard. Nor is Indonesia a signatory to the International Whaling Commission which regulates catches. Nor does the Commission object to genuine aboriginal whaling. But there are foreign pressure groups who would ban whaling of any sort. Then I would also have to explain that motor ships equipped with scout helicopters and guns that fired exploding harpoon heads had decimated most species of great whales, just as the Taiwanese trawlers had recently stripped the bay of sharks. And I thought of the American buffalo being reduced to near-extinction by men with rifles who took the tongues and pelts and left the rest to rot. To try to explain this to a man for whom whale hunting was as hard and desperate a life today as the buffalo hunt had been for the Plains Indians would have baffled him. He would have been right to conclude that he and his community were living in the shadow of contradictory and overwhelming forces, and that the people of Lamalera were as vulnerable — and had as little control over their survival — as the whales themselves.

Sperm whales, when agitated, swim with their mouths wide open.

An angry or distressed sperm whale surging towards you makes a terrifying sight. Trondur thought so, as he floundered in the warm water, and a bull sperm whale came straight at him. A second, even more anguished sperm whale was already heaving and thrashing less than two metres away to his left. 'If you take me,' Trondur silently implored the advancing open-mouthed whale, 'please take me all, and leave nothing behind.' It was a reasonable plea. A sperm whale's lower jaw hangs down to display as many as fifty massive, yellowing teeth. Each tooth can be up to eight inches long, though only the upper third of the tooth cone protrudes above the gum. The gullet behind this row of sharp studs is an expandable tunnel of carmine pink. At the last moment, Trondur clearly felt the animal sense his presence. The whale swerved with delicate precision. The inky black body, as big as a dozen elephants, raced past. Trondur felt the increase of water pressure. For a moment the gap between the two whales on each side of him was so narrow that he could have reached out and touched either animal. There was a quick buffeting swirl, and the whale was gone, leaving Trondur to deal with another problem. He is a very clumsy swimmer.

It was three days after the village had taken the five whales, and — to general incredulity and exultation — almost the same events were being repeated. Another pod of whales had surfaced right in front of the *tena* fleet, just when the tide, wind and current were favourable. The crews could scarcely believe this double bounty. Veteran hunters could hardly recall when two major whale encounters had happened in such quick succession. Some of the villagers, I learned later, considered that the presence of Trondur, his son Brandur, and me in Lamalera was playing some mysterious role in calling the whales into view.

Trondur had gone out with the fleet, bringing along sketchpad and pencils and a camera to take photographs that he would later work up into drawings. The harpooner of the boat in which Trondur was riding struck his whale, and the maddened animal dashed off. It swam directly towards a neighbouring boat. This boat had already harpooned a whale, and its crew were fully occupied in fighting the big creature which had surfaced alongside. As a highly experienced seaman, Trondur saw at once what was going to happen: the fleeing whale would dive and drag Trondur's boat underneath the neighbouring boat. Trondur's companions, the Lamalera men, also realised the danger and promptly abandoned ship. They jumped into the sea and began to swim as hard as they could in the opposite direction, to get clear of the collision. They swam without hesitation, as they had grown up in the warm tropics where children play and frolic in the water's edge. But Trondur is a sailor of the northern tradition. As a boy growing up in the Faeroe Islands he had not learned to swim. The older fishermen of the Faeroes believed that a sailor who did not know how to swim paid more attention to staying on the boat and was a better seaman for his caution. And if a man did fall overboard in his heavy clothes and work-boots, and tried to swim, then either his struggles were useless or they brought a lingering death from exposure. It was better to drown quickly. Years later, Trondur had learned the rudiments of swimming while on my expeditions in more hospitable seas, but he could only manage a few metres at a time. So now he waited, alone aboard the hurtling boat, until the whale dived and the line began to drag his boat under. Then Trondur jumped for his life.

As he spluttered to the surface, he hoped that he would be able to swim far enough to the closest boat, the one with an enraged whale alongside, and cling on before he sank and drowned. He managed to dog-paddle the few yards — this was when the loose, onrushing whale gave him space. But to his dismay, as he approached the boat it was towed out of reach by its captive whale. Trondur looked around. The boat he had been forced to abandon now wallowed back to the surface. It was floating upside-down. Trondur just managed to reach it and hang on until the crew members swam up and turned their boat right side up and began to bail out the water. Trondur was astonished to find that the vessel had suffered only superficial damage. The matting sail was torn. There were some small dents and splinters in the woodwork. But there was nothing like the major breakage he expected. The only explanation that Trondur could imagine was that something large and soft had acted as a huge fender during the under-water passage. That something soft must have been the second whale. His boat had been pulled beneath a sperm whale and another *tena* on its abrupt submarine journey. 'Good the water is so warm,' Trondur commented to me when he came ashore that evening. 'But I lost my camera. No trouble, I will always remember the picture!'

I had stayed ashore. The earlier five-whale catch had been enough for me. At close range I had seen how the whale hunters worked. I respected their skill and bravery, and appreciated their need for the hunt. But I did not relish the sight of wounded whales and blood in the water, and there was a clue to the white whale which I wanted to investigate.

The clue came from a casual remark made to me by a small, dark-skinned fisherman whom I had met on the beach. He was Paulus Ebang, a member of the clan whose ancestors are said to have arrived in Lamalera riding on the back of a baleen whale. Paulus mentioned that he had been a crew member aboard *Baka Tena* on the day a white sperm whale had deliberately attacked the boat. His remark was the first hint I had heard of the white whale being aggressive, of behaving in the belligerent way of the mythical Moby Dick. According to Paulus, the attack had taken place the previous year. The whale had been pure white, and had appeared from a westerly direction, about ten minutes after the *tena* fleet had enagaged a large pod of sperm whales. Paulus suggested that I talk to the assistant harpooner of *Baka Tena*, Marinus Lelaona. He had been standing up in the boat during the attack of the white whale, and had seen exactly what happened.

Marinus was a rather nervous 24-year-old with a habit of twisting his hands together as he talked. He sat on the edge of a whaleboat in its shed and lowered his head shyly, looking up between sentences, to see if I was following his story through Camillus's translation.

'It was on the 31st of April, just before the start of the full whaling season. Someone saw sperm whale in the bay and shouted, "Baleo! Baleo!" and we put to sea in *Baka Tena*, heading south. After some time we saw three sperm whale. They were coming from the west so we turned toward them, rolled up the sail and began paddling. Our harpooner — his name is Alfredus — put the head on the harpoon shaft and moved forward to his place. When we came near the whales, Alfredus turned round and asked the crew, "Which is our ancestor? Where is he?" and the crew replied, "That one, close to the tip of the harpoon." And he called, "Hurry, hurry, paddle faster, straight ahead, and come close to him." Then Alfredus struck the whale, and the whale pulled out the rope faster and faster, dragging us first to south, then again to the west. After that the whale became tired, came to the surface, laying there, floating.'

'What about the white whale? When did you see the white whale?'

'Alfredus was going to harpoon our whale the second time. He prepared his second harpoon, and was standing on the platform ready to strike the blow when the white whale attacked.'

'Did you see the white whale arrive? Or had it been there all the time?'

'I did not see the white whale in the beginning, only when it attacked,' answered Marinus. 'I was watching Alfredus. But some of the other crew say that they saw the white whale swimming quickly towards us from the south. It came from in front of us and swam past the boat, and we

289

thought it had gone. It was very big whale, much larger than the *tena,* maybe three metres longer. Its colour was not white like a bone, but the same white as when a piece of pale driftwood has been left in the sunshine for many years and turns white. Maybe the whale, also, is white from old age. The white whale turned round after he passed our boat and came back. It swam right alongside our boat, along the right-hand side, and when it came where the harpooner was standing, ready to use his harpoon, the white whale struck with its tail. It struck up at Alfredus, and hit him sideways. The tail hit Alfredus so hard that the blow knocked the harpoon out of his hand and shattered the bamboo. The harpoon pole broke in splinters. One splinter flew back through the air and hit a crew man on the head and opened a bad cut. By coincidence the wounded man was Alfredus's father. Alfredus himself was knocked right off the harpoon platform by the tail, and fell into the water. As he fell, he hit his head on the side of the boat, and he too was wounded in the head. We pulled Alfredus back on the boat, and bound up his head with a cloth. First we put some tobacco on the wound to help it heal. Afterwards Alfredus said he was able to tackle the whale he had harpooned earlier.'

'What happened to the white whale? Did you see it again?'

'No, after it had struck our harpooner with its tail, the white whale swam away and we did not see it again that day.'

'Do you think that the white whale knew wha it was doing when it hit the harpooner? Do you think it attacked deliberately, or was it just by chance?'

'Oh, the white whale came to strike us, and to help the ordinary black whale,' said Marinus without hesitation. 'Among the crew we talked about the attack afterwards. We said that the white whale attacked us because we had been quarrelling among ourselves. Sylvester, who was in charge of the boat, had been angry with his brother Jacobus. They were arguing about who would get the whale's teeth. The old people tell us that if there is a quarrel in a crew, the sperm whales will know and they will not join us. Instead they will punish us.'

Here was an intriguing mix of observation, folklore and superstition. Had the white whale really known where to strike with its tail? Did the animal understand that the most effective attack was to disable the harpooner? Such well-thought-out action seemed far-fetched, though there was no doubt that the white whale was behaving as a *kea* by coming to the assistance of another whale in distress, and so the white whale's behaviour was true to type. I recalled how, on the day of the five-whale catch, I had seen a harpooned sperm whale put its head out of the water to inspect what was tormenting it No doubt the white whale had similarly assesse the situation when it arrived to help. So the was a possibility that it had identified the harpooner as being the main threat. There was no way of knowing.

The idea that the white whale was punishing the *tena* crew for quarrelling invoked the belief — found among most aboriginal hunting peoples — that the prey will only allow itself to be caught if the hunters behave correctly and observe all the proper ritual preparations for the hunt. In a sense the sperm whales of Lamalera are guardians of this belief. The whales are ancestors who hold ancient knowledge, and they have the power to impose sanctions if tradition is flouted or ignored. The sperm whales could simply disappear and the villages would go hungry, but the sperm whales can also — and this is unusual among hunting peoples — punish the hunters for their transgressions by physically attacking them or their boats.

Where did the white whale fit into this lore? Petrus Beliko Lolong supplied me with the answer. Petrus was a smaller, more thoughtful version of Rufinus Keraf, retired harpooner and maker of harpoon heads. Both men were much the same age, in their late sixties, and both were immensely experienced whale hunters. The community respected them as men whose entire lives had been devoted to the pursuit of whales, who had never thought to emigrate from the village, and who knew of the old ways from their first-hand experience. Physically the two men could not have been more different. Rufinus was tall and lanky, with long arms and legs and a slight stoop. Petrus was a bobbing sparrow of a man. Perhaps five feet two inches tall, he was light boned, with small hands and feet, and stood bolt upright. His head was shaved close, and he moved with short quick motions. His resemblance to a small foraging bird was enhanced by the fact that he had quick, bright eyes, and when he finished a statement, Petrus cocked his head to one side and looked as if he was about to chirrup.

I asked Petrus how long he had been hunting whale. 'All my life,' he replied simply. He had been born in 1931, he said, one of five children of a fishing family. He received only an elementary school education, just four years in school, and already by the age of nine was going to sea on a *tena*, though only as an observer and to help bail out the boat. All his family worked on that same vessel, *Dato Tena*, and at that time the harpooner was a man called Bapak Getan.

'That means you've been hunting for sperm whales for nearly sixty years,' I said.

'Yes.'

'Have you ever seen or heard of a white sperm whale?'

Petrus replied without a moment's hesitation: 'Oh yes. The white whale has visited us many times. Sometimes it can be a wicked fellow.'

Petrus was still going out each day on a *tena*, and we were talking aboard *Praso Sapang* as she cruised for whales. Petrus was far too old to

293

throw a harpoon; he was an ordinary paddler now. But every morning he was among the first to arrive at the boatshed, his straw hat perched jauntily on his head. And when it came to launch the boat, no one flung himself more enthusiastically into the job of pushing and heaving than this little gnome of a man, as active and energetic as any of the twenty-year-olds on the crew.

He also had a tenacious memory. He remembered the names of the boats which were damaged on the very first occasion he met the white whale, forty-nine years earlier. One casualty had been his own clan boat, *Dato Tena*, wrecked by the white whale itself. The other had been *Dolu Tena*. 'The harpooner of *Dolu Tena* had harpooned a young whale, and the mother whale was so angry that it beat *Dolu Tena* violently and broke the boat. After the boat was broken, the mother whale struck again, but hit only the rope on the stern, and the bows of *Dolu Tena* survived. It was a great shame that two boats were damaged that day, though we took six whales.'

'Were you surprised or frightened when you first saw the white whale?'

'Well, the old people had already told me about the white whale. When we were small boys on the boat, if someone saw the white whale, the old people told us to be quiet, be still. We were not allowed to catch anything if the white whale was in the area because the white whale is very brave and dangerous. The old people explained that the white whale was

294

from the clan of Tufa Ona.

'On the day it hit our boat, I did not see the white whale. It came up from underneath the water, striking the keel. It was the people in the other boats who saw the whale and said that it was a white whale. A black whale had been harpooned, and we were paddling to get close and harpoon a *kea* if one appeared, and suddenly the white whale hit us from underwater. After that, we were all swimming in the water, waiting for the other boat to finish hunting whale and pull us to the land. *Nara Tena* was the boat which pulled us ashore.'

Petrus provided a clear picture of how the white whale behaved. 'Sometimes the white whale is there. But we cannot see him,' he said. 'The white whale swims with the other whales, but to one side. Often he is swimming deep, down below them. He does not like to come to the surface often. He likes to stay down for a long time. And sometimes he comes to check our boats to see that all is correct. If the boat is correct, then there is no trouble. But if he sees that the boat is not properly made, that the joints are not made in the correct way, or that the wooden pins are wrong, then he will strike the boat at that spot, and break it.

'The white whale can be very dangerous. When he surfaces, that means he is very angry. He moves his head up and down on the sea, and waves his tail, throwing up water. When he does this, it is a signal for us to start paddling, to run away. Not to get near him. The reason why we have never harpooned the white whale is because he never comes to the surface in the normal way like the black whales. The white whale always moves violently, and this is very dangerous for us. For this reason, no one has ever killed the white whale, neither the old people, nor the young people today. They have never succeeded in taking the white whale.'

I asked Petrus how often he had seen the white whale, and how recently. It turned out that he had been sunk twice by the animal. The second time had been in 1970, and the circumstances had been very similar to the first sinking: one boat had harpooned a whale, and the other *tenas* had clustered in the vicinity, waiting for the arrival of a *kea*. But the victim had been the *tena* on which Petrus sailed at that time, *Boko Lolo*. The white whale had burst up from the sea and struck the boat, capsizing it, so that the crew could take no part in the action. The crew had righted their vessel, and — again Petrus's memory for detail was exact — *Soge Tena* had come to their assistance and brought them to shore.

The last time that Petrus himself had been close to the white whale was on 3 June 1992. On that day the white whale had attacked *Soge Tena*, and damaged the boat. Petrus remembered the incident quite clearly because two tourists were riding in the vessel at the time. They must have had the shock of their lives.

I now had a list of sightings of the white whale extending over more than half a century. Petrus, Marinus, Rufinus, one-legged Bernardus, Paulus — they had all met the white whale and their accounts were remarkably consistent. There was no question in my mind that somewhere in the waters off Lamalera swims a white sperm whale.

TAILPIECE

'It's a white whale, I say,' resumed Ahab, as he threw down the top-maul; 'a white whale. Skin your eyes for him, men; look sharp for white water; if you see but a bubble, sing out.'

HERMAN MELVILLE, *Moby Dick*

My quest for a white whale had taken me 6,000 miles from my starting point in Nuku Hiva. By the time I reached Lamalera I was in a place Melville could not have known. The name of Lamalera is missing from the logbooks of the Yankee, English and Australian whaleships which cruised the Gulf of Ombay, north of Timor, in the years before Melville wrote *Moby Dick*. One of his favourite sources, surgeon Bennett, visited Timor aboard the *Tuscan* in 1836. He mentions that he could see Pantar Island, Lamalera's close neighbour, across the gulf, and that the Timorese wanted to buy whales' teeth from their visitors. But neither Bennett nor anyone else of the foreign whale-hunting fraternity writes of Lamalera itself, which is odd, because the foreign vessels prowling the gulf for sperm whale must have glimpsed the yellow flecks of the sails of Lamalera's *tenas* on the horizon hunting the same prey. The villagers of Lamalera were pursuing whale and other large sea animals long before the Europeans arrived. When I stood on the clifftop beside

Guru Ben's home and watched the *tena* fleet returning from patrol, I was conscious that the same spectacle was already unfolding at Lamalera when the first Europeans to hunt whales offshore, the Basques, were venturing off the north coast of Iberia on the other side of the world. For hundreds of years the *tena* fleet had come home in the same fashion every midafternoon during the whaling season, until each vessel had become part of the collective awareness of the village. As soon as the boats were close enough to distinguish the rectangles of their sails, any villager beside me on the look-out point was able to identify which boat was which, and — as often as not — tell me whether the boat had had any success that day. Sometimes it was easy to tell — several of the *tenas* displayed a black flag if they were bringing home a significant catch. But often the observer could inform me what had happened to a particular boat because other watchers from the land had been tracking the fleet all day. Wives at home in the upper village could see out over the bay; children climbing toddy palms to gather *tuak* used their vantage points; women making salt in the salt-pans on the shoreline had a limited horizon but an unobstructed field of view. All of them kept a vigilant eye on the *tenas* and spread news of any activity. This boat had chased manta ray but failed; another boat had taken a shark; and, most suggestive of all, the boat that was coming back with its sail a darker shade had been capsized. The matting sail was still wet.

When the breeze favoured them, the *tenas* came home in a dramatic charge. They ran downwind, towards the declining sun. The low-angled rays turned their sails to the colour of fresh wheat straw. The sails were tell-tales of progress. They bellied to the breeze, then flapped, drooped and hung slack as the boats rounded the point and came into the wind shadow of the mountain. Men rose from their rowing benches to lower, roll and stow the sail, and pivot back the bipod mast. Then they returned to their seats and picked up their paddles and ran the boat ashore stern first.

Melville had never described a scene remotely like this. The men of Lamalera hunt the sperm whale in their own special way. Their equipment is unique, and their concept of hunting is distinctive. The sturdy hand-lashed *tena* and the long bamboo whale-harpoon are found nowhere else. The stimulus of the chase is not the individual's skill or luck or tenacity. There is no Ahab, Queequeg or Fedallah to prosecute the hunt with a singular zeal. In Lamalera the clan and the boat itself are the key elements, and they endure. If a boat is sunk, its replacement bears the same name. If it is totally rebuilt from the keel up, nothing alters the spirit of the boat. When a harpooner switches vessels, he leaves behind all the equipment. Rufinus, the gaunt maker of harpoon heads and former harpooner, described the day he left *Tena Ana* and moved on *Kebako Puka* to replace his father who was retiring. Rufinus went to *Tena Ana* in its shed and lifted out the harpoon heads, the special ropes and the bamboo poles and laid them carefully on the sand. He and the new harpooner recited prayers over them. They sprinkled holy water, and then the new man gathered up the tackle and returned them to the boat, their permanent home. They were now in his trust.

So how is it that the sea hunters of Lamalera have a concept of the white whale so similar to Melville's vision of his imaginary Moby Dick? They are steeped in a different tradition of whaling, yet their white whale could have swum through Melville's pages side by side with Moby Dick. The two animals have many similarities. The Lamalera whale is also a bull sperm whale and very large. He is a leader among sperm whales, and their protector in times of danger. He is a lone creature, swimming on his own, though in distant company with his fellows. He appears again and again over the span of years, and in the same haunts. Above all, he is a sentient animal. The white whale of Lamalera *thinks*. He knows the correct formula of the whale hunt, how the *tenas* should be constructed, how the crews should behave, how the traditions run. And if he finds that these traditions are flouted, the white whale will intervene. He has a violent streak. He can be *galak* (a nasty or wicked fellow). So he must be respected, and he evokes a feeling of awe in those who meet him. When he attacks, boats sink and human life is put in peril.

The villagers could not have imported elements of Melville's tale to describe their own white whale. They do not know the Moby Dick story. Their world is too isolated. They are literate but they possess few books. Melville would have said that the whiteness of their whale had affected their point of view, making the animal seem eerie and supernatural in their eyes. In Pamilacan I had found that the white whale shark and the white manta ray did awake a blend of respect and apprehension. But it is puzzling that a white coloration should make a sea animal mysterious and awe-inspiring. White is such a common feature of a seascape. There are legions of white seabirds, and white is the colour of water, however it is disturbed. There are white-caps of waves, the white of a boat's wake, the white foaming streak of a fish moving fast underwater, the white of spindrift in a gale, the tumultuous white of a great roller breaking and its summit tumbling down in a rumbling welter of foam. White at sea is natural, not freakish. A fisherman or lookout on a ship is informed by the quality of white. The white of small waves has a certain rhythm, so do the white streaks laid across the surface of a gale-torn sea. What catches the seaman's attention is the sudden contradictory sort of white, the break in a pattern with the sudden white flash when a fish leaps, or a gannet plummets into the water, or a whale spouts its white spray.

A more essential reason why the sea hunters regard the whale as so special is the origin of the animal. Whales breathe air and suckle their young. The traditional sea hunters appreciate that the whale stands closer to man the mammal than any fish ever could, and they have no need for the theory of evolution to explain the process of how the whales adapted to marine habitat. The native peoples of the Pacific produce their own versions of how the whale first went to sea. The shaman of the mountain in Lamalera evoked for me the picture of the sperm whale as a sort of giant cow, walking down the mountain-side and swimming out into the ocean. In Tonga a collector of folk tales, Philippe Tonga, recited a tale worthy of Aesop. The Tongan demi-god Maui was invited to go to an important feast but had no gift or food to bring with him, so he gathered all his animals around him and told them that he was going to kill one of them to take with him. There was a humpback whale, a turtle, a pig, an earthworm, a rooster and a dog. He immediately looked at the whale, but the whale pointed out that he was too big, he wouldn't fit in the *umu* (earth oven) and there was too much meat on him and it would go bad in the hot Tongan sun. Maui thought about it and realised the humpback was right. He then looked at the earthworm who tried to make himself look even smaller and said, 'You wouldn't want to take me to the feast, Maui, I am very gritty and earthy and anyhow there's not much eating on me.' Maui agreed and turned to the turtle. The turtle lay peacefully in the sun and pointed out how difficult it would be to open his shell, his tough leathery skin, and how salty his flesh tasted, so Maui decided against him. Then he looked towards the dog who wagged his tail and said, 'Maui, if you kill me, who will bark and tell you when people are coming and guard you?' Maui agreed, and so decided not to bring him to the feast. He considered the rooster, who pointed out that Maui would be at a loss without the rooster to wake him up in the mornings; Maui agreed that it was important to get up early and that the rooster certainly helped.

Finally he looked at the pig. 'Yeah, take the pig, kill the pig,' all the other animals called. The pig flew into a terrible rage and charged at them. The earthworm just dug himself into the ground as the pig chased him with his snout, and this is why the pigs of Tonga today root around in the ground still chasing earthworms. The turtle just lay where he was and pulled his legs and head into his shell while the pig ranted and cursed telling him to go into the ocean where he belonged. The dog just barked, showing his teeth at the pig when he ran towards him, while the rooster flew up into the nearest tree and let out a mighty cock-a-doodle-doo. The pig finally charged at the humpback whale and chased him to the water's edge, telling him to go to the ocean and never come back on land again.

Maui killed the pig and wrapped him up in a *ngatu* (unpainted tapa cloth) and took him to the feast.

'This is why when you are invited to an important feast in Tonga you will be served roast pig and also why you should bring tapa as a gift,' concluded Philippe Tonga. 'It also explains why the humpback whales of Tonga, though they swim close to the edge of the reefs and breathe air like land mammals, remain in the seas surrounding Tonga and are no longer found on the land.'

If whales had once dwelled on land alongside Man, then it was natural that they should still be capable of interacting with humans. Many sea-faring peoples believe this is true. Until the late nineteenth century the Icelanders still referred to a whale they called 'God's gift'. They also knew it as the 'fish driver', and Icelandic fishing law forbade any fisherman to molest the animal because it was believed that this whale helpfully shepherded the shoals of cod and capelin into their nets. If the whale was harmed it would drive the fish away — almost exactly what Tonio and his colleagues of Pamilacan feared would happen if they harmed the white manta ray and the white whale shark. The Icelanders also believed that the friendly whale — it was almost certainly the fin whale — protected fishermen from other, malicious, breeds of whale. And, like the Lamalera sea hunters, the Icelanders recommended that fishermen at sea should be of good temper and never quarrel. Otherwise 'God's gift' would chase the fish away.

Such notions were not entirely fanciful. A small town called Eden in south-east Australia shows off the skeleton of a killer whale called Tom. Eden was once a shore station for part-time whaling. The prey was mainly humpback whales, intercepted as they moved along the coast on their winter migration. When whales were seen, small boats went out, manned by oarsmen and hand-harpooners, much like Lamalera. Within a few years a pack of killer whales found out how to assist in the chase. Like hounds, the orcas would locate and corner the passing humpback whales. They detained the migrating humpbacks at the entrance to the bay, and announced the availability of the prey by slapping their tails on the water. It is said that the local aborigines regarded the orcas as their ancestors — a curious parallel with Lamalera, if true. The boatmen rewarded the orcas with scraps from the carcasses, and gave names to individual members of the orca pack — Humpy, Hooker, Jackson, Old Ben, Stranger. The orcas' undisputed leader was Tom. He died in September 1930, apparently of old age. The whalers found his corpse floating in the sea and towed it to their try-works, then cleaned his bones and wired them together, and put him on display in the town museum.

Recognised to be intelligent, the great whales

are also sufficiently elusive by habit to encourage fantasy among their traditional hunters. Samson Cook in Tonga was aware that humpback whales migrate. He had no idea where they came from nor where they went when they left the Tongan shore. He thought they might go to the North Pole or Europe, and then return 'to born a baby'. On Camiguin in the Philippines the harpooner Ramon saw a lone, huge black sperm whale cruise past his house in the same season almost every year. His neighbour, another harpooner, witnessed the same sight. Neither had any idea where the whale came from nor where it was going; only that the creature was so vast that it had to be the same animal, and that it disappeared into the unknown. The hook jumpers of Pamilacan had the same vision of the whale sharks. The enormous fish loomed up from the deep a week after the full moon. Then most of them mysteriously turned and sank back into the depths after a day or two. What happened during those long intervals — months on end, when whales or whale sharks or any of the big sea creatures are lost from view — was a mystery. And mystery provokes a response from humans — they seek to explain through science or to invest with a panoply of legend and myth.

Happily, mystery remains a feature of sperm whales even for scientists. It is a pleasing twist that marine biologists, trying to solve the enigmatic behaviour of sperm whales, have come up with explanations as colourful as the centuries-old ideas of the men in rowing boats. A much-discussed problem is how a sperm whale manages to catch its food. Sperm whale eat squid, mostly, in vast quantities. They take the squid at depths ranging from a few feet to hundreds of fathoms. In the lower depths daylight does not penetrate, so how does a bulky sperm whale, swimming in the pitch-dark, catch an agile squid which can twist and turn and dart about by pumping water through its body like Nature's water jet? The hungry whale cannot even see its fleeing meal. And should the whale succeed in overhauling the fugitive squid, there is another difficulty: how can the sperm whale grip anything in its mouth? The sperm whale's impressive teeth erupt only in the lower jaw. The teeth of the upper jaw are much smaller, and only a few of them show above the gum. The sperm whale has no real bite. The nineteenth century whalemen had a theory that the sperm whale does not chase its prey but simply sinks down to the 'squid level' in the sea. There the animal hangs, motionless and quiet, with its mouth agape. In the deep-sea gloom the squid are attracted by the ghostly, light pink cavern, and swim in. The whale closes its jaws and swallows.

In a broad leap of imagination, two Russian whale scientists proposed that the sperm whale is a living stun-gun. In their underwater scenario, the sperm whale comes up to the unsuspecting squid and looses off a sound burst of such intensity — water being a far more efficient conductor of sound than air — that the unfortunate squid is virtually paralysed. Then the whale sucks up the inert prey. Another theory proposes that the sperm whale can catch swiftly moving squid because there is very little oxygen in the far depths where the hunt takes place. The sperm whale chases the squid until the prey runs out of energy, while the sperm whale still has a reserve tank — the vast stores of oxygen in its blood.

Yet neither the open-jaw idea, nor the stun-gun notion, nor the theory of oxygen reserves explain why the teeth of elderly sperm whales are noticeably worn down. In theory, they have never been able to chew.

A world authority on sperm whales, Malcolm Clarke, calculated that a single male sperm whale requires fifteen tons of food every day, and the smaller females need five tons. So how do the world's sperm whales find enough squid and other food to sustain their huge bulk? Clarke estimated the sperm whale population at 1.25 million animals (in 1973), and worked out that 100 million tons of squid would be needed to keep them fed for a year. This is a biomass of such gargantuan proportions that no one has imagined where so many squid could exist. Neither has anyone yet seen those monstrous squid whose tentacles have been found floating in chunks on the sea, vomited up by harpooned sperm whales. Nelson Haley, harpooner aboard the whale ship *Charles W. Morgan* at the extraordinarily young age of seventeen, said that some of the pieces were 'almost if not quite as large as a whaleboat'. The entire squid must have been at least fifty feet long overall. Such giant cephalopods could be the source of sailors' stories of seeing battles between sperm whales and giant squid, where the whale thrashes on the sea, its huge head enveloped by the flailing tentacles of its foe — a glimpse of two semi-legendary beasts, the Kraken and the Great Whale.

So it is little wonder that fact and fiction, myth and truth, intertwine in their combat for survival when sperm whales are involved. At least my search for a white whale had validated several of the 'wild legends of the South Sperm Whale Fisheries', as Melville had called them. I had seen for myself how *kea* whales rush in to help their fellows under attack. Those reliable chroniclers of the whaleships, Beale and Bennett, had said that sperm whales swam to the rescue and deliberately tried to sever the harpoon line and free the victim. The Lamalera whalers told the same thing: more than once they had seen a *kea* take the harpoon rope in its mouth and try to snap it. Beale and Bennett had written about the strong maternal instinct of the mother whale. Tongans, Filipinos and Indonesians all said that special care was needed when tackling a mother whale and her calf. The Tongans deliberately harpooned the humpback calf, knowing the mother would follow faithfully and could be taken later. But all agreed that it would be foolhardy to try this technique with a sperm whale.

The enraged parent was likely to attack the boat with no regard for her own safety, and the whalers should cut the line and flee. Samson Cook had an extra word of advice: if the calf was male, then the other whales might swim away. But if the harpooned calf was a female, then the mother — and probably the whole pod as well — was certain to attack.

The Lamalera whale hunters had brought the nineteenth century to life for me. I had seen the notorious 'Nantucket sleigh ride' with a Lamalera *tena* pulled away by a whale 'when first pierced by the harpoon' as Bennett had put it, towing 'the attached boat at the rate of more than fifteen miles an hour'. I had observed the dramatic impact of a sperm whale bursting up beneath a *tena* and tossing it into the air — a milder version of that favourite artist's theme with the whaleboat in the air, bouncing off the whale's back and the men cartwheeling into the sea. In my yellow dinghy I had been within yards when the sleek black snout of a sperm whale rose out of the sea, and slid against the wooden planks of the whaleboat, and I heard a high-pitched creaking sound and wondered whether the noise was whale skin sliding against timber, or the desperate clicks of a dying whale calling for a *kea*. Then the whale rolled slowly over, its head still rubbing the boat, and the strange sharp-jawed mouth opened wide, its lower gum studded with teeth. I feared that a whaleman would slip and fall into the maw as he leaned for-

314

ward to try to finish off the animal with a knife. That had happened too, I learned. But it was not a fatal slip. One clumsy man fell right into the whale's mouth, the jaws closed slightly and he received a puncture wound in his stomach. But the whale then let him go, and the man survived to live another fifteen years, a near-Jonah.

When Marinus was describing how a blow from the flukes of the white whale shattered the harpoon and the splinters flew back and injured the father of *Dolu Tena*'s harpooner I thought of Frank Bullen, the adventure-seeker aboard the *Cachalot* a century earlier. He saw a whaleman killed by a flying boat-spade, the instrument used for cutting blubber and sometimes for severing a whale's tendons near the tail to cripple it. The whale flicked its tail, struck the boat-spade from the harpooner's hand, and the spade had flown through the air and split open the head of an oarsman. The whaling writers — Beale, Bennett, and the Reverend Henry Cheever, who wrote *The Whale and His Captors*, another Melville source — had set out a litany of such mishaps: whaleboats capsized, or towed under, or beaten to pieces with great blows from the sperm whale's tail. It was all verifiable. I had seen the heavy smack of the sperm whale's tail defending itself. I had observed the crew of a sunken *tena* standing waist-deep in the water on their boat, waiting for help, much as the six man crew of a Yankee whaleboat had been accustomed to sit, oars lashed across the gunnel to keep their vessel

315

afloat until rescue came. And I had witnessed something which I did not find in any book: the sperm whale, when harpooned, turns and looks at the tormentor.

Not everything matched the old whaling lore. I was startled when the Lamalera hunters chanted and thumped their paddles loudly on the sides of the boat as they raced down on a sperm whale wallowing on the surface. From what I had read, the nineteenth-century whalemen took great care to be as silent as possible when approaching the whale in light weather. They crept upon the animal like pygmies stalking an elephant in the forest. They muffled the oars in the rowlocks, forbade anyone to talk in the boat, and during the final approach on their target often stowed their oars and took up paddles which they dipped soundlessly in the water. They would have been puzzled to see that the Lamalera whales ignored the din kicked up by their hunters — and astounded by the outcome of a recent experiment conducted in the Azores where the islanders in open boats hunted sperm whales in the Yankee style until the 1980s. The modern Azoreans wanted to protect the sperm whales from being run down by the inter-island ferries. Someone suggested clearing the whales away from the ferry routes by blasts of underwater sound. Several sounds were tried, of varying intensities and frequencies. The whales took not the slightest notice. Like birds who learn to ignore the gas-powered bang guns which farmers leave in fields, the sperm whales seemed to have learned to disregard submarine cacophony.

Other claims by Melville and the nineteenth-century whale authors were beyond my experience. Does the whale really turn its head sunwards when it is about to die? I was not sure. Nor is it always the case that the dying whale goes into its 'flurry', the final spasm before death when the whale is supposed to swim round thrashing in a tight, dangerous circle. From what I witnessed and was told, the whale sometimes expires passively and slips quietly beneath the sea, head up. And the Lamalera people would have disagreed with Robert Coffin, a member of the extended family which included the unlucky lad eaten by the survivors of the *Essex*. Robert Coffin described the foolish joy of gorging himself on ship's biscuit soaked and softened in boiling whale oil. He took the 'great square crackers, so hard you need a hammer to break them, and held them in the boiling oil. They immediately became as tender as pie crust, and I gorged myself with them. But O! didn't I pay for my feast! It brought out boils all over me. I had twenty-six on me at once and thought of Job!' No one in Lamalera that I asked had ever suffered from an excess diet of blubber.

Can the white whale of Lamalera be a descendant of Mocha Dick, the fighting white whale and real-life inspiration for Moby Dick? Sperm whales can have much the same lifespan as humans, about seventy years, so the two white whales cannot be the same animal. Mocha Dick was first recorded off the coast of Peru in 1810, and he would have died long ago, even if his first chronicler, J. N. Reynolds, is wrong in claiming in 1839 that Mocha Dick had already been hunted down and despatched. Mocha Dick — or a rogue whale very like him — kept appearing for at least another twenty years after Reynolds alleged that the monster had been rendered into one hundred barrels of oil. On 5 July 1840, according to the Detroit *Free Press*, the whale Mocha Dick destroyed two boats from the English whaleship *Desmond*. The *Desmond*'s crew did not know which animal they were tackling when they lowered their boats some 215 miles west of Valparaiso, though this was Mocha Dick's home territory. Instead of fleeing his attackers, Mocha Dick swam aggressively towards them. He rammed the first boat head-on, wrecking it. He then dived, waited in ambush for fifteen minutes, and came surging upwards to strike the second boat under the keel, tossing it into the air. 'Chewing the planks of the boat with lordly leisure,' wrote Howard Vincent, a leading Melville scholar, 'Mocha Dick at last swam off in a northerly direction, leaving behind him two dead whalemen. The men aboard ship reported him to be the largest whale they had ever seen, easily identifiable by an eight-foot scar across his head.'

Vincent noted that this story was printed half a

century after the attack on the *Desmond*, and that Mocha Dick had achieved his own legendary status without the need for association with Moby Dick. Eight weeks after the tussle with the *Desmond*, two boats from the Russian ship *Sarepta* killed a whale and were getting ready to tow the carcass to their mother ship when Mocha Dick surfaced nearby, and charged down at them. One whaleboat took refuge from the onslaught by dodging behind the dead whale. But Mocha Dick caught the second boat in his jaws and crushed it. The surviving boat sneaked back to the *Sarepta* without being molested, and the Russian vessel stayed in the area for three hours hoping to retrieve the dead whale. But Mocha Dick stood guard, and the *Sarepta* was forced to abandon her catch. A lucky Nantucket ship found the dead whale adrift two days later and by whaling custom claimed possession. Mocha Dick was nowhere in sight.

Mocha Dick then appeared off the Falklands. A huge sperm whale brazenly breached so close to the English whaleship *John Day* that the backwash made the *John Day* roll 'as if in a gale'. The whaler launched three boats against this audacious newcomer, and one boat managed to get a harpoon into Mocha Dick. The boat was dragged for three miles before the 'fighting whale' turned round and swam right over the boat like a sea-going juggernaut, pausing only to thwack the wreckage with his vast tail, reputed to be twenty-eight feet across. This left two men dead.

The whale then sank down into the ocean and lay doggo until one of the remaining boats came up and unwisely tried to pick up the whale line still trailing from the harpoon in Mocha Dick's side. At that instant Mocha Dick came bursting up from the sea, overturned the boat, smashed it, and killed two more men. Wisely, the *John Day* withdrew from the skirmish.

Mocha Dick's final and most rambunctious challenge was on an international scale. He defeated no less than three whaleships, the Scottish *Crieff*, the English *Dudley*, and the American *Yankee*. If reports are to be believed, these vessels came upon the white whale off the coast of Japan, as Mocha Dick was battering an unfortunate merchant ship carrying a cargo of timber. Apparently from sheer malice the whale had charged the merchant vessel and knocked off her stern so she had settled in the water, her decks awash. Determined to put an end to the menace of Mocha Dick, the three whaleship captains agreed on joint action. Each lowered two whaleboats, the first to attack the whale, the second to act as a rescue craft. The crews drew lots to decide who would lead the onslaught, and the choice fell on a boat from the *Yankee*. That boat advanced warily to the spot where Mocha Dick had last been seen and waited, fully alert. After twenty minutes Mocha Dick surfaced within range, and the mate of the *Yankee* succeeded in planting his harpoon. For the next five minutes it seemed that Mocha Dick had lost his fighting spirit or was badly hurt. The great whale lay still. But then he turned and, swimming at a furious pace, first bowled over a Scottish whaleboat, then took up an English boat in his jaws and crunched it to shreds, crushing two men. Those who had been tipped into the water swam for their lives to avoid the great tail as it deliberately flailed the sea near them. Two men did not get away fast enough, and their deaths brought the carnage to four. Mocha Dick now returned his attention to the waterlogged timber ship. Still towing the *Yankee*'s boat behind him, he swam straight at her and rammed. The force of the blow was so great that the vessel turned keel up. By now the *Yankee*'s men had seen enough. They cut their line and began to row back to their mother ship. But Mocha Dick still had his grand finale to deliver. He swam underwater towards the *Crieff*, and suddenly shot up just beneath her bow in a thunderous arc. He missed the ship by inches, and carried away her jib boom and bowsprit with his enormous bulk. Splashing back into the ocean, he raced towards the *Yankee*'s boat. The crew took one look and promptly jumped into the sea to save themselves. They looked on aghast while Mocha Dick took their twenty-eight-foot whaleboat in his mouth, and calmly 'chewed it as a horse does his oats.'

Vincent cites one terminal report of Mocha Dick. In August 1859, far away from the Pacific, a Swedish whaler took a huge sperm whale off the coast of Brazil. It was said to be a hundred feet long, with a jaw that measured twenty-six feet. The animal was old and exhausted, and did not put up a fight. On closer inspection the veteran was found to have a badly scarred head and to be blind in his right eye, the results of countless battles. On such evidence the immense creature was claimed as the true Mocha Dick.

The *Acushnet*, the real-life whaleship on which Melville gathered his whaling experience, had disappeared from the scene while the legendary Mocha Dick was still careering through the oceans. *Acushnet* was wrecked on St Lawrence Island at the entrance to the Bering Strait in August 1851 while on another whaling voyage. A passing brig, the *Wyandott*, picked up her captain, crew and 250 barrels of oil from her cargo, and brought them to Honolulu. Two months later Melville published his masterpiece and immortalised *Acushnet* as the venerable *Pequod*. He may not even have known the fate of the original. He had, however, found out what had happened to the ship's company he deserted nine years earlier on Nuku Hiva. A former shipmate, Henry Hubard, visited him while he was writing *Moby Dick*. Hubard had completed *Acushnet*'s four-year voyage and returned to the home port of Fairhaven. Melville jotted down a list of what Hubard could remember had happened to the rest of the crew. It was a grim roll-call. Hubard knew of only nine foremast hands who had 'come home'. Six others had run away at various ports, mostly on the coast of South America. One of them later committed suicide when he got back to the United States. Four more had been put ashore due to sickness, including two men who were suffering 'with disreputable disease'. They were dropped off in Hawaii. Significantly, only one of the ship's officers — second mate John Hall — had come back with Captain Valentine Pease. Both the first and third mates abandoned the voyage midway. The first mate left the ship after he 'had a fight with the Captain' and the third mate apparently supported him because the two officers both quit the *Acushnet* while in Patya in Peru. Their fates are not known. Captain Pease, Melville notes dourly, 'returned & lives in asylum at the Vinyard'.

Captain Pease clearly ran an unhappy ship, and he may have been a part-model for Melville's creation, the half-crazed, obsessive Ahab, whose pride turns to blasphemy and brings ruin. Melville makes much of the God-fearing nature of his Quaker Nantucketeers, and I had noted how Christianity still plays a role among the whale hunters I met. Pamilacan and Lamalera are both very devout Christian communities, and this is against the general pattern. Muslims make up the crews aboard most of the traditional trading craft of Indonesia, and the 'sea peoples' of the Philippines are either animist or Muslim. Tonga is a special case. In the island kingdom there are few opportunities for anyone to be other than Christian, and Samson Cook had emphasised his devotion by becoming a minister of the Tongan church. Christian faith, it seems, still sustains the whale hunters, offering a shield against the dangers of their work. I recalled how the fishermen of Pamilacan always came ashore on the way to the whale shark reefs to light candles in the Church of San Isidoro and pray for a safe return. In Lamalera there is scarcely a gesture or custom during the whale hunt which does not have its Christian gloss — the holy water sprinkled on boat and crew before the launch, a paternoster after the sail is hoisted, another prayer if the fishing is bad and to ask the Lord to intervene to improve the catch. The anthropologist Bob Barnes has shown that many of these Christian formulae are grafted on earlier pagan customs, but the graft has succeeded to an astonishing degree. Twenty-five kilometres to the north-west of Lamalera is another coastal fishing village, confusingly called Lamakera. It is entirely Muslim. Until recently the men of Lamakera also hunted whales, using a design of boat which the Lamalera men jealously say was copied from their own. The Muslims hunted baleen whales, not sperm whales. Now they have given up taking whales except when they meet a whale by chance when hunting manta ray. Their lack of success, say the Lamalera men, is because they are Muslims, foul-mouthed and blasphemous. They do not have the pure heart which comes from Christian prayer. Sperm whales, they contend, deliver themselves only to Christians.

Two antique harpoons provide a link between Lamalera and the world Melville described. The two harpoons are kept carefully stored as clan property in the house of *Kena Puka*. The keeper of these relics brought them out to show me. They are surprisingly lightweight, no more than three or four pounds. Each has a long slender shaft of wrought iron, with a broad two-flanged arrowhead. The men of Lamalera have never made or used harpoons of this shape and suppose that they must have come from some foreign ship. Melville would have recognised them at once. There would have been dozens of them shipped aboard the *Acushnet* when she sailed from Fairhaven, and the ship's blacksmith would have been able to forge replacements when they were lost. Normally each harpoon was stamped with an identifying mark, but the antiques in the possession of the *Kena Puka* clan are plain. There is no way of knowing which ship once carried them or where and when they were thrown. Their keeper could only tell me that an earlier *Kena Puka* had seen a dead whale floating on the sea. The crew hauled alongside the carcass and found the two harpoons embedded in the flesh and retrieved them. He could not tell me when this had happened, except that it was a very long time ago. If the harpoons did come from a Western whaleship, then she may have been cruising for whales about the time that

Moby Dick was written. That classic broad arrow-pattern of harpoon head went out of common use 150 years ago.

Mocha Dick, it will be remembered, carried twenty rusty harpoons in his blubber when he was finally caught and rendered down, according to Reynolds. And Melville has Queequeg recognise Moby Dick as the whale which has 'Oh! Good many iron in him hide . . . all twiske-tee betwisk . . .' The tattooed South Sea islander falters for a word and turns his hand round and round 'as though uncorking a bottle' until Ahab cries, "Corkscrew! . . . aye, Queequeg, the harpoons lie twisted and wrenched in him.' Losing harpoons was commonplace. Melville was familiar with shipboard tales of harpoons lost and harpoons recovered, though he took his detail from his favoured whaling authors. Captain Bunker from New Bedford, 'of whom almost everybody has heard' according to Henry Cheever, threw a harpoon into a whale in 'north latitude thirty degrees and thirty minutes, and east longitude one hundred and fifty four degrees'. The whale broke the line, and the harpoon was gone. Five years later the captain was sailing in precisely the same latitude but fourteen degrees farther to the west, when 'he made fast to a noble whale, and after a hard struggle succeeded in getting him alongside. And lo! When cutting him up a harpoon, rusted off at the shank, was found fast anchored in the old fellow's "cutwater". "Hallo!" said Captain Bunker jesting, "here is my missing old iron." What he said proved to be very truth, for the blubber-kept harpoon was the identical one he had lost five years before, having on it the ship's name, and his own private mark.'

These lost harpoons served, by chance, as tracker tags. When they were recovered, the whalemen began to glean some idea of the migrations of the sperm whale. Stone lances and bone harpoons found in whales caught in the Davis Strait between Greenland and Canada led Captain William Scoresby Jr, another of Melville's sources, to guess they were the hunting weapons of Eskimos who lived on the northern edge of the New World and had not yet encountered Westerners and obtained iron from them. Scoresby theorised that the whales had swum the length of the North American coast, perhaps from the Pacific Ocean itself, and that meant there was a north-west sea passage. Nearly two hundred years later we still know little about the migrations of sperm whales. They are such sea-wandering creatures that their distribution and movements are difficult to track. Separate populations of sperm whales are scattered around the world's oceans, each inhabiting its own range. But it is a mystery whether these populations intermingle from time to time, and to what extent, or if some sperm whales — the lone 'emperors' in particular — travel huge distances from one ocean to the next. The whalemen long ago recognised 'nursery herds' of cow whales and their calves, and now it is appreciated that a 'nursery herd' is the primary social unit. An older female leads and each mother whale teaches her child the pod's distinctive vocabulary of clicks and grunts. When a pod splits up, and one group swims away to find another territory, some scientists claim to detect a similarity of language between the two halves, generations later.

So the sperm whales of the Gulf of Ombay can be said to be descendants of the whales which swam there in Melville's time. 'A large whale called Timor Jack is the hero of many strange stories, such as his destroying every boat sent out against him,' wrote Beale, and Melville underlined the words 'Timor Jack' in his copy of Beale's book. Perhaps Melville thought of choosing Timor Jack as his model for Moby Dick, or he might have been tempted to select 'New Zealand Tom' who destroyed nine whaleboats 'before breakfast' one day in 1804. The fighting whale of New Zealand was distinguished by a 'white hump'. But in the end Melville apparently preferred Mocha Dick as his main inspiration. Timor Jack was left to the mercy of the real-life whalers. They determined to be rid of him. A whaleman craftily attached a floating cask to the line of the first harpoon, to distract Timor Jack's attention. While the whale watched the cask, the whaleboats closed with him and killed him.

What drove the Western whalers to these acts of deliberate slaughter? Sailing halfway round the world for profit, they arrived in the whale's natural arena with the rampant spirit of the gladiator. They had to conquer the great sea beast; nothing less would do. This is one of the messages which Melville may have meant us to understand. There are as many interpretations to his tale as there have been readers, but time and again the white whale is taken as a symbol of vulnerable Nature at the mercy of Man the predator. On the last and fatal day of the chase, First Mate Starbuck implores Captain Ahab to stop his insane pursuit and leave the whale alone. 'See!' he cries. 'Moby Dick seeks thee not. It is thou, thou, that madly seekest him.' But Ahab presses on to his own destruction. It is exactly what the sea hunters of Pamilacan and Lamalera would have warned: harm the white sea beast, and general disaster will follow. The hook jumpers of Pamilacan do not attack the white manta ray, nor the white whale shark, and in Tonga Samson had told me that the Cook family never took such risks. The whale hunters of Lamalera go farther: they revere the white whale as much as fear it. The white whale is an ancestor. It has its proper place among the creatures of the sea, and is not a selected target for their harpoons. The whale hunt is a matter of survival, not of conquest. And more than a hundred years after Melville's tale, the story still belongs to a survivor — and that survivor, tragically or justly, may or may not be Man.

After what I had seen on my travels in search

of the white whale I had come to appreciate the plight of the whale hunters themselves. In Tonga Samson no longer hunts whales by the edict of his king. The President of the Philippines banned the hunting of the whale sharks soon after my visit there in an effort to preserve the remaining stocks. On Pamilacan today no one knows for certain how the community will survive. Already in Lamalera the crews of the *tena* are mostly old men. With the passing of the generations — or a whale-hunting ban — a way of life, a skill, a diversity of culture will inevitably vanish. What consolation there is remains the same as the grand outcome to Melville's story of Moby Dick — the wondrous survivor is, still, a white whale.

'. . . and knowing that after repeated intrepid assaults, the White Whale had escaped alive; it cannot be much matter of surprise that some men go further in their superstitions; declaring Moby Dick not only ubiquitous, but immortal.'

HERMAN MELVILLE, *Moby Dick*

ACKNOWLEDGEMENTS

I wish there had been some way in which those people who generously helped me to accomplish my quest for the white whale could have participated in some of the high points of my experiences. David Brettell and his colleagues at Henshaw Inflatables Ltd had taken particular care in preparing the bright yellow dinghy which allowed me to accompany — and film — the *tena* fleet of Lamalera while it was in action offshore among the sperm whales. David Allen OBE, Chairman of DHL WorldWide Express, Cecilia Lawrence, and the team at DHL. Cork airport — who have helped me on previous expeditions — made sure that the dinghy got safely to Indonesia and back again, with the assistance of the DHL staff at Denpasar, Bali. Tony O'Connor of RTE Dublin arranged the loan of lightweight video equipment from which the still images for the book are taken, and another long-standing ally and friend, George Durrant of Ampair Ltd, donated solar panels to recharge the camera batteries. Malaysian Airlines helped with travel, and before I set out for eastern Indonesia Dr

Robert Barnes was liberal with his advice about Lamalera's culture and most thoughtful in allowing me to benefit from his own extended visits to the area. In the field I was fortunate to meet by chance Karl-Heinz Pampus to help me with any problems of the Lamaholot language. Richard Hardiman of Amerada Hess was munificent in arranging for Trondur Patursson to join me in Indonesia so that this book could be illustrated with Trondur's superb drawings.

In the Philippines Lory Tan and Juni Binamura were my expert mentors. They steered me in the right direction to find and appreciate the island of Pamilacan and its 'hook jumpers'.

In Tonga Allan and Lynn Bowe, ably assisted by Nosa Luis, demonstrated how entertaining and hard-working hosts can improve even an island paradise.

I hope that by describing my search of Moby Dick I have been able to share with these friends and supporters my enjoyment of tracking down the white whale.

A NOTE ABOUT THE AUTHOR

Acclaimed adventure writer and explorer Tim Severin has made a career of retracing the storied journeys of mythical and historical figures in replica vessels. These experiences have been turned into a body of captivating and illuminating books, including *The Brendan Voyage* and *In Search of Genghis Khan*. When not travelling, he lives in County Cork, Ireland.

1	28	121	192	250	308	351	386	417
2	35	123	193	251	310	352	388	418
3	39	124	195	252	311	353	390	419
4	40	132	198	257	312	354	392	421
5	41	136	203	258	317	355	393	422
6	42	148	208	259	318	357	394	423
7	54	149	212	262	320	359	395	425
8	55	154	216	263	321	360	396	427
9	61	157	220	268	322	361	397	428
10	64	160	224	269	324	362	399	429
11	68	164	227	272	326	363	400	431
12	69	166	232	273	327	364	401	432
13	78	167	233	274	328	366	403	433
14	79	168	234	279	331	368	404	435
15	80	169	237	285	333	372	405	436
16	84	172	238	288	336	373	406	437
17	85	174	240	295	337	374	407	438
18	90	175	241	297	338	375	408	440
19	99	180	242	299	341	376	409	441
20	100	182	243	301	344	377	410	442
21	101	183	244	303	347	379	411	443
22	110	188	247	304	348	380	413	444
23	119	189	249	307	350	383	416	445

447	470	493	516	539	562	585	608	63
448	471	494	517	540	563	586	609	63
449	472	495	518	541	564	587	610	63
450	473	496	519	542	565	588	611	63
451	474	497	520	543	566	589	612	63
452	475	498	521	544	567	590	613	63
453	476	499	522	545	568	591	614	63
454	477	500	523	546	569	592	615	63
455	478	501	524	547	570	593	616	63
456	479	502	525	548	571	594	617	64
457	480	503	526	549	572	595	618	64
458	481	504	527	550	573	596	619	64
459	482	505	528	551	574	597	620	64
460	483	506	529	552	575	598	621	64
461	484	507	530	553	576	599	622	64
462	485	508	531	554	577	600	623	64
463	486	509	532	555	578	601	624	
464	487	510	533	556	579	602	625	64
465	488	511	534	557	580	603	626	64
466	489	512	535	558	581	604	627	65
467	490	513	536	559	582	605	628	65
468	491	514	537	560	583	606	629	65
469	492	515	538	561	584	607	630	65